AF333946

ALBERT PALEY
ON PARK AVENUE

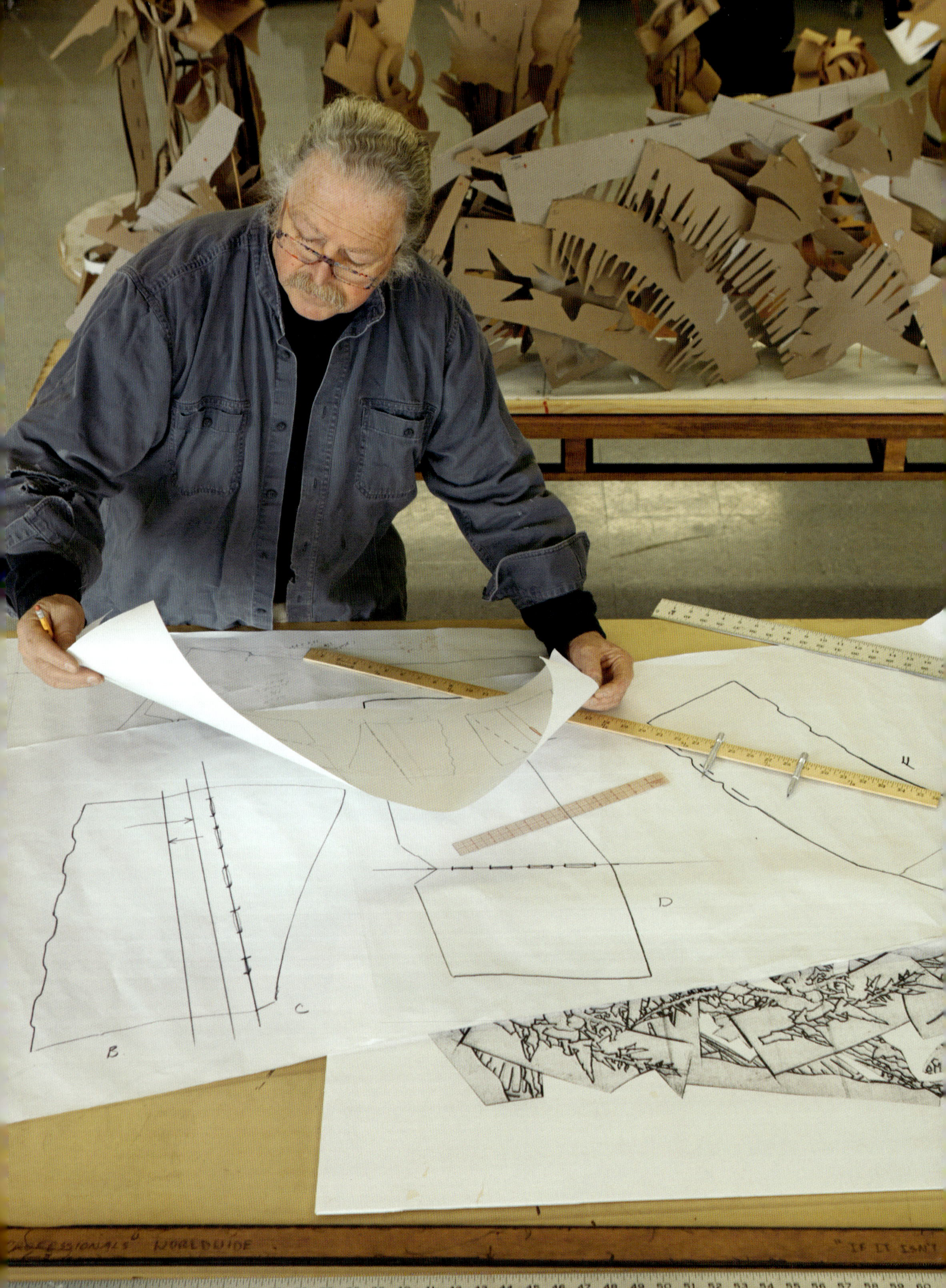

ALBERT PALEY
ON PARK AVENUE

Edited by
Paola Gribaudo

SilvanaEditoriale

ALBERT PALEY

Paley on Park Avenue
June 29 – November 8, 2013

Celebrating New York City's eminence as an art world center, the Park Avenue malls on the upper east side of Manhattan provide a dramatic and unique location for a wide range of large-scale outdoor sculpture. Under the auspices of the Sculpture Advisory Committee of The Fund for Park Avenue and the Public Art Program of the City of New York's Department of Parks & Recreation, periodic one-artist installations of recent sculptures have created a changing and exciting creative panorama along this venerable thoroughfare since 2000.
The focus of the program has been on living artists who either select recent work to show or, as Albert Paley has done with an ambition unparalleled in the history of the program, create an entirely new body of work. Funding for these exhibitions comes from the artists themselves, arts organizations, galleries and private philanthropy.
The creation of the Sculpture Advisory Committee was a natural extension of The Fund for Park Avenue's ongoing beautification efforts which are supported annually by the buildings along Park Avenue, private individuals, corporate contributions, and foundations. The Fund for Park Avenue oversees and ensures that the trees, plantings, flowers, and seasonal decorations on the Park Avenue malls are properly and beautifully maintained.
The Sculpture Advisory Committee of The Fund for Park Avenue is thrilled that Albert Paley has joined the distinguished group of sculptors (listed on the next page) who have exhibited on Park Avenue.

Charles C. Bergman
Chairman
The Sculpture Advisory Committee
of The Fund for Park Avenue

2013
Albert Paley
Alexandre Arrechea

2012
Niki de Saint Phalle
Rafael Barrios

2011
Brian Hunt
Will Ryman

2010
Yoshimoto Nara
Mia Westerland Rosen

2009
Les Lelannes
James Surls

2008
Sui Jianguo
Jun Kaneko

2007
Robert Indiana
Donna Dennis

2005
Deborah Butterfield
Beverly Pepper

2004
Bernar Venet

2003
Jean Dubuffet
Robert Indiana
Tom Otterness

2002
Manolo Valdes

2000
George Rickey

Charles C. Bergman
Chairman
and the Sculpture Advisory Committee of The
Fund for Park Avenue
Linda Blumberg
Mary Ceruti
Stuart Alan Levy
Richard Oldenburg
Samuel Sachs II
Richard Schwartz
Patterson Sims
Ronald D. Spencer, Esq.
John P. Stern

Ex officio:
New York City Department of Parks & Recreation
Jonathan Kuhn
Jennifer Lantzas

The Fund for Park Avenue
Barbara McLaughlin

Cover
Envious Composure, 2013

p. 2
Paley with *Progression* patterns
Paley Studios, Lyell Avenue
Rochester, New York

pp. 32-33
Design area
Paley Studios, Lyell Avenue
Rochester, New York

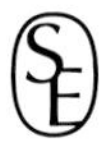

Silvana Editoriale

Produced by
Arti Grafiche Amilcare Pizzi S.p.A.

Direction
Dario Cimorelli

Art Director
Giacomo Merli

Production Coordinator
Michela Bramati

Editing
Lorena Ansani

Layout
Nicola Cazzulo

Editorial Assistant
Emma Altomare

Photo Editor
Alessandra Olivari, Silvia Sala

Press Office
Lidia Masolini, press@silvanaeditoriale.it

CONTENTS

9   Foreword
GERALD PETERS

11   Albert Paley Interview
PATTERSON SIMS

Works

34   Progression
44   Between the Shadows
54   Reflection
62   Encore
70   Jester
76   Counter Balance
84   Variance
92   Tilted Column
100   Ambiguous Response
108   Cloaked Intention
114   Composed Presence
120   Languorous Repose
126   Envious Composure

133   Biography
134   Albert Paley

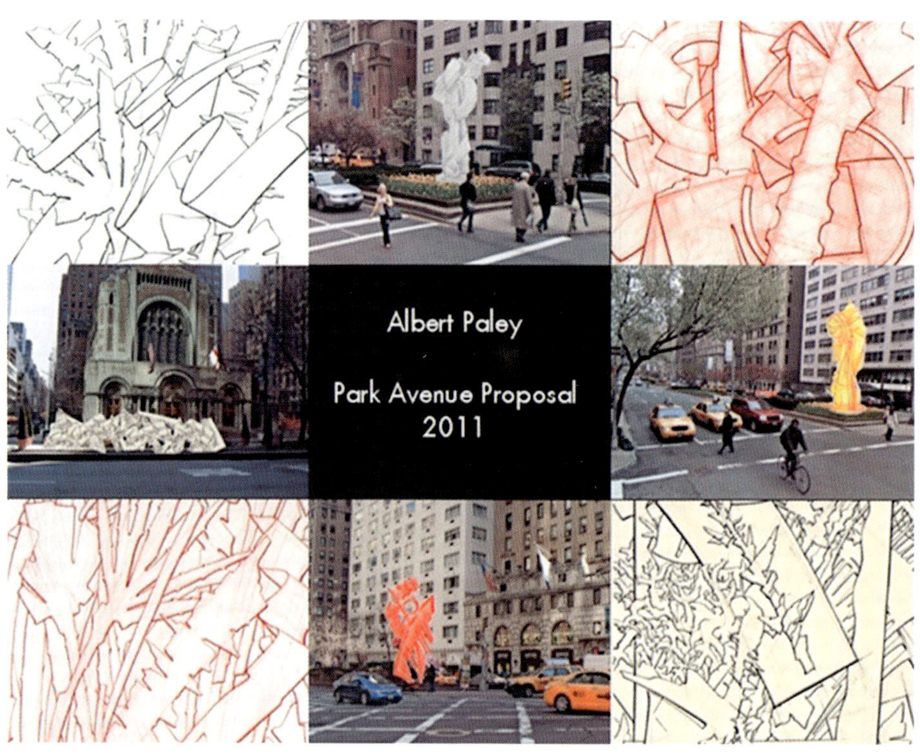

Project Proposal
Paley on Park Avenue
2011

FOREWORD

G E R A L D   P E T E R S

I have long admired the work of Albert Paley and am so pleased that he has been chosen as the featured artist on Park Avenue for summer 2013. One of his greatest talents lies in his ability to integrate his monumental sculptures with their surroundings, and the fifteen blocks that he occupies on Park Avenue between 52nd and 67th Streets offer a beautiful and varied backdrop for him to work with.

Since 2008, I have had the honor of representing Paley in both my New York and Santa Fe galleries, although we have had the pleasure of working with his pieces since the late 90s. He is a unique talent among sculptors and continues to expand what it is possible to achieve with metal on a large scale. One of the most telling indications of Paley's incredible talent is the numerous commissions, both public and private, he has completed throughout the United States and beyond. Each unique, and perfectly suited to its surrounding architecture and landscape, his work awes and inspires all who encounter it.

Paley first began working with metal as a jewelry designer. Creating one-of-a-kind ornamental pieces that allowed him to test the boundaries of his medium, he eventually transitioned into large scale works, including decorative arts and furniture. In 1973, Paley was awarded a commission from the Smithsonian to design portal gates for the Renwick Gallery in Washington DC. An immediate critical and public success, this commission would mark his arrival as a sculptor of large scale works and remains today as one of his most well-known and celebrated works. At present Paley has completed over 50 site-specific commissions, and with the exposure that he will gain with this installation on one of New York's busiest thoroughfares, there is no doubt that number will continue to rise.

With these fifteen blocks on Park Avenue Paley has a perfect and diverse setting to showcase his incredible skill, creating intricate and organic sculptures in the unforgiving medium of steel. This expansive venue allows him the opportunity to incorporate his vision with the distinct architecture of the city, while also creating a visual dialogue with the numerous people who will discover the work whether passing by on foot or in a vehicle. A truly successful site specific sculpture will enhance its environment as well as be enhanced by it, and without a doubt Paley's sculptures will bring new life and vibrancy to the landscape of Park Avenue, while the city will likewise bring Paley's steel to life.

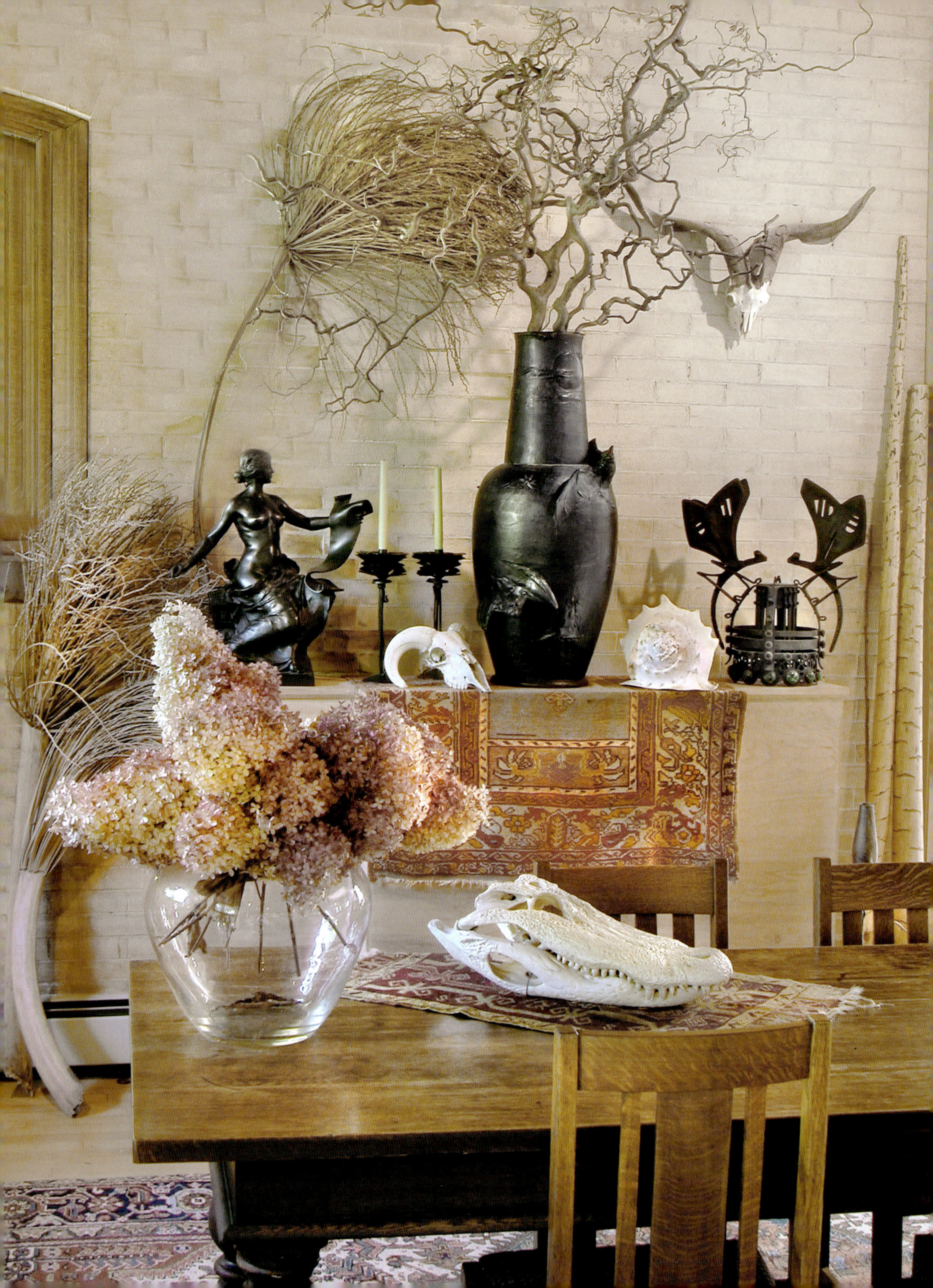

ALBERT PALEY INTERVIEW

PATTERSON SIMS

P rodigiously talented and productive, the artist Albert Paley (b. 1944) attained a new level of ambition and visibility with his series of thirteen monumental metal sculptures installed on the median malls of Park Avenue in New York City from 52nd to 67th Streets in the summer of 2013.

Born and raised in Philadelphia, Paley was also educated there, receiving his Bachelors (1966) and Masters degrees (1969) at the Tyler School of Art of Temple University. From the start of his artistic career in the mid-1960s, Paley has focused on working in metal. He swiftly established his prominence as a goldsmith and for his jewelry, exhibiting these first aspects of his metalworking frequently through the late 1970s.

In 1969 Paley moved to Rochester, New York to take a teaching position at the Rochester Institute of Technology, where he now holds the Charlotte Frederick Morris endowed chair at the College of Imaging Arts and Sciences, and Rochester has remained his base for nearly 45 years.

In 1974 Paley turned to forging curvilinear ironwork. His involvement with iron and the subsequent commissions for the portal gates for the Renwick Gallery, Smithsonian Museum, outdoor ironwork for the Hunter Museum in Chattanooga, Tennessee, and the New York State Capital in Albany made him quickly and widely recognized for his capacity to powerfully meld sculpture and architecture.

In Rochester Paley has had a succession of four increasingly large studio spaces. In the early 1980s Paley and his wife, Frances, a former psychotherapist and now a photographer, renovated and repurposed the stable and carriage house of Dr. James Sibley Watson, Jr. (1894 –1982), the famed medical doctor, philanthropist, early experimenter in motion pictures, and publisher and editor with Scoffed Thayer of *The Dial* magazine. This handsome building serves as Paley's drawing and planning studio and houses the Paleys' extensive library and significant collection of European Art Nouveau decorative arts, which they have installed with great style and artistry. There is much to be learned about

View of the Paley's living room in Rochester, New York, showing Paley, *Ginko Candleholders*, 1994, Hans Stoltenberg Lerche, *Vase*, 1891, and Alessandro Mazzucotelli, *Dragonfly Lamp*, 1906

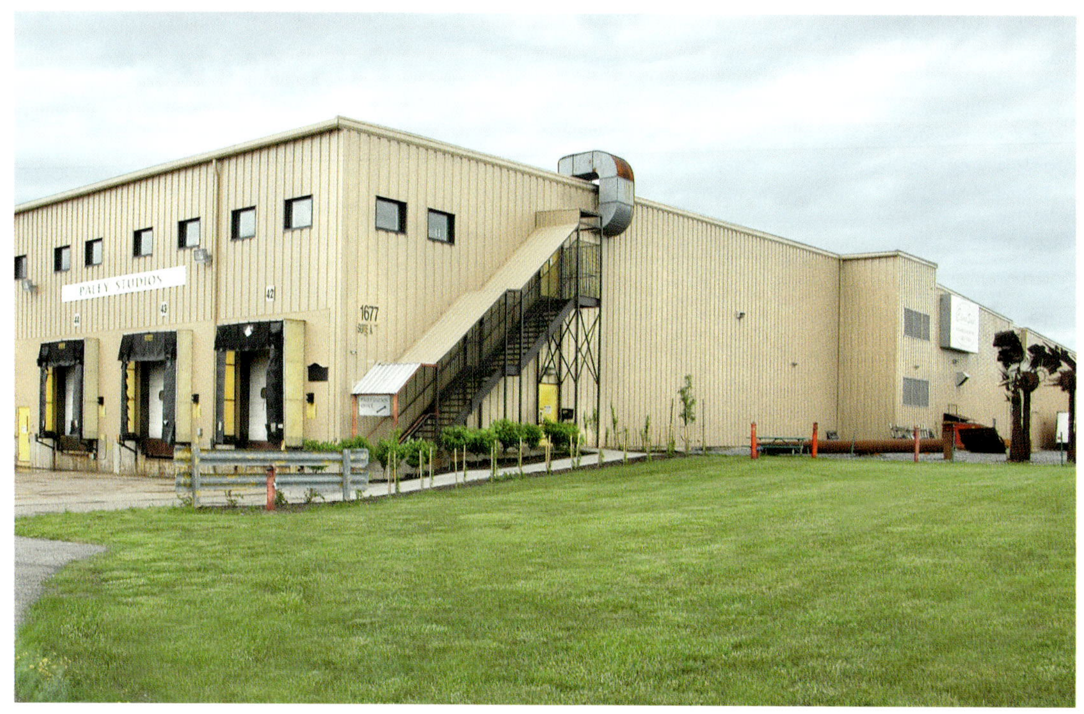

Paley Studios, Lyell Avenue
Rochester, New York

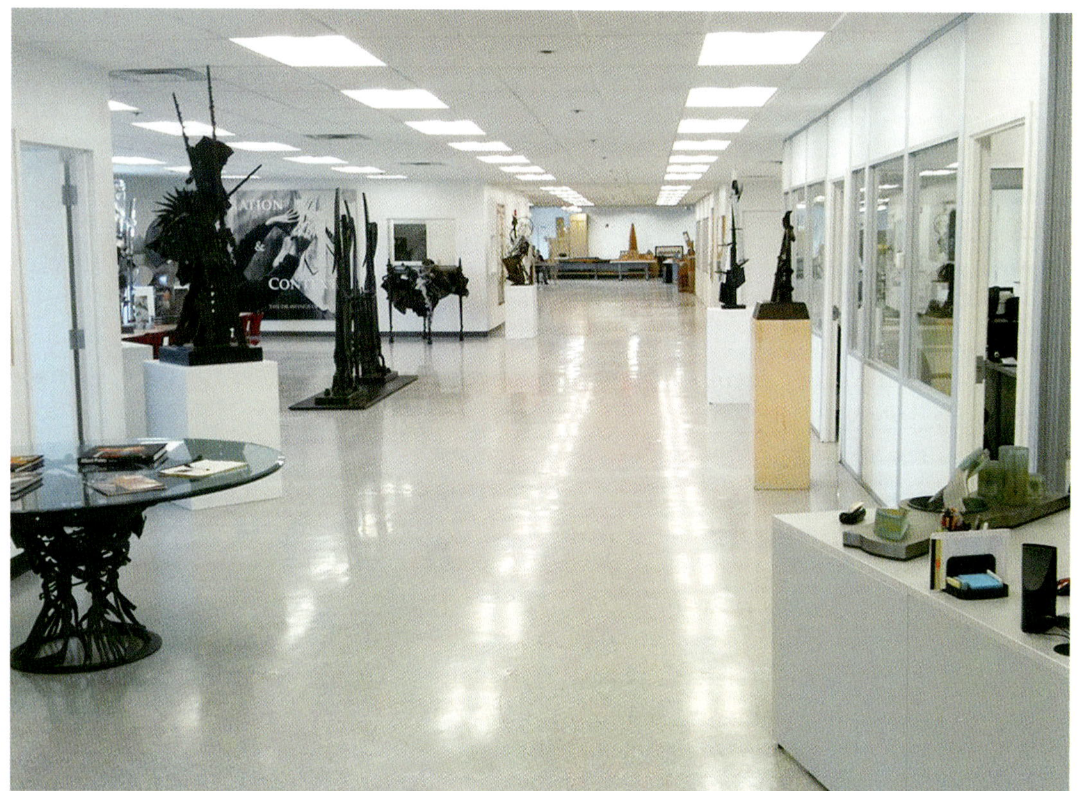

Offices and display area
Paley Studios, Lyell Avenue
Rochester, New York

Paley's baroque and festive sensibility by seeing this collection and how he and his wife have chosen to live with it.

By 1982, his focus shifted to fabricated steel sculptures within the architectural arena, which has lead to his current independent focus on large public sculpture. Primarily in the continental United States with commissions in Australia, Canada, England, Mexico, Germany, and Japan he has completed over sixty site-specific works. Since 1998 Paley and his wife have spend part of the winter at their residence and studio in Carmel, California.

This interview occurred at Paley's current, 50,000 square foot studio outside Rochester, which he and his staff and crew of fifteen moved into in 2011. Retaining his long ponytail and relaxed warmth from the 1960s, Paley presides over a highly industrious and efficient operation with quietly commanding leadership. This new studio space also serves as an informal museum of his sculpture and decorative art with an outside viewing area for larger sculptures. It has an extensive, meticulously well-ordered archive of the files and papers of his now almost fifty-year career and a separate storeroom for his multiple studies and unique works on paper and numerous print editions. Though new technological and manufacturing resources, AutoCAD, ever-improving computer software, and specialist consulting engineers have increased the sophistication, scale, and speed of production, it is ultimately a formidable, personal fusion of intuition, craft, and exuberant, unfettered, and celebratory spirit that fuels Paley's creativity.

P.S. *How does it feel to be installing your sculpture on Park Avenue in New York City?*

A.P. Though since my teenage years I have visited New York City periodically, I have never lived there. Since I moved to Rochester N.Y. from Philadelphia in1969, I have chosen to lead a relatively cloistered studio and academic life. Even before stopping teaching full time in 1985, I have been totally consumed with making my art. I have lectured extensively in the US and internationally. Except for occasional group exhibitions in galleries and museums my involvement with NYC has been occasional and brief.

Therefore, I saw the possibility to exhibit sculpture on Park Avenue as a truly great opportunity. Although my smaller sculpture and decorative art have been shown in the city, I have never had a gallery that had the capacity to present large-scale sculptures.

Of course, New York City is one of the cultural capitals of the world: a city and axis of economic, cultural, and symbolic importance. Having my sculptures installed along the grand thoroughfare of Park Avenue is deeply gratifying. Park Avenue has its own specific status and magic. It is one of the broadest streets of the city and the reality that trains run beneath it increases its allure and mystery. The medians provide a green space that plays off of its proximity to Central Park with its large expanse and orchestration of urban nature.

Although Park Avenue is punctuated by several iconic structures, it is not a particularly progressional street. It is primarily a transit environment. Within its commercial and residential homogeneity the Park Avenue sculpture installations offer a diverse, fresh, and unexpected visual experiences for pedestrians and those in vehicles.

Relatively numerous and widely located, my large-scale sculptures have been the result of site-specific competitions and commissions for public, individuals and corporate, educational and religious institutions. Only at my new studio in Rochester, have I ever been able to assemble a significant grouping of large-scale sculptures. This is the first time I have been afforded the opportunity to create a group of sculptures to be seen together in such a visible public environment. This is all the more significant in this economy with the drastic reduction of government and corporate funding for the arts there are fewer opportunities for public commissions or exhibitions of large-scale sculpture.

P.S. *There was an opportunity for you to make a large permanent piece in New York City in the Central Park Zoo in the mid 1980s.*

A.P. Not being able to realize the Central Park project was one of the real disappointments of my career. It would have been in the spirit of my earlier work for the State Capitol in Albany and the Smithsonian's Renwick Gallery.
The impetus and realization of commissions has always resulted in a growth mode for me. The piece for Central Park was far more ambitious than anything I had done before. Costs were higher than expected, and at that point in my career, I didn't know how to negotiate. My inability to adjust lost me the important chance to have a public sculpture permanently installed in middle of Manhattan.
Fortunately, 25 years later, in 2004, the concept for the Central Park Zoo prototype - in an

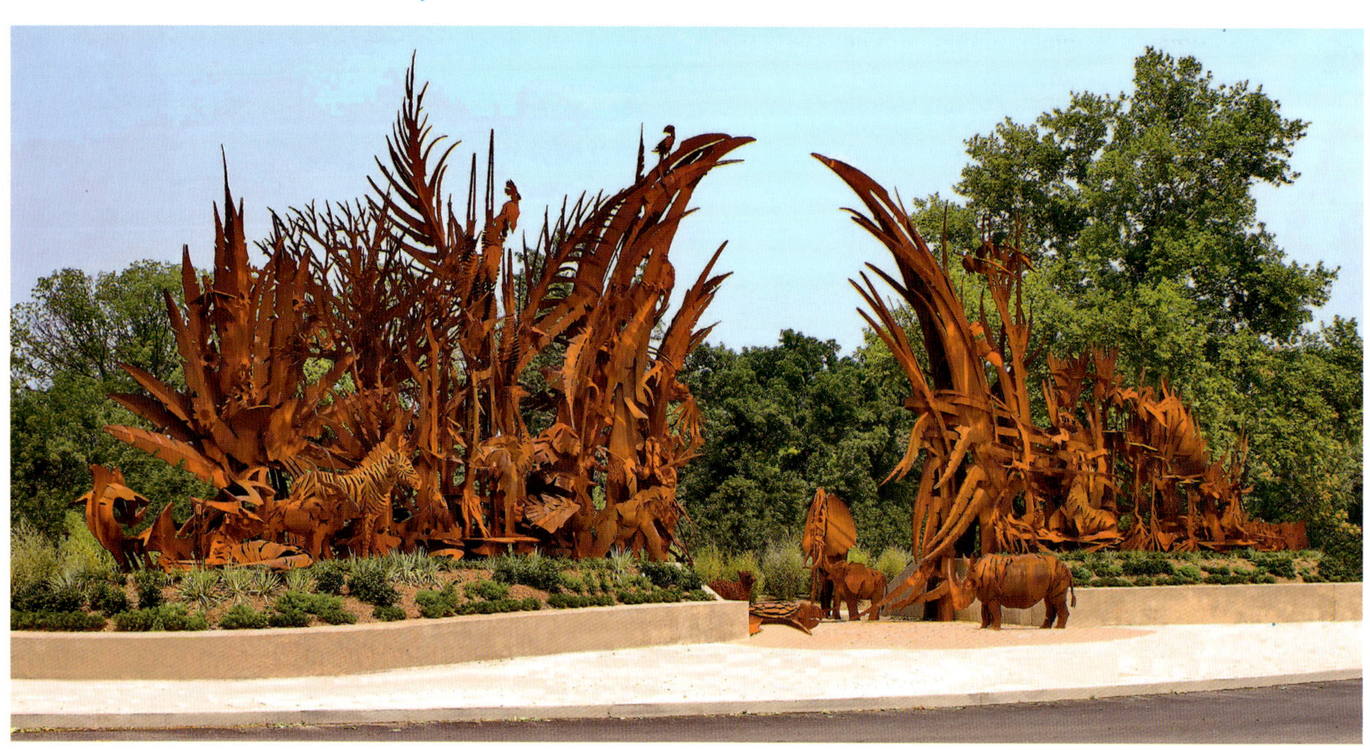

Animals Always, 2006
Forged, and fabricated weathering steel, 36' x 130' x 8'
Forrest Park, St. Louis Zoo, St. Louis, Missouri

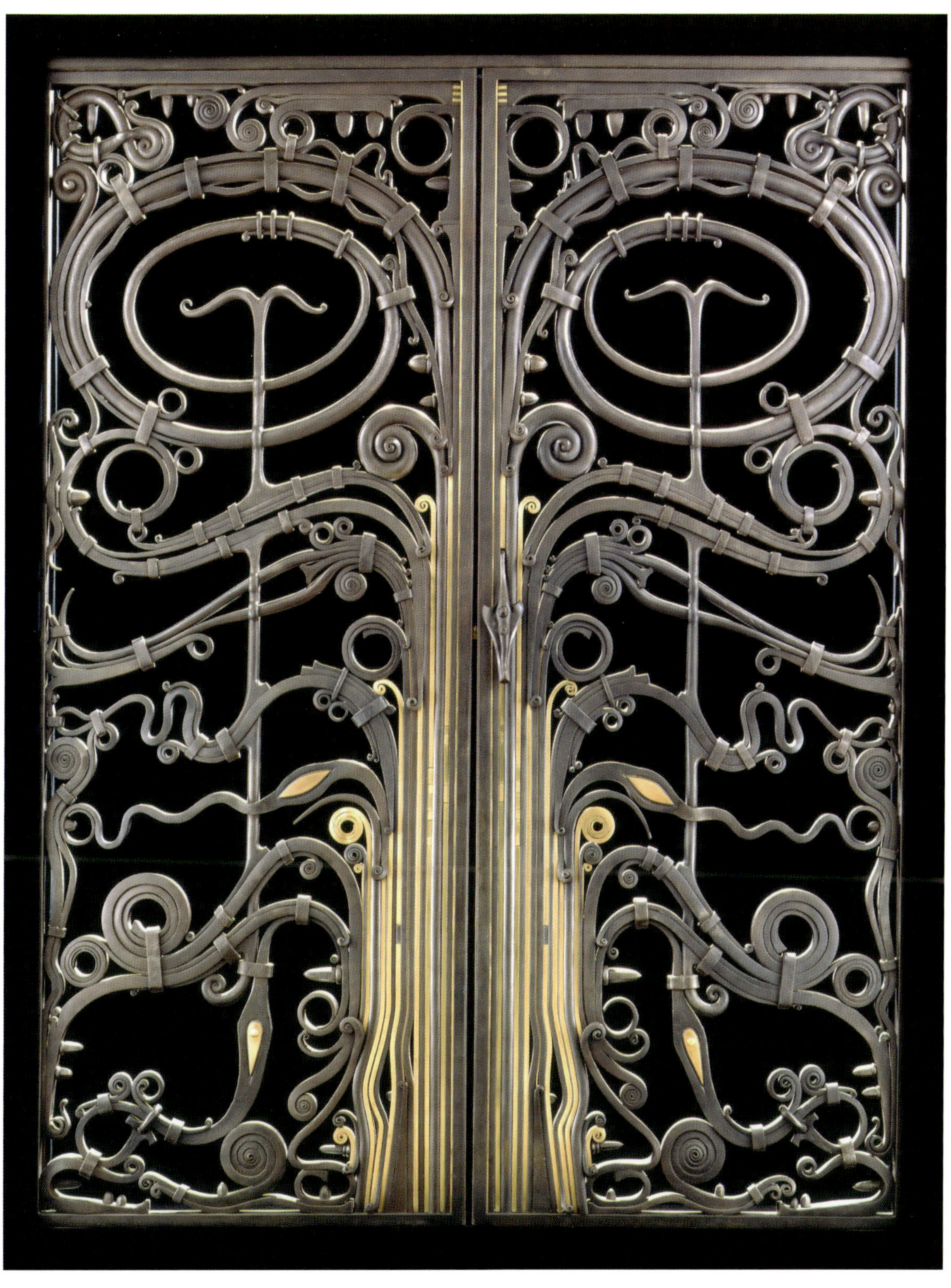

Portal Gates, 1974
Forged and fabricated steel, brass, bronze, and copper, 7'6" x 6' x 3"
Renwick Gallery, Smithsonian Institution, Washington, DC

even grander scale – was realized with the *Animals Always* plaza sculpture, in St. Louis, which was created for the St. Louis Zoo.

Over those years, my approaches to using metal have changed dramatically – from intricate jewelry to forged functional ironwork to complex compositions of fabricated cut steel plate. All this work with metal emerged from my early stone and wood figurative sculpture. Founded in representation, my art still maintains a dialogue between figuration and abstraction, but formal, material, and color relationships now prevail.

P.S. *The Park Avenue Sculpture Committee of the Fund for Park Avenue in concert with the Department of Parks and Recreation invited you to consider installing your sculpture on the median malls along Park Avenue. With this invitation there was no mandate of the number of works, which aspect of your sculpture to show, or what malls you should use. How did you decide what you wanted to do and what were your overarching considerations for what became thirteen new sculptures?*

A.P. First of all, as an artist and a sculptor one is always looking for opportunities to show and present your art. You need a stage and a forum to do so. If I just do what I know I can do, it's not exciting to me. Being able to do something that I've never done before is what drives me. This unexpected invitation generated the most public context and potential for the most numerous production of large-scale sculptures that has ever been possible for me. The timing was totally propitious. I had just moved to a new and much larger studio space, which has the fullest range of equipment and the best team of skilled fabricators and other associates I have ever worked with. Many things happen here, from sculpture to drawing to printmaking. For the first time ever I have the space and capacity to work on a number of large-scale sculptures simultaneously. Though I have the reputation and experience of doing site-specific work and commissions for permanent installations, I have had many sculptures I have wanted to make for a long time. The Park Avenue series gave the studio the chance to create a group of large-scale works to be exhibited in such a prominent yet temporary setting that allowed me to works more freely than I have ever been able to a public sculptor.

Taking on this project has involved a substantial financial commitment, but fortunately we were able to secure sponsorships from various institutions and individuals in advance, that gave the studio the financial capacity to make the Park Avenue installation possible.

Because of the scope of what I envisioned for Park Avenue, my studio's prior commitments, and realizing I had less than two years to prepare, I knew it would be a challenge. As always, I wanted to put maximum effort into the Park Avenue project and came up with a highly rigorous and detailed schedule for designing and fabricating thirteen sculptures.

My previous public commissions were always site specific. However the Park Avenue sculptures, although every piece was sketched, planned, and conceived for their particular location on Park Avenue, were also temporary and will eventually be installed elsewhere. So these sculptures were conceived to be site-sensitive, not site-specific.

I initially spent a lot of time walking up and down Park Avenue as I honed in on where I wanted to site works. I was highly attuned of these thirteen works' spatial and architectural context, the height, width, and ambiance of surrounding buildings and streetscape, the complexity or simplicity of the architecture and natural elements that they were to be seen within along these blocks of Park Avenues. I considered the purposes, history and functions of the buildings near where I wanted the sculptures to be placed.

Each of the Park Avenue median malls has very specific circumstances and logistics that required separate consideration. I wanted to create both synergies and contrasts. If, for example, there is a site where the surrounding façades was very uniform, I created a more complex sculpture that accentuated the contrast. Yet sometimes I sought to harmonize and not to contrast.

When people are experiencing the sculptures, they are concurrently responding to the buildings, the landscaping, and the changing traffic and dynamism of the urban environment. For example, the two most prominent sculptures of the thirteen are placed at the 57th Street intersection. 57th Street is the widest cross street therefore the sculptures needed to be particularly assertive to galvanize the site. Though it is upper Park Avenue's most trafficked arterial intersection, my primary concern was for the pedestrian experience. I realized the sculptures would first be seen from vehicles from a distance. I wanted them to be landmarks. I also considered the pedestrian reality and its more personal and intimate experience, which was achieved through detailing and spatial relationships that can only be seen with extra time and in close proximity.

In my previous sculpture installations, created for a wide diversity of sites from religious institutions to athletic stadiums, museums to libraries, corporate settings to private collections, I have endeavored to create an ambiance that enables the viewer to experience the specific sense of place, symbolism, history and emotional context of the commission.

New York City and, in a more stately and refined way, Park Avenue, is full of complexity and subtle shifts in its mix of residential, cultural, religious, and commercial functions and structures. It has a gravitas, history, and aura quite unlike any setting in which my work has been placed. Trying to assess the right way to address and respect Park Avenue's distinctly urban and urbane realities and demographics of its buildings occupants and users and passersby was the challenge.

Many Manhattan streets are strikingly narrow in relation to the high canyons of buildings at their edges, but Park Avenue affords unusual vistas and sight lines. Obviously the city and Park Avenue residents and the Fund for Park Avenue have made a serious commitment to keeping the street medians a vital and pleasing experience with the well maintained plantings of flowers, shrubs, and trees. These efforts beautify and humanize the avenue and are the platform and most immediate context of the changing sculpture program.

Working on the Park Avenue project caused me to reflect on the city and its history more deeply than I had before. In the 1870s when Park Avenue was first opened and was being developed people would walk or be on horseback or in a carriage. They passed through their surroundings more slowly and with fewer distractions. Then the motorcar emerged and the greater speed and visual and emotional complexity that ensued in this new worldwide urban chapter is vividly expressed in Cubist and Italian Futurist art. This zeitgeist is very much the foundation of our present urban environment with its speed and constant construction and destruction. That said, Park Avenue's stability and reserved pace makes it strikingly unusual mid-town urban street. No buses run on Park Avenue, and it sidewalks are almost never crowded. Its expensive corporate and residential structures cause it to not be particularly frequented by tourists or shoppers, who can be found on the adjacent Madison and Lexington Avenues.

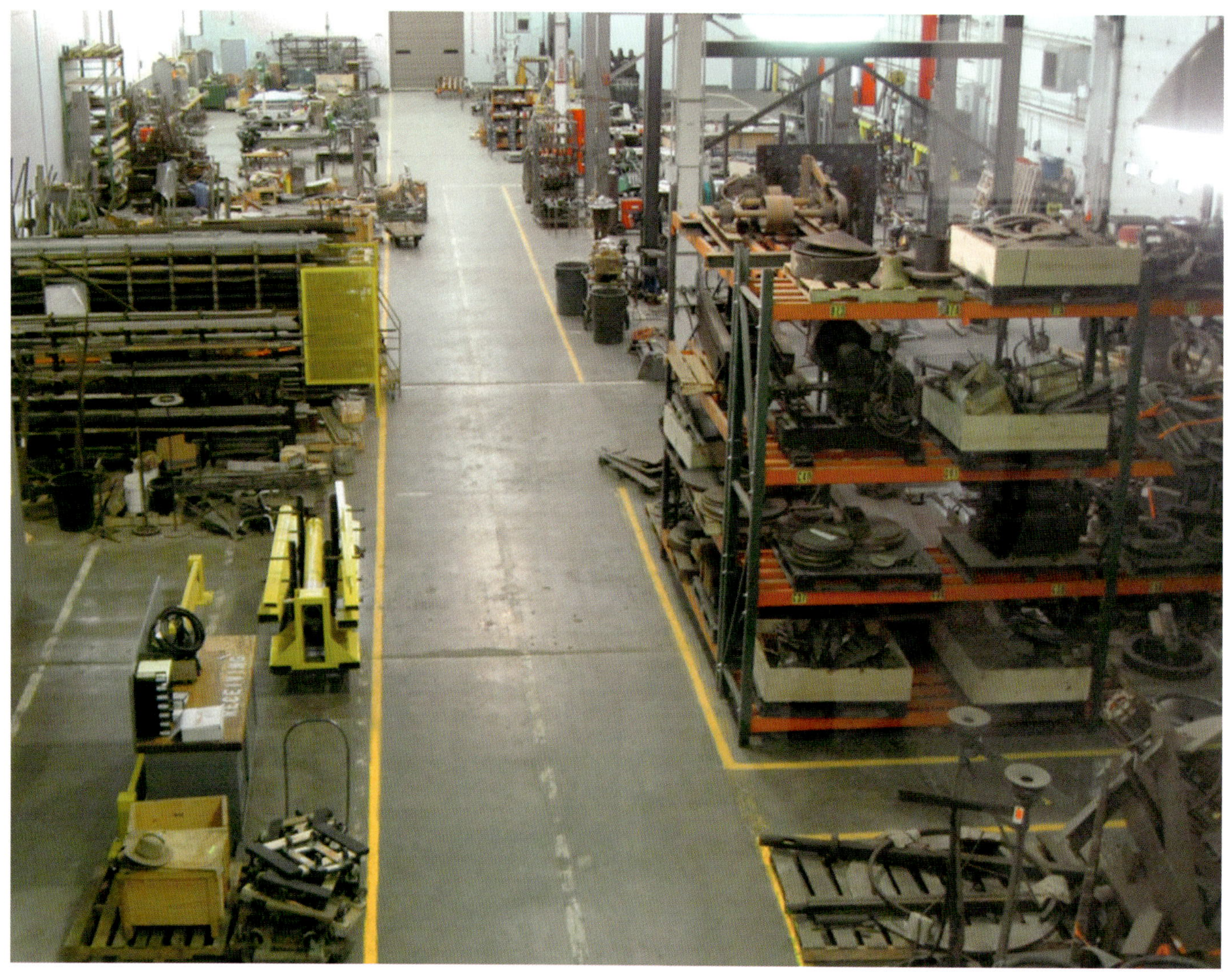

Fabrication area, Paley Studios
Lyell Avenue, Rochester, New York

Park Avenue's changing sculpture installations over the last fifteen years have given this restrained and refined street new and changing visual experiences and layers of associations and memories. Giving people the opportunity to see ambitious art and the chance to confront a variety of sensibilities within a fixed environment as part of their daily life is important. The serendipity of art on Park Avenue reminds me of Henry Moore's concept of "selective vision". He would walk on a beach and always be looking at stones washed up on the shore. He would pass thousands of pebbles, and then, all of a sudden, he'd pick one up. His eye was seeing all those pebbles, but then he'd see one that somehow drew him to select it. There was something innate and profound that propelled him to pick up that particular pebble. I would hope that the presence of my sculptures would likewise engage that "selective vision" of the passersby and find a place in their memory and striking a similar intimate and deep bond of connection.

P.S. *So you have never worked on such an extensive group of large-scale public sculptures before?*

A.P. Not of this magnitude. I have created many public sculptures, several that are much larger, but completing these thirteen sculptures in such a condensed time period is unparalleled for me. After the exhibition on Park Avenue they will go into other public and private collections, therefore they were made for Park Avenue yet will exist independently in situations that do and could not replicate the Park Avenue environment.

P.S. *How did you go about developing the thirteen new sculptures at the same time?*

A.P. After receiving the invitation from the Park Avenue Sculpture Committee I had a very short period of time to get a proposal together. I went into my archive, looking for studies and drawings of sculptures I've always wanted to make but had not realized. I sought to create a spectrum of new work, varying in composition, scale, imagery, materials and finishes, not variations on a theme.
The financial requirements necessary for this project required the studio to generate considerable funds to bring this undertaking into a reality. The studio reached out to various collectors and institutions that were supportive of my work and developed a sponsorship program. This enabled the studio to pre-sell eight of the Park Avenue sculptures. For this first, essential step due to short time I had we could only present the drawings, not even models, for the thirteen new works. Fortunately this financial program was successful. In part, I feel, this was due to the importance accorded by buyers for the Park Avenue Project.

P.S. *That you were able to get these works sold before they were made impresses me. On top of that, it is not a great period for sales of large-scale sculpture by living artists.*

A.P. There is a real problem right now for sculptors because of the financial volatility and crises in the US and globally. I am especially aware of this as my current studio operation is structured towards making large-scale work. The number of public art commissions have been dramatically reduced as corporations and cities do not want to spend on art what they have in the past. Galleries have reduced their exhibition programs and refined the number of artists they represent. Fortunately interest in my work by private collections remains high in a time when there are more artists competing for fewer opportunities. It is a challenging and demanding time to say the least.

P.S. *What were the Park Avenue series other specific issues?*

A.P. My sculptures go through various phases, from drawings to models, to the computer to address pattern development and structural engineering before fabrication. There is also the involvement of subcontracting for the material supplies and services. Besides the actual design and fabrication, there is a labyrinth of technical and legal concerns and paperwork that include calculations of weight loads, sub-foundation requirements, installation permits, insurance, loading and transport, staging areas, cranes, trucks and crews. The processes of installation and de-installation on Park Avenue are an extremely complex affair.

P.S. *How have the new technologies impacted on your creative process and the fabrication of your work?*

A.P. Obviously technology now plays a significant role in the development of my sculpture. One of the main reasons I embrace metal as a means of expression is because of the diversity of technology that is available for this medium. My studio adopts all of the technological advancements in metallurgy and fabrication techniques. But technique is only a means to an end, what drives the process is my visual vocabulary, establishing the relationship of forms and composition, and the processes of creativity.
Computer technology has certainly allowed for easier calculations, record keeping, and communication. Software technology has streamlined the conversion of drawings to the cutting of linear patterns as well as our interface with our subcontractors for structural engineering documents and installation finishing. Services such as forming and some structural joining are worked out as hybrids of a physical model and computer applications.

P.S. *Your work started at a much more intimate scale. You made jewelry, then the forged iron gates, and then decorative, functional objects in the mid-1970s again from the 1990s on. By the late 1980s you really has become a sculptor of larger and larger pieces: did you always know that you would be a monumental sculptor?*

A.P. Many times when lecturing on the evolution of my work people ask me, what do you really want to do? People often seem to see a disconnect between the different aspects of my art. I have been involved in making art for over fifty years. When I was goldsmithing, I was totally committed to that discipline. When I was forging steel that process equally consumed me. As my opportunities and options evolved, my focus demanded the development of different skills and resources to progress.
In addition to personal development, I have always been responsive to my audience. Exploring different ways to draw the attention and engagement of the viewer is a primary concern. As my work developed, I have always been aware of its social context and how it might enrich one's experience. From the start I have wanted to make work that people respond to. I asked how do the wearers of my jewelry want to present themselves? Or in the architectural arena, how can my metalwork coalesce with and enhance the architectural experience?
I have always been concerned with aspects of ceremony and rituals of living. This is most obvious in my forged iron tables, candlesticks, lights, and other furniture. I create objects that add formality, solemnity, and excitement to public and private spaces to elaborate the ceremonial aspects and rituals of life. A key theme of my work has been the act of passage. I have specialized in gates, portals, and thresholds that are both functional and symbolic to enhance and ennoble space. I seek artistic statements

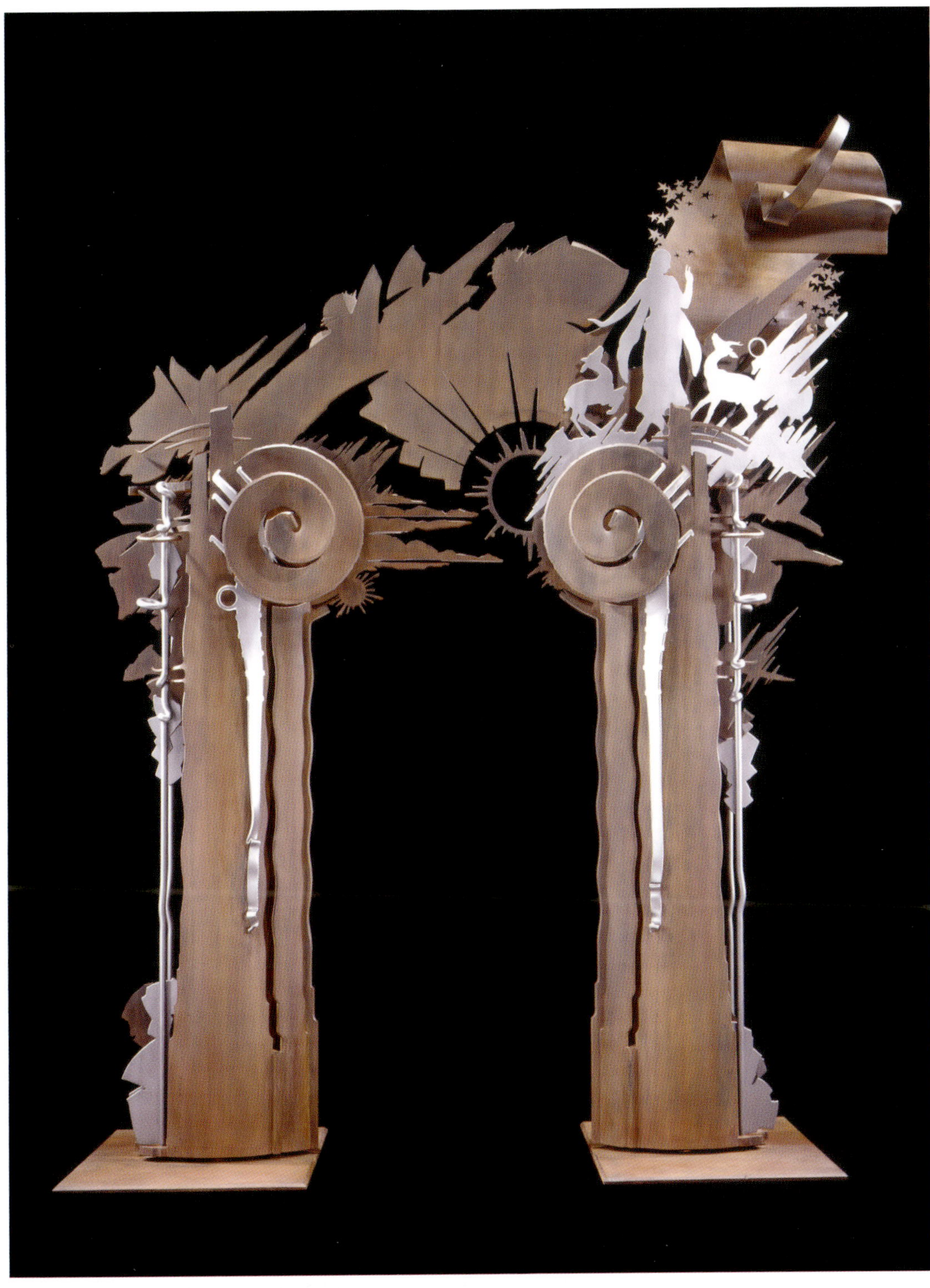

Penumbra, 1996
Formed and fabricated stainless steel and weathering steel, 15'1½" x 11' x 4'8"
Paley Studios, Lyell Avenue, Rochester, New York

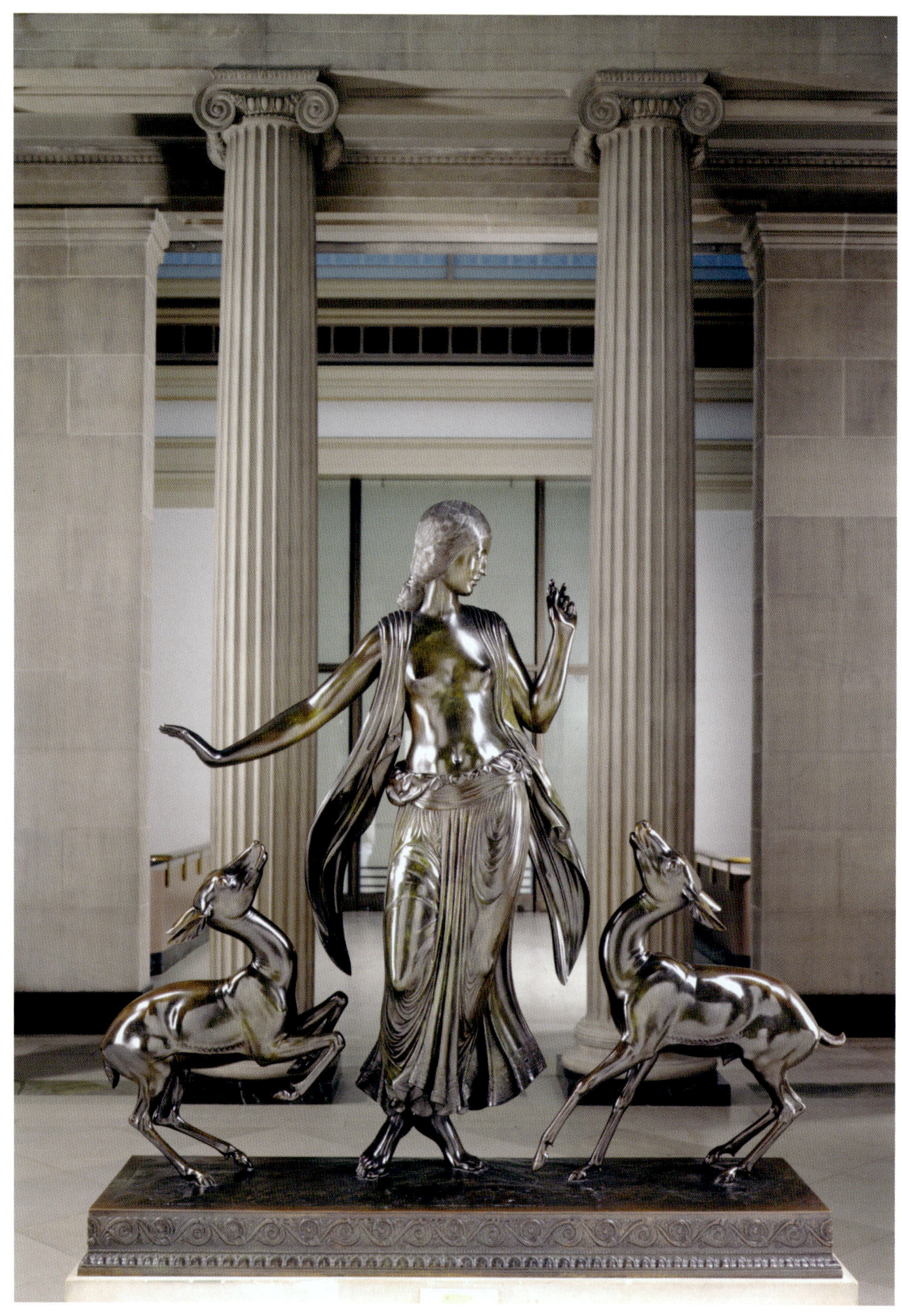

Paul Manship, *Dancer and Gazelles*, modeled 1916, this cast ca. 1922
Bronze, 72" x 73½",
Toledo Museum of Art, Frederick B. and Kate L. Shoemaker Fund, Toledo, Ohio

that are of course personal expressions yet respond to their public and social context. My work comes from an emotional base; it does not derive from theory or an intellectual or literal context.

P.S. *I see an unfurled, floral, and almost patriotic and triumphal quality in your art, with intimations of banners, swags, bunting, flagpoles, Greek Doric columns, and even confetti. Is that an accurate reading?*

A.P. That's an interesting perception. In the early 1980s when I started being invited to speak at international conferences, I would often hear that "Paley's work is so American." I had thought that I was dealing with a formal, universal language – the square, the sphere, curves, and color, but I kept hearing, "this is American work."
Then I began to perceive other national identities. These are, of course, gross exaggerations; Swiss work is very rational, Italian and French artists' works were markedly florid, and the Scandinavian art appears more restrained and emotionally cool. I could see others' national identities in art, yet I could not comprehend these distinctions in my own and what made American art American. My foreign colleagues would describe US artists as expansive, exuberant and highly optimistic. And they were probably right. By being so much of my own culture, I was totally unaware of it.
As I have thought more about it I see the core of America and its artistic identity as "manifest destiny", an intense belief and a right to assert one's will. You may see flags, banners, swags, and confetti in my sculpture, but for me it is a quality "manifest destiny" filtered through Abstract Expressionism. In the most practical terms I seek for my sculptures to function like time-lapse photography, where energy and the process of movement and gesture is frozen, as exemplified in Edward Muybridge's sequenced photographs.
My sculptures combine gestural or folded metal within an otherwise rational or geometric structure. I equate it with the way cloth drapes, delineates, covers, and reveals the human figure in classic Greco-Roman sculpture. I also feel it has a kinship to the way sixteenth century Dutch still life paintings celebrates the profusion of form and color in bouquets of flowers and also includes the few fallen flower petals to express the transitory reality of beauty, nature, and life. I seek to arrest both the physical and emotional ephemerality of time and motion.

P.S. *As well as manifesting the American and global post-1945 abstract expressionist sculptural energy and vision spanning from David Smith to Mark di Suvero to John Chamberlain, your work encompasses the American figurative legacy of Daniel Chester French, Gaston Lachaise, Hunt Dietrich, and Paul Manship, one of whose works,* Dancer and Gazelles, *1917 is directly replicated on your piece,* Penumbra, *1996.*

A.P. I admire figurative and the non-objective sculptors. My use of gestured and structured geometry is based on the human body, contrapposto, and movement, which I see as exemplified by the grace and torsion of Manship's figures and animals. My work exists within a continuum, a product of art history extending into the 21st century. As well as western

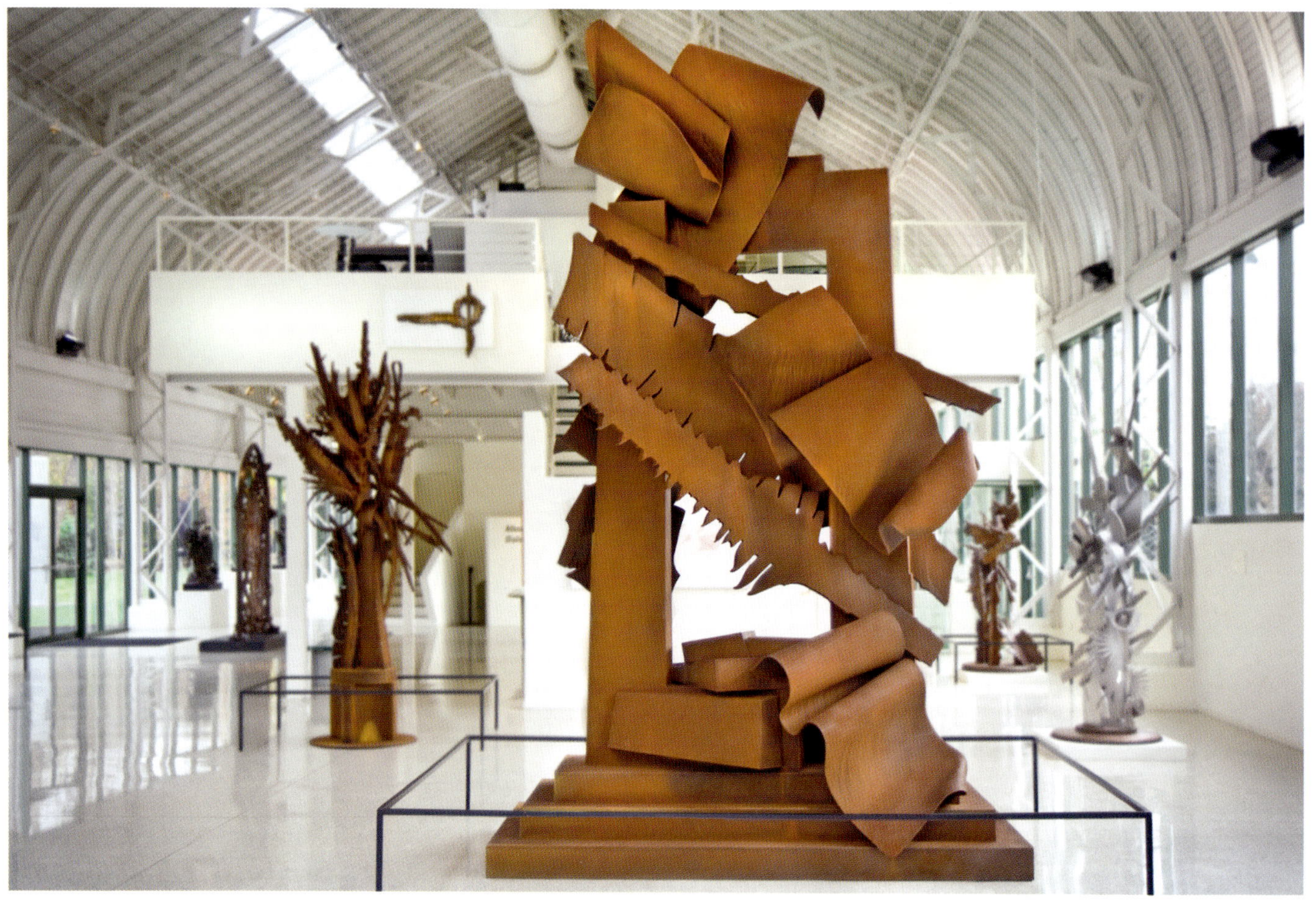

Proscenium, 2009
Formed and fabricated weathering steel, 13'10" x 8'8" x 4'3"
Albert Paley, Grounds for Sculpture Exhibition, Hamilton, New Jersey

art, I am drawn to other cultures and sculpture traditions such as seen in Angkor Watt and Machu Picchu, Oceanic and Celtic art, and particularly and most obviously in European Art Nouveau, which I have collected in depth. Another obvious influence is the complexity, dissonance, and paradox of Baroque art.

In this information age an incredibly broad range of history envelopes us. In my home I have an extensive library that supports my various avenues of exploration around art history.

P.S. *I see your art as located between the public allure and panache of Dale Chihuly's installations and the iconic power and weight of Mark di Suvero's monumental sculpture.*

A.P. I understand your comparisons. My work, even to me, is a highly complex amalgam. Its specific ingredients and their quantities are deeply relevant to me but probably irrelevant to the experience of the viewer.

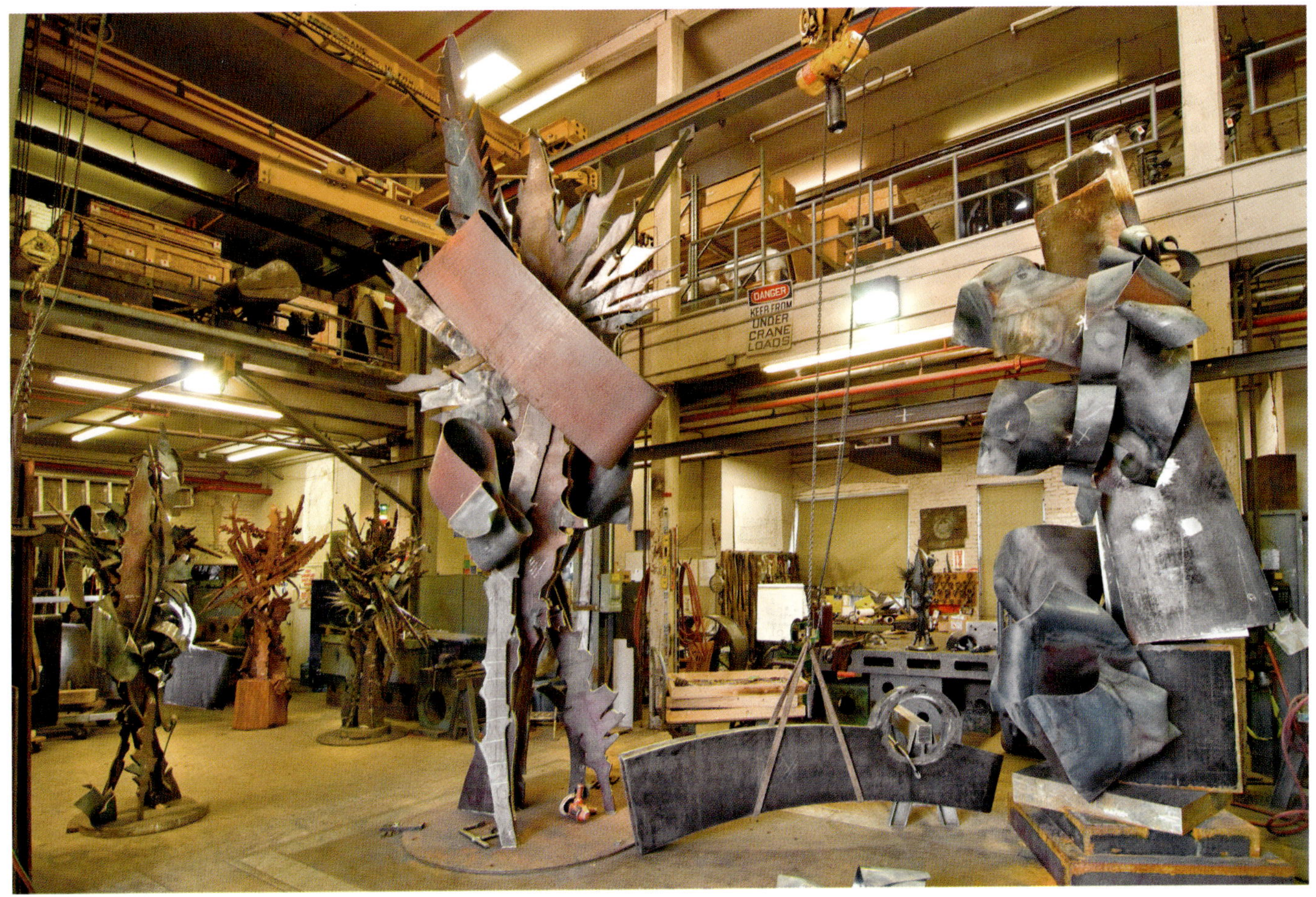

Sculpture fabrication, Paley Studios
Lyell Avenue, Rochester, New York

P.S. *Your current studio in Rochester definitely reminds me of Dale Chihuly's mammoth hotshop in Seattle and his similar capacity – with a dedicated cadre of artisan fabricators – to create almost staggering amounts of art that can be intimate or huge and traverse seamlessly from craft to art. Specifically, the opulent appeal and baroque functionality of his chandeliers has a clear kinship with the bravado of your sinuous gates, tables, and lamps.*

A.P. I have visited Dale in Seattle and seen his studio spaces. In the context of large studio environments and the high demand for our art there is a connection between us. But my gates and decorative arts starting in the 1970s are a relatively small part of my studio's activities. My artistic efforts now are directed to making large-scale public sculptures.

P.S. *You and your work were described by Edward Lucie-Smith, whom I consider your most penetrating and thoughtful chronicler, as "the American maker who has most successfully straddled the related fields of fine art and craft". Do you think that statement still applies to you?*

A.P. For some reason my work has seemed to reside between the cleavage planes of culture and has been difficult for others to categorize. Before my involvement in jewelry I carved wood and stone within the figurative tradition. When I became involved with ironwork, it was at that time a dormant 19th century medium and aesthetic. Forging iron-fences, gates, and various architectural elements allowed me to increase the scale and thus embrace and interact with architecture.

P.S. Can you speak about your use of color and mixing metals, which became a more defining aspect of your work after 1990?

A.P. Three-dimensional forms emerge more emphatically when color is added. Color inserts an emotional dimension to form. The play of shadow and color together enrich the complexity of the form. Color however changes balance and composition by its expansive or recessive quality – as well as by its emotional context. As with Picasso's blue period, he wanted the viewer to feel – his imagery and color were inseparable. Three-dimensional form without color deals with the concrete nature of form in space, as soon as color is added, it, like music, releases emotion.

P.S. *Overall the aesthetic of your work seems to be an additive rather than a reductive one.*

A.P. That is true. Rather than eliminating elements to arrive at a singular statement or elemental form, I create a context that hopefully brings ambiguity into equilibrium and fuse ssynergy and tension. I compare this process to the distinct but integral processes of composing and performing music.

P.S. *Your work has been well documented in many texts and catalogues. What do you feel that writers about you and your work have missed?*

A.P. So many writers have said to me, "I just can't get a handle on you. I can't figure where you fit in." That seems to be the overriding concern that I don't seem to align with any particular school or signature philosophy. Even for me it is not an easy explanation. My experience is within a wide spectrum of opposites. My activities might be separately categorized however it all originates from a singular history and vision: seeking new experience coupled with the persistence of past knowledge. Bringing my invisible realities and sensibilities into tangible forms has been the basis of my activities.
Recently I have started writing poetry. It is another way of probing that reality. Language that everybody fundamentally understands is perceived as concrete, then in a poetic context can convey a perception and understanding that is totally different.
As I have already said, working on thirteen major sculptures in a two year period was a totally demanding and exhilarating experience for the studio and me. The Park Avenue series was approached with an urgency that it mandated more pre-planning, organization, and quick decision making than anything I have faced thus far in my life as an artist.

The sculpture *Progression* is sited at the end of the median mall between the International Style modernist icon of Seagram Building and the restrained façade of the New York Racquet Club. Its composition was based on a collage I made from the parts of one of my lithographs. The title refers to the evolution from drawing to print to collage to sculpture, as well the visual cause and affect of its elongated and interrelated forms. This is the most horizontal sculpture I have ever made. I sought to translate the ceaseless movement of New York City in an almost Futurist way. Resting upon a contrasting CorTen base, its formal unity is further accentuated by the play of light and shadow across its white surface.

Between the Shadows is the only piece that's polychromed. Made of CorTen its yellow and blue color sections are of intersecting vertical planes. I used these colors to intensify the slicing of its forms and complicate the interplay of light and shade and the slicing of its forms.

Reflection, at the 54th Street intersection, is fabricated of stainless steel. The title refers to the luminosity play and the way its material both mirrors and abstracts its surroundings.

Encore, is on the south end of the 57th Street intersection. It is made of stainless steel and Cor-ten. Painted red, *Jester* is installed across from it on the north side of 57th Street.
There is a simpler, unfolding, and gestural quality to it. In this busy intersection of commerce starting to give way to the upper, residential Park Avenue, I sought a sense of celebration and drama both in the way the pieces are composed and how they establish a relationship and subtly reach out to one another across 57th Street. They are quite distinct and were conceived as separate pieces, but I see them as complementary opposites. *Encore* is both lyrical and compressed, folding into itself. *Jester* is angular, jagged, and active. Its circle of empty space finds a match in the ovoid loop at the top of *Encore*.

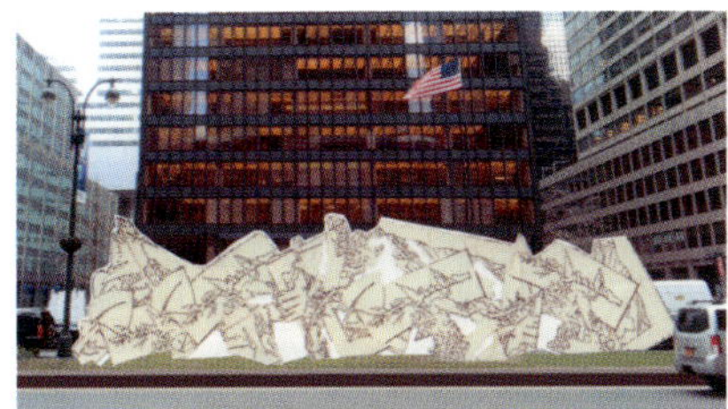

Progression

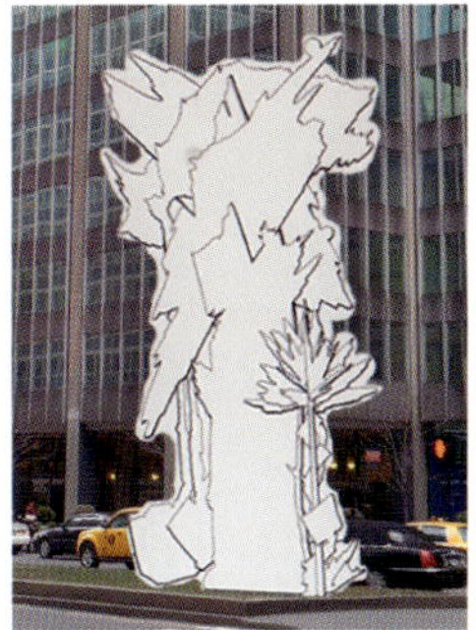

Between the Shadows

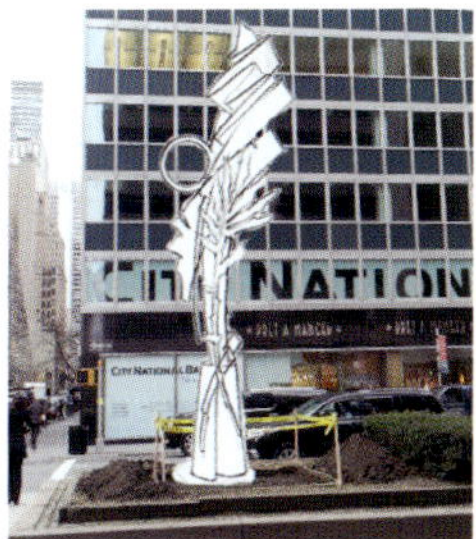

Reflection

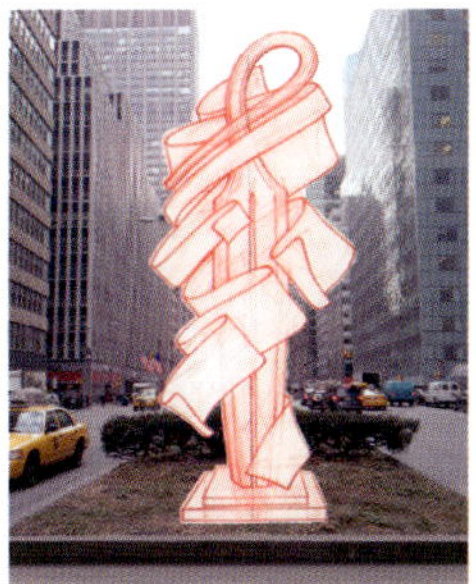

Encore

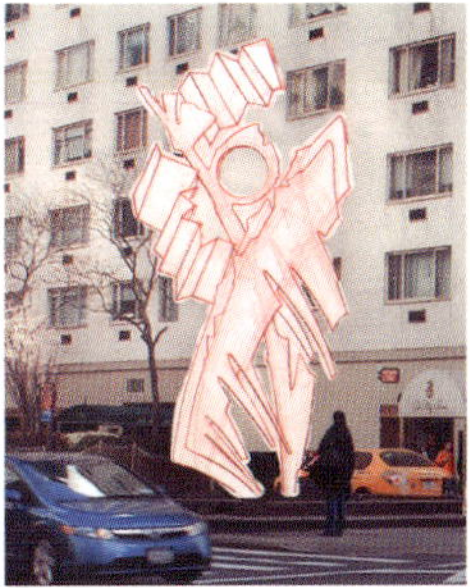

Jester

Counter Balance at 58th Street is unified by its CorTen patina. The composition is for me the most balanced of the thirteen pieces with its fusion of curvilinear and geometric forms. I wanted with this work to establish equilibrium among disparate elements.

Variance, located at 59th Street, is composed of many tightly massed and interwoven lengthy elements. I wanted the lightness of the stainless steel defy its physicality and create a staccato interplay of delicate elements. It rests upon a wedged geometric base.

Tilted Column, on corner of 60th Street, deals with another mode of balance and gesture. I envisioned that this broken and tilted column and its folded metal shapes defy gravity and remain erect, held together by the cascading ribbons of steel.

Ambiguous Response was placed at 61st Street. Long banners of steel wrap around its central telescoping shaft. The sculpture reaches out at the top across the street towards *Cloaked Intention*.

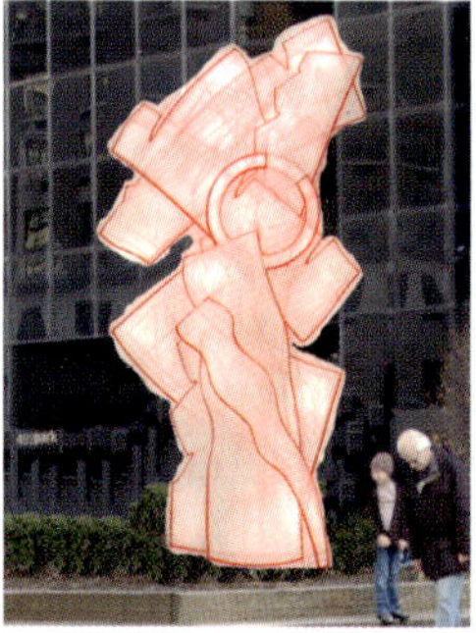

Counter Balance

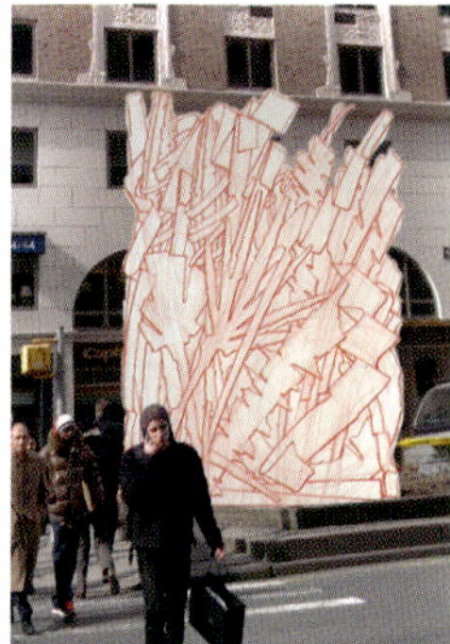

Variance

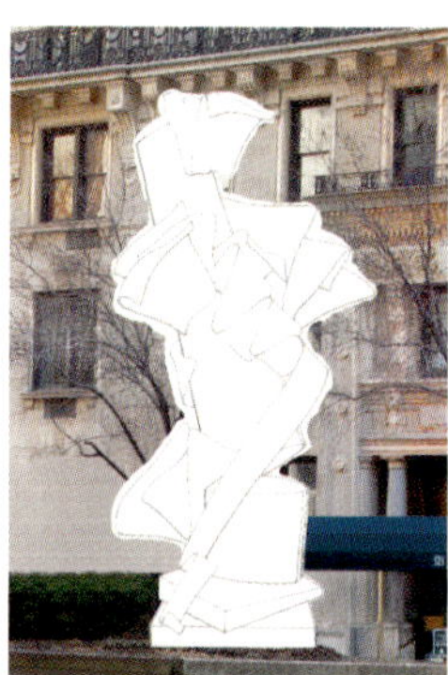

Tilted Column

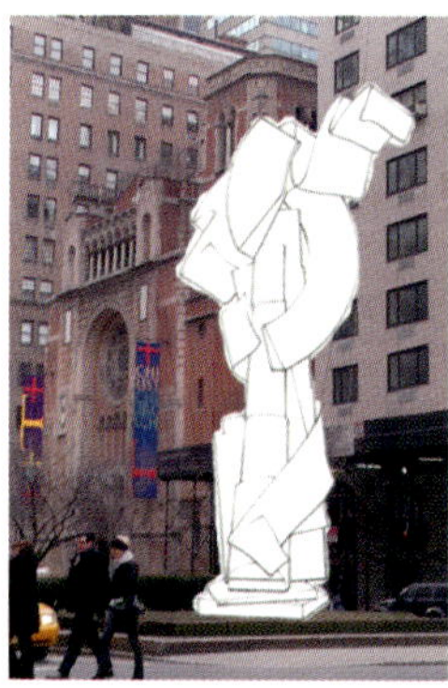

Ambiguous Response

Cloaked Intention also has folded metal ribbons of steel; that gesture towards *Ambiguous Response* across the 61st Street intersection. I see these two works as forming a ceremonial archway.

Positioned in the middle of the mall between 63rd and 64th Streets, *Composed Presence* is seen against a trio of distinctively shorter buildings; the Central Presbyterian Church, an apartment building, and the Third Church of Christ, Scientist. Painted red, *Composed Presence*, is the smallest and most compact work in the series. It folds into itself and does not, unlike all the other works in the series, extend into space.

The two sculptures on 66th and 67th Streets, *Languorous Repose* and *Envious Composure* flank the Park Avenue Armory. The work on 66th, *Languorous Repose,* is stainless steel. As with *Encore* and *Ambiguous Response,* the geometric blocks it rests upon give way to the organic, curvilinear mélange of elements above. Placed on 67th Street, *Envious Composure* is the most lyrical of the sculptures, it wraps in upon itself in a glistening curvilinear cohesion of metallic bronze.

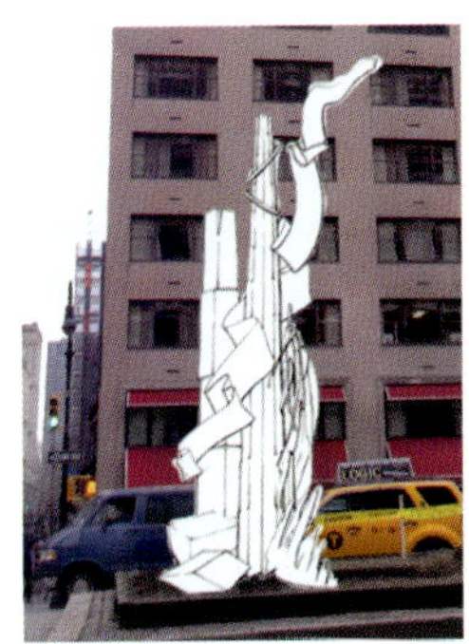

Cloaked Intention

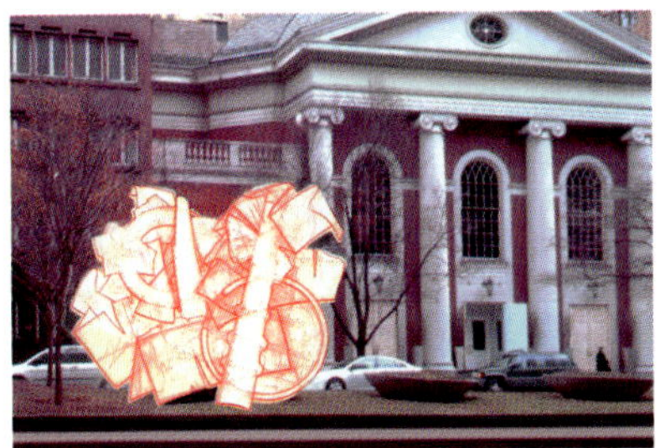

Composed Presence

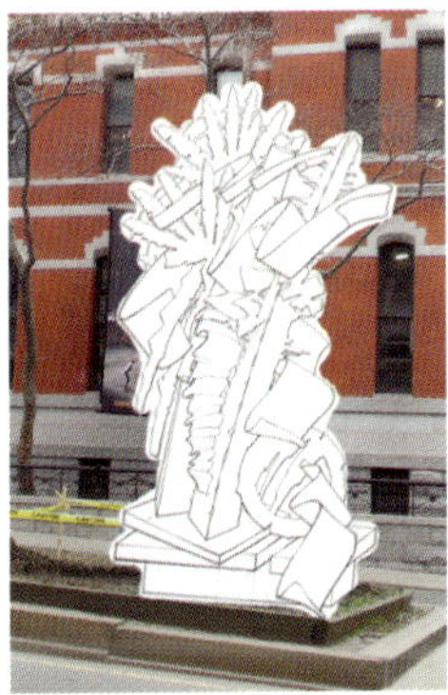

Languorous Repose

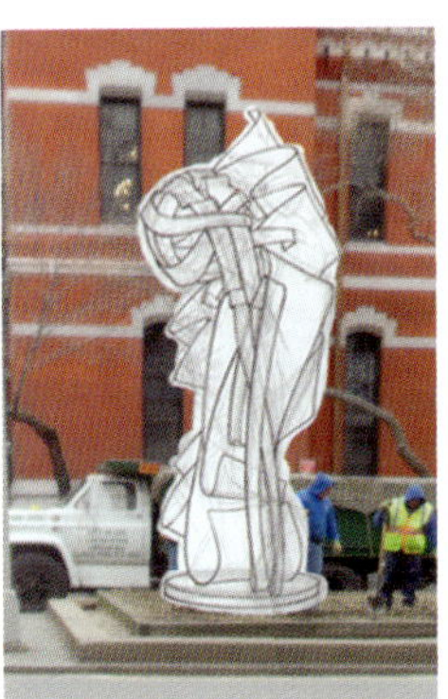

Envious Composure

Envious Composure   67th Street   ______________________

Languorous Repose   66th Street   ______________________

Composed Presence   64th Street   ______________________

Cloaked Intention   61st Street   ______________________

Ambiguous Response   61st Street   ______________________
Tilted Column   60th Street   ______________________

Variance   59th Street   ______________________

Counter Balance   58th Street   ______________________

Jester   57th Street   ______________________

Encore   57th Street   ______________________

Reflection   54th Street   ______________________

Between the Shadows   53rd Street   ______________________

Progression   52nd Street   ______________________

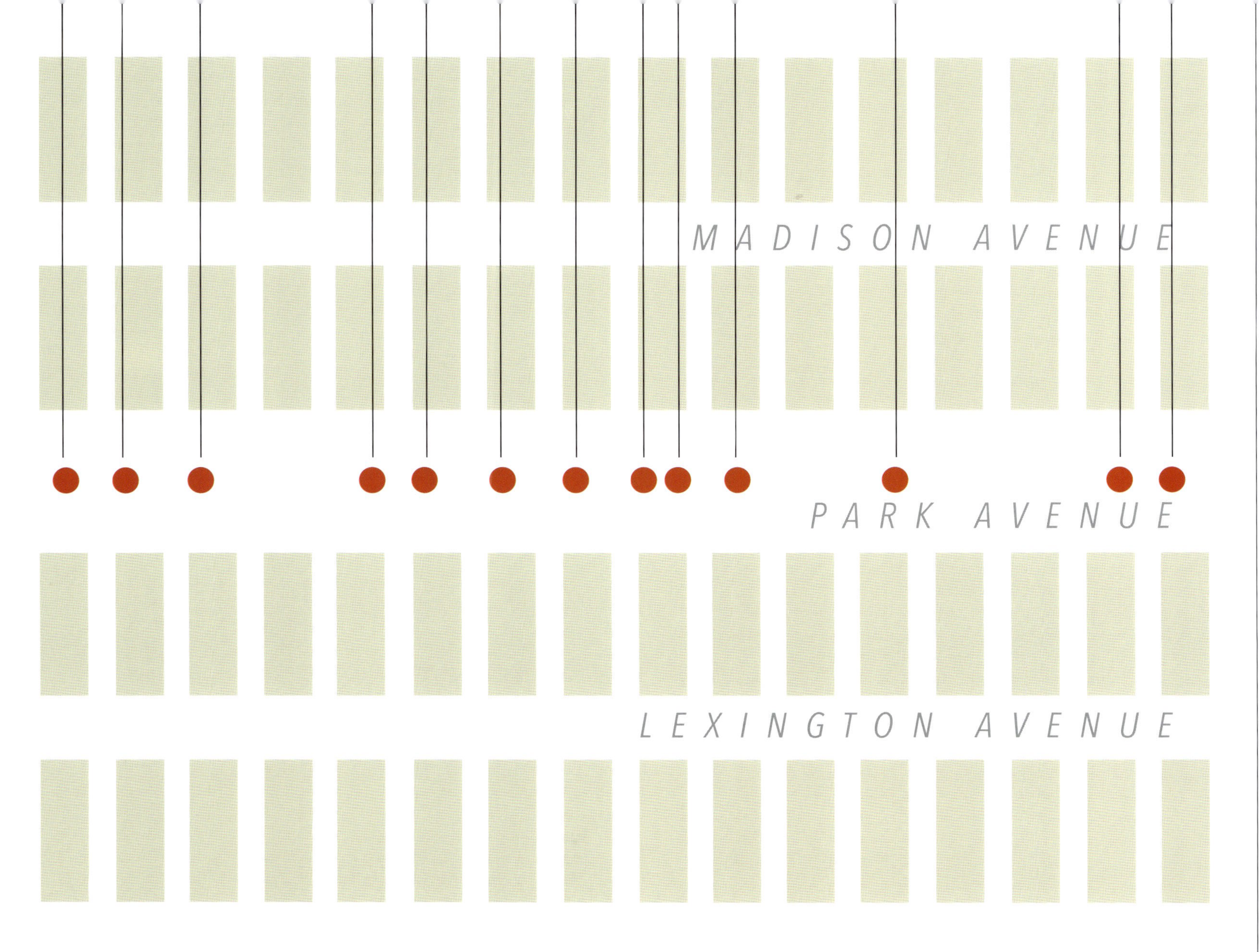

MADISON AVENUE
PARK AVENUE
LEXINGTON AVENUE

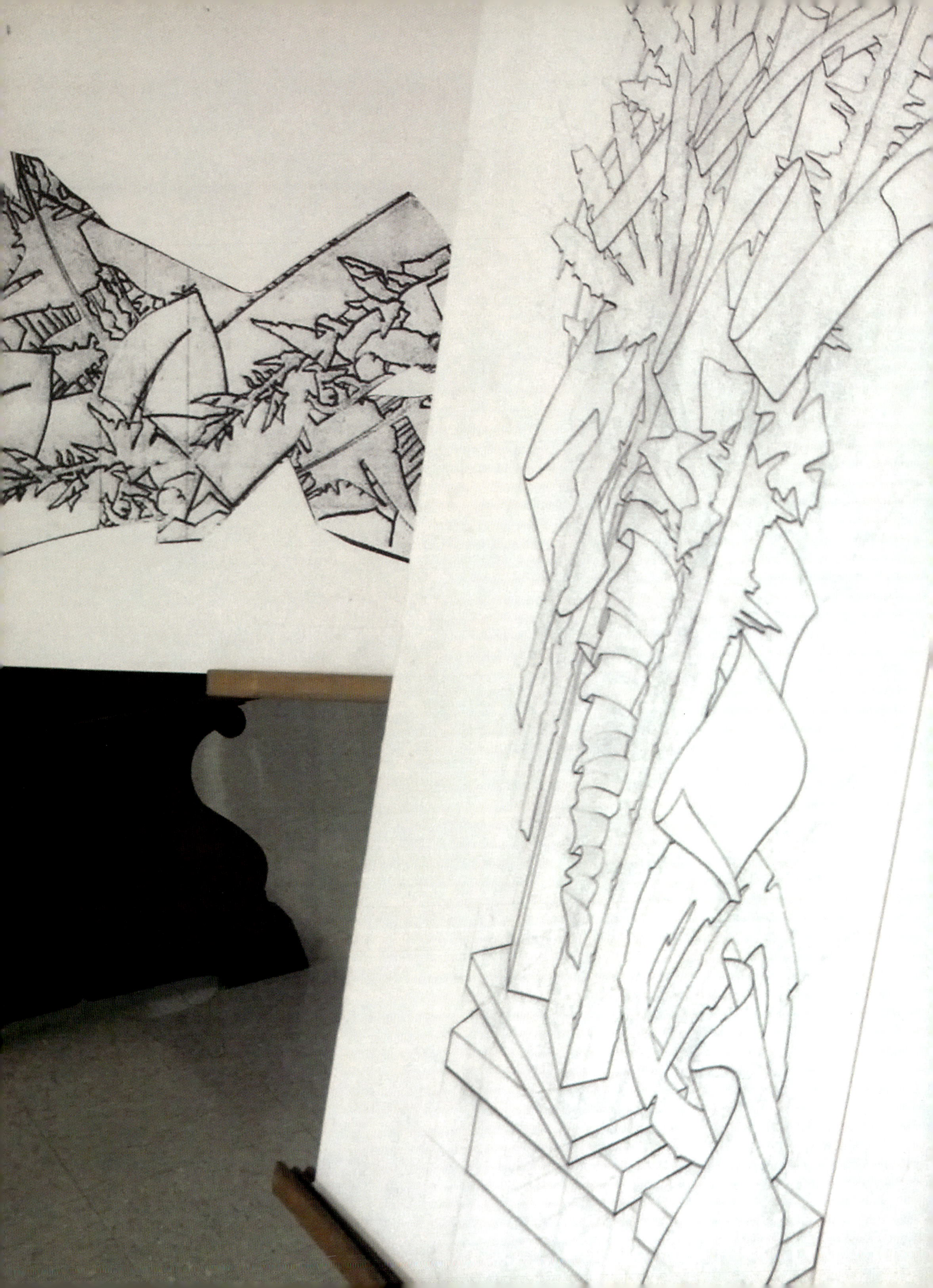

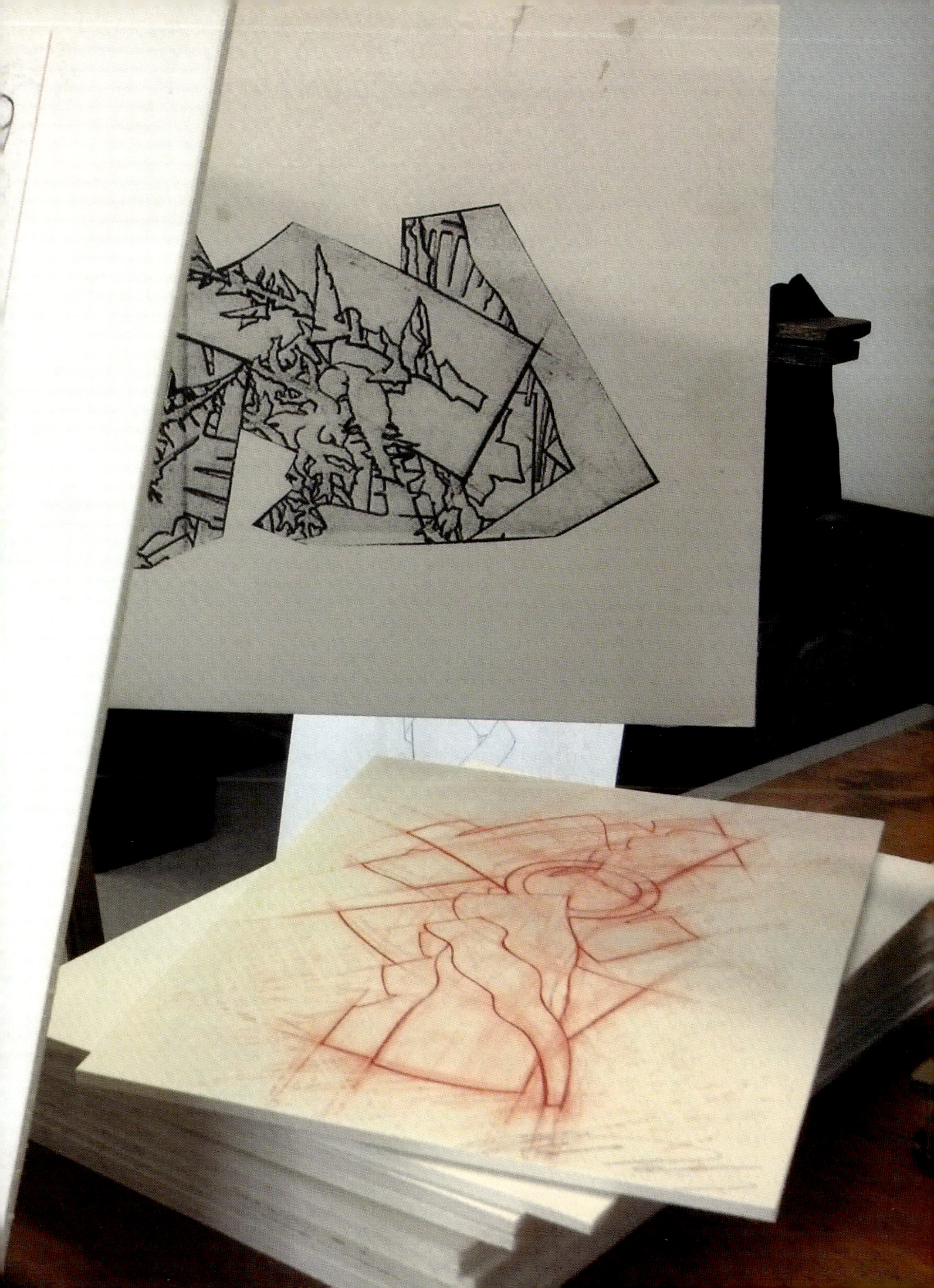

52ND
PROGRESSION

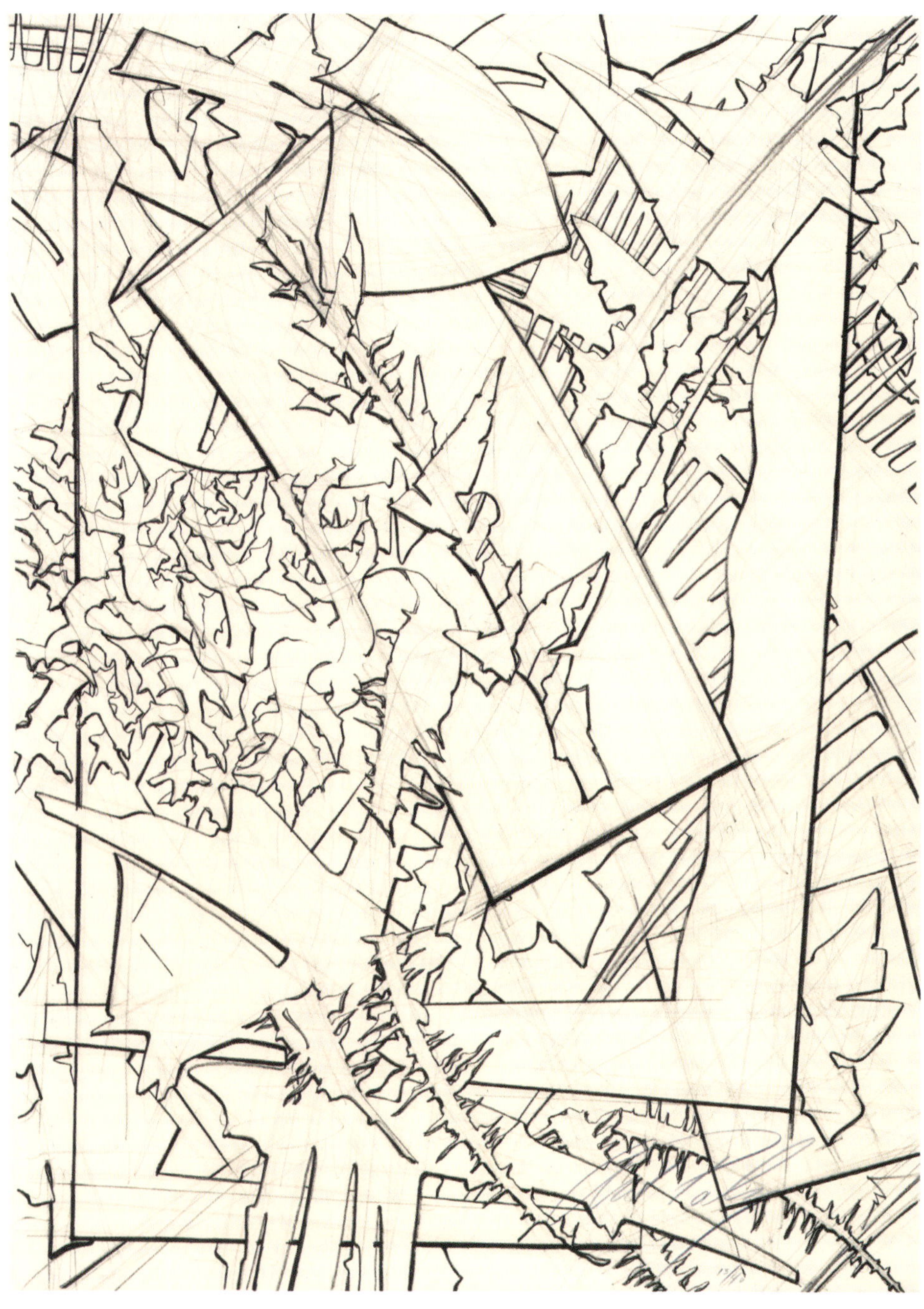

52nd Street – *Progression*
San Jose edition, 1999
Lithograph
29″ x 23″
Paley Studios Archive

Progression
Concept drawing
Graphite on paper
32″ x 50¾″
Paley Studios Archive

Progression
Photographic montage
10″ x 48″
Paley Studios Archive

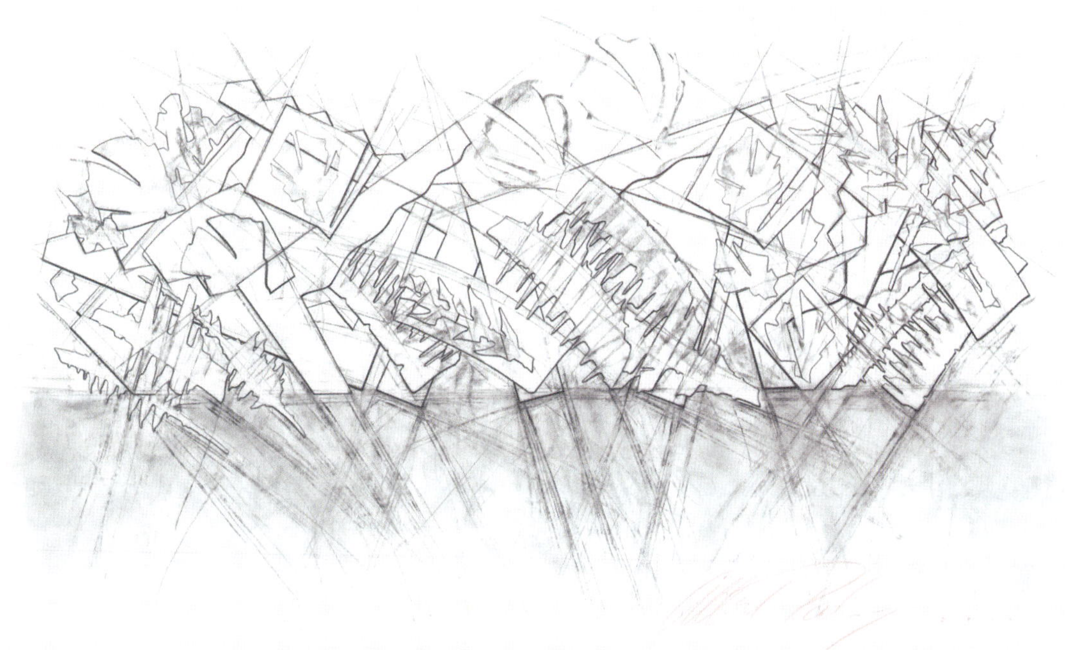

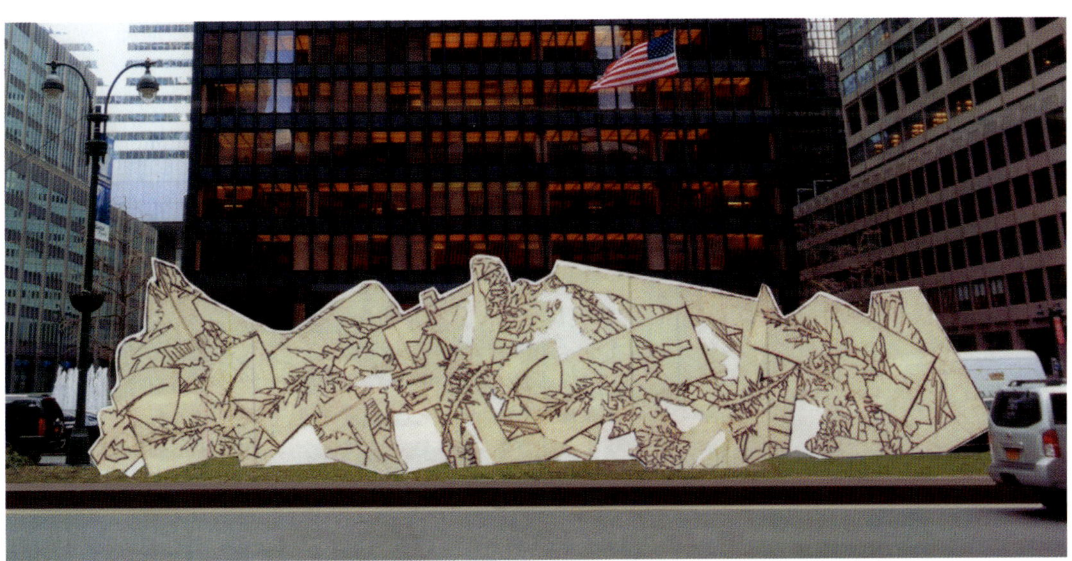

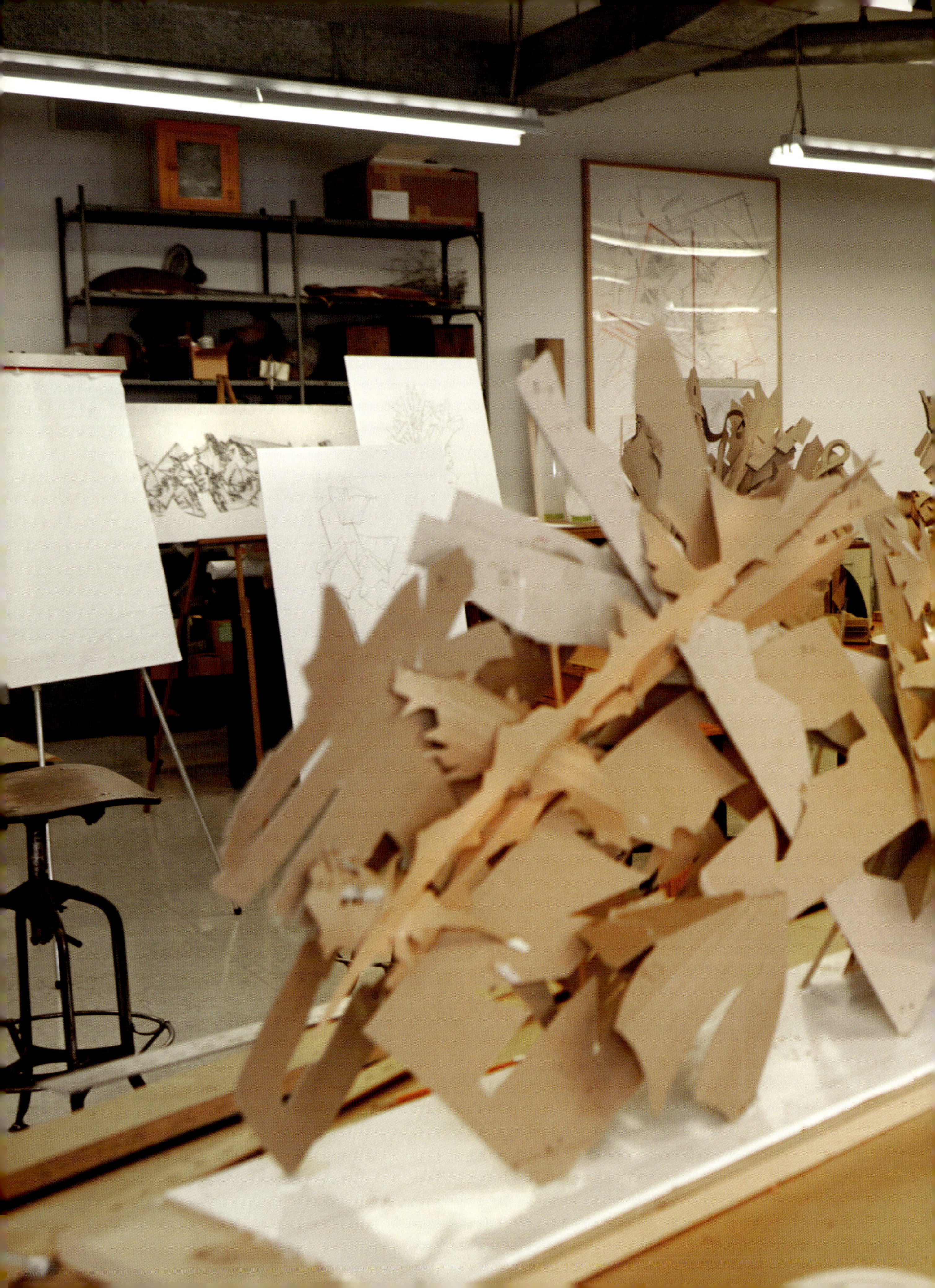

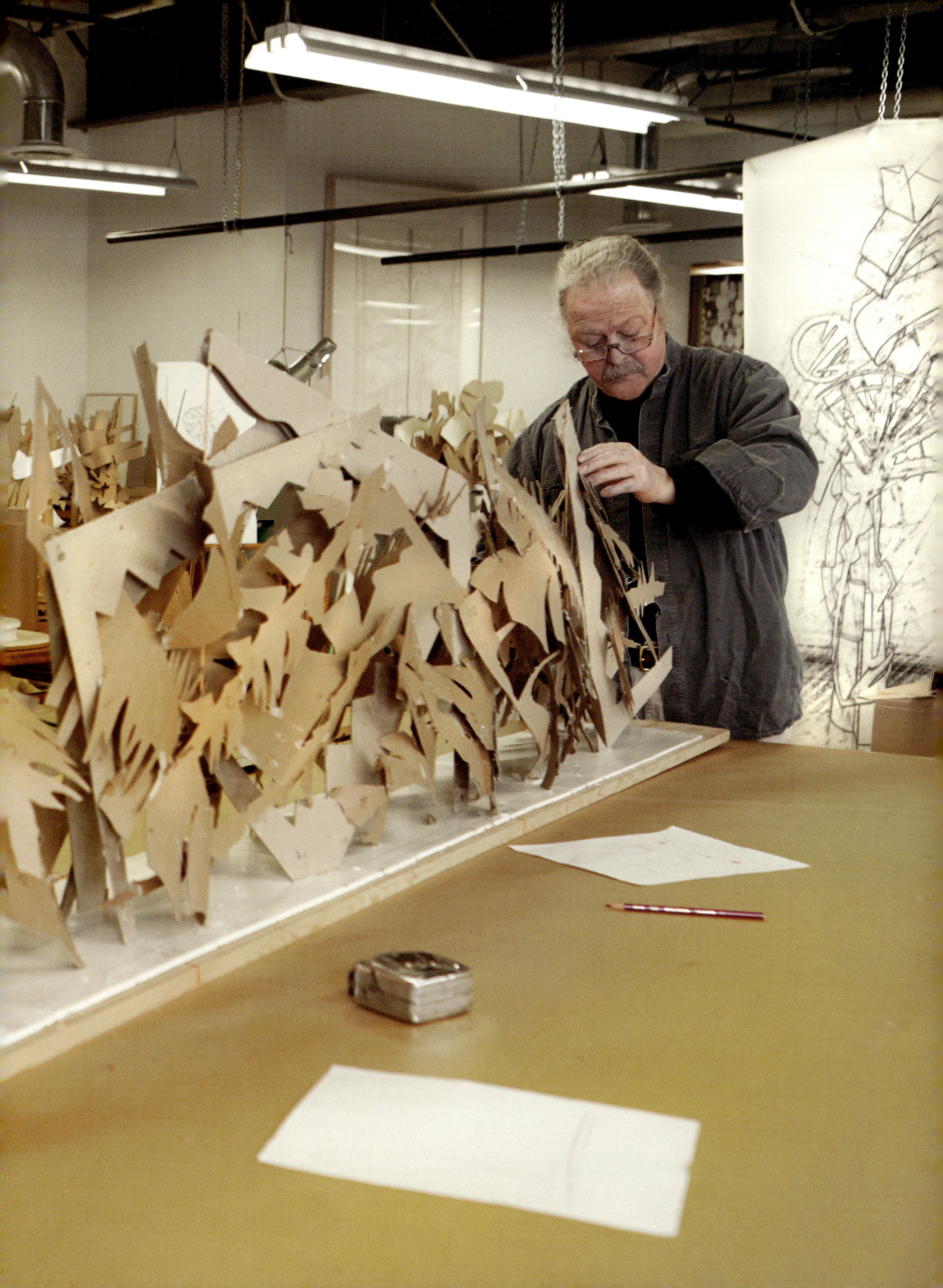

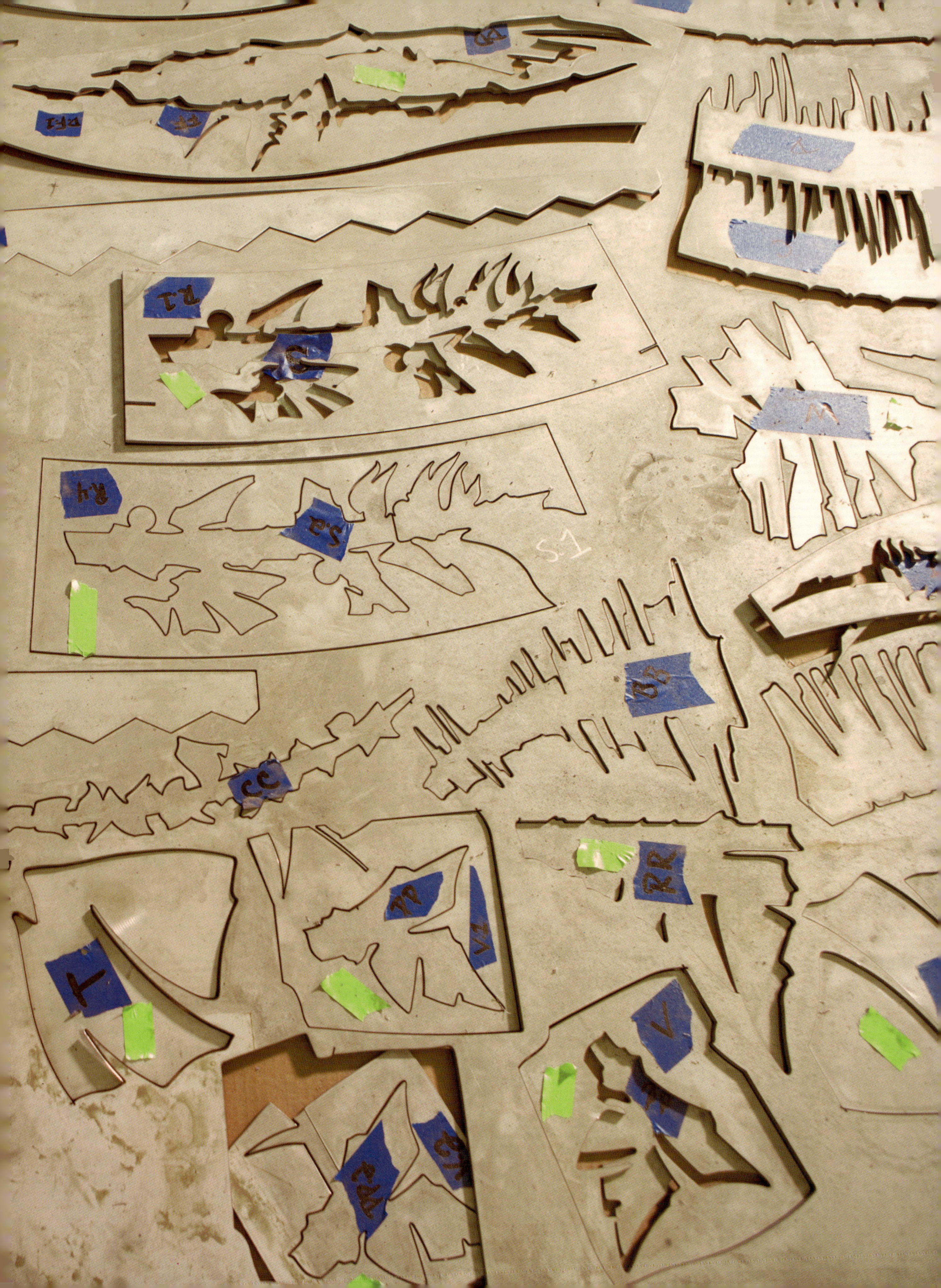

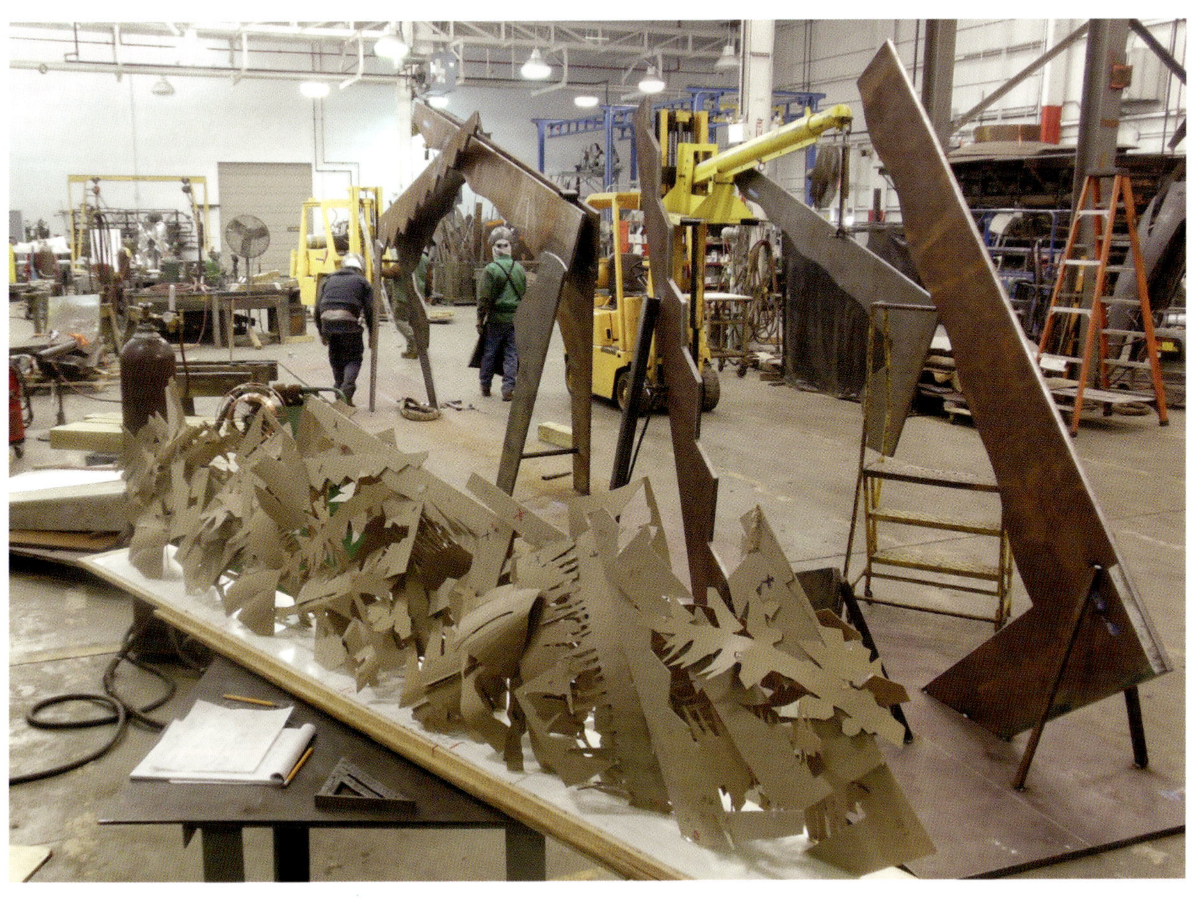

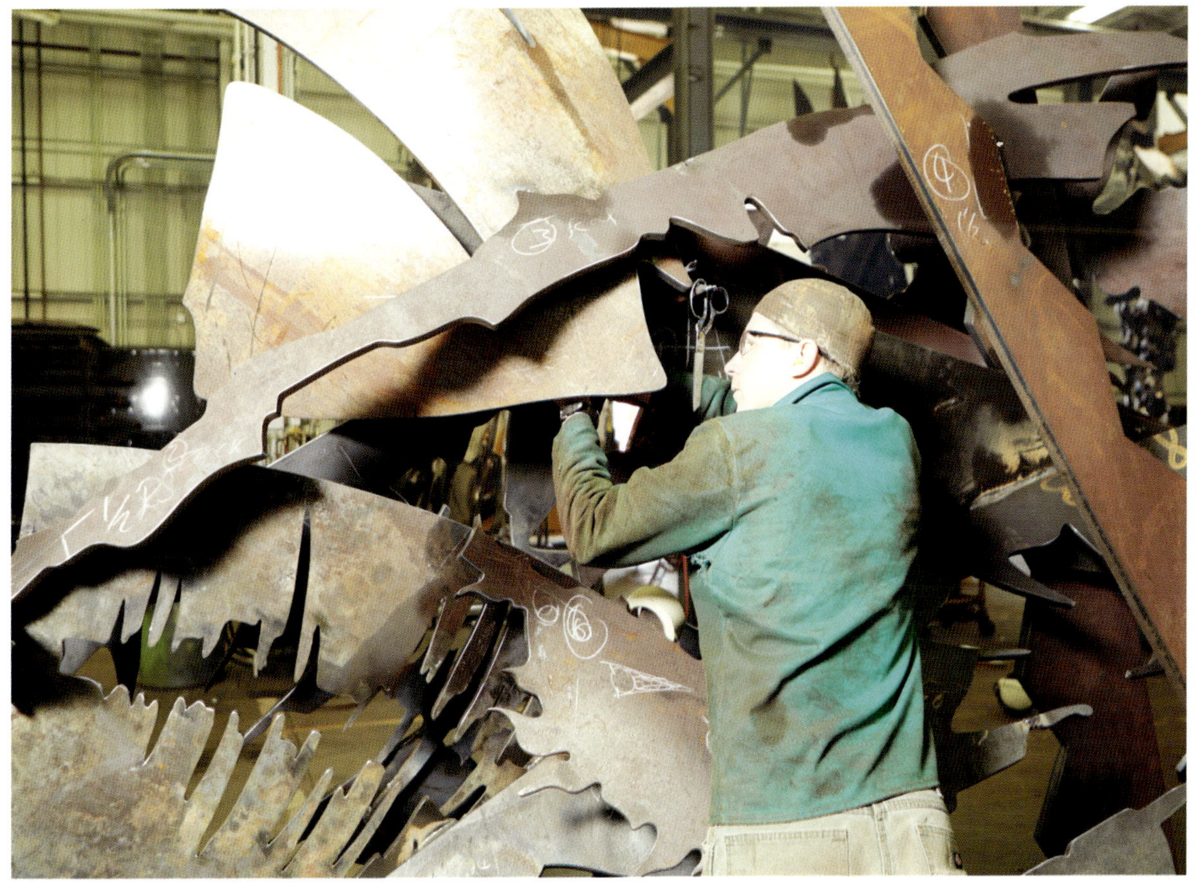

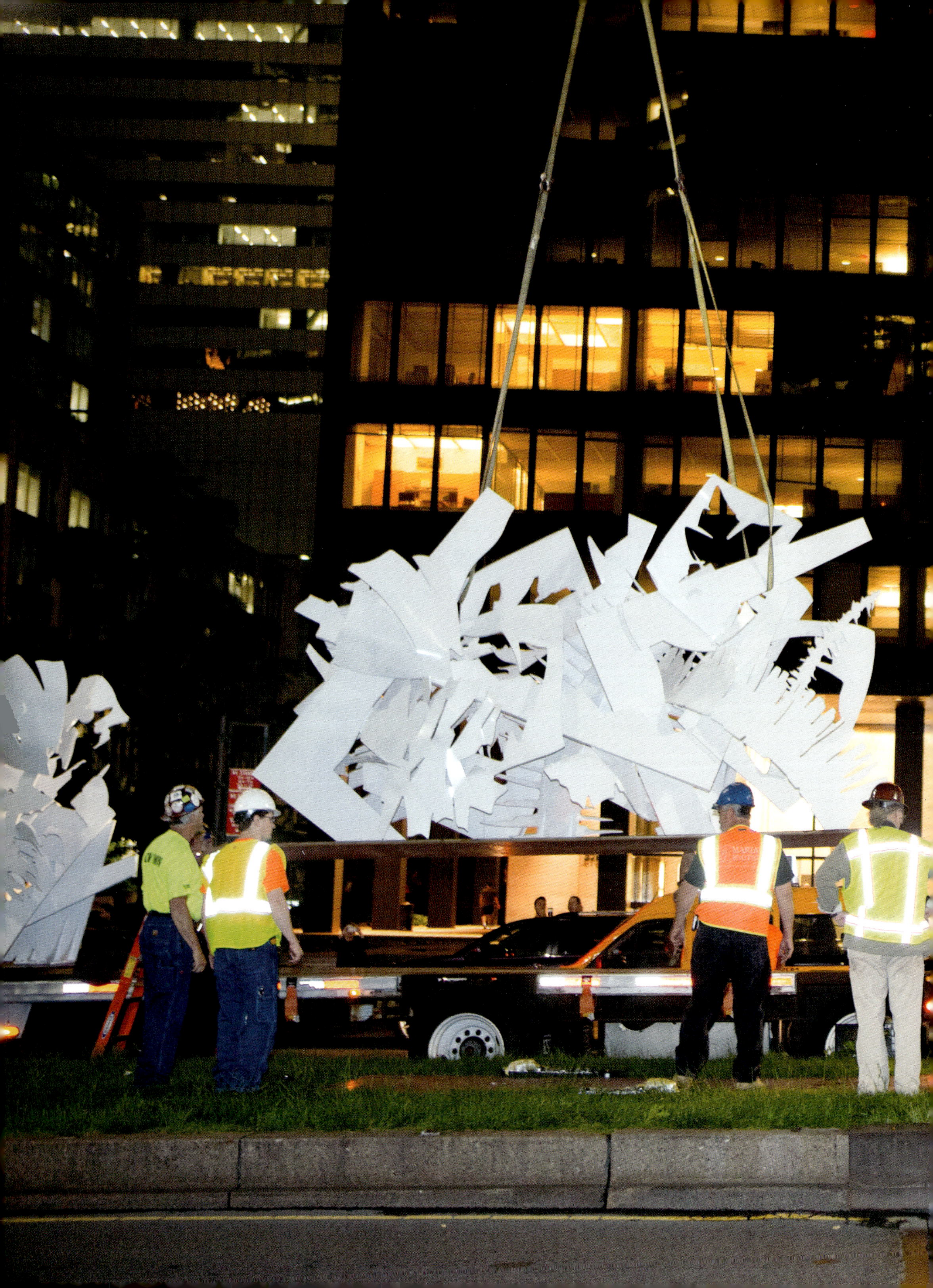

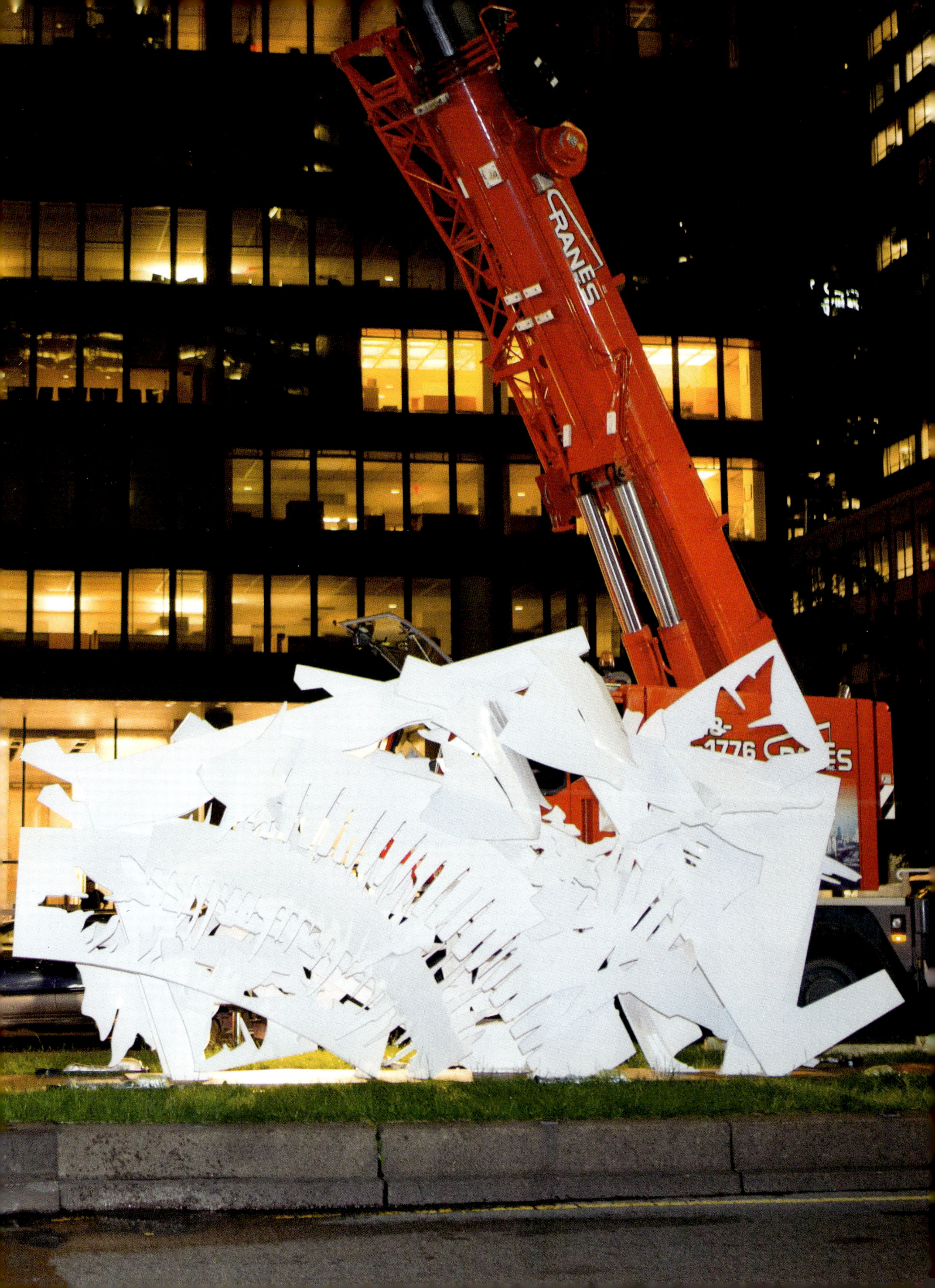
CRANES
CRANES
4776

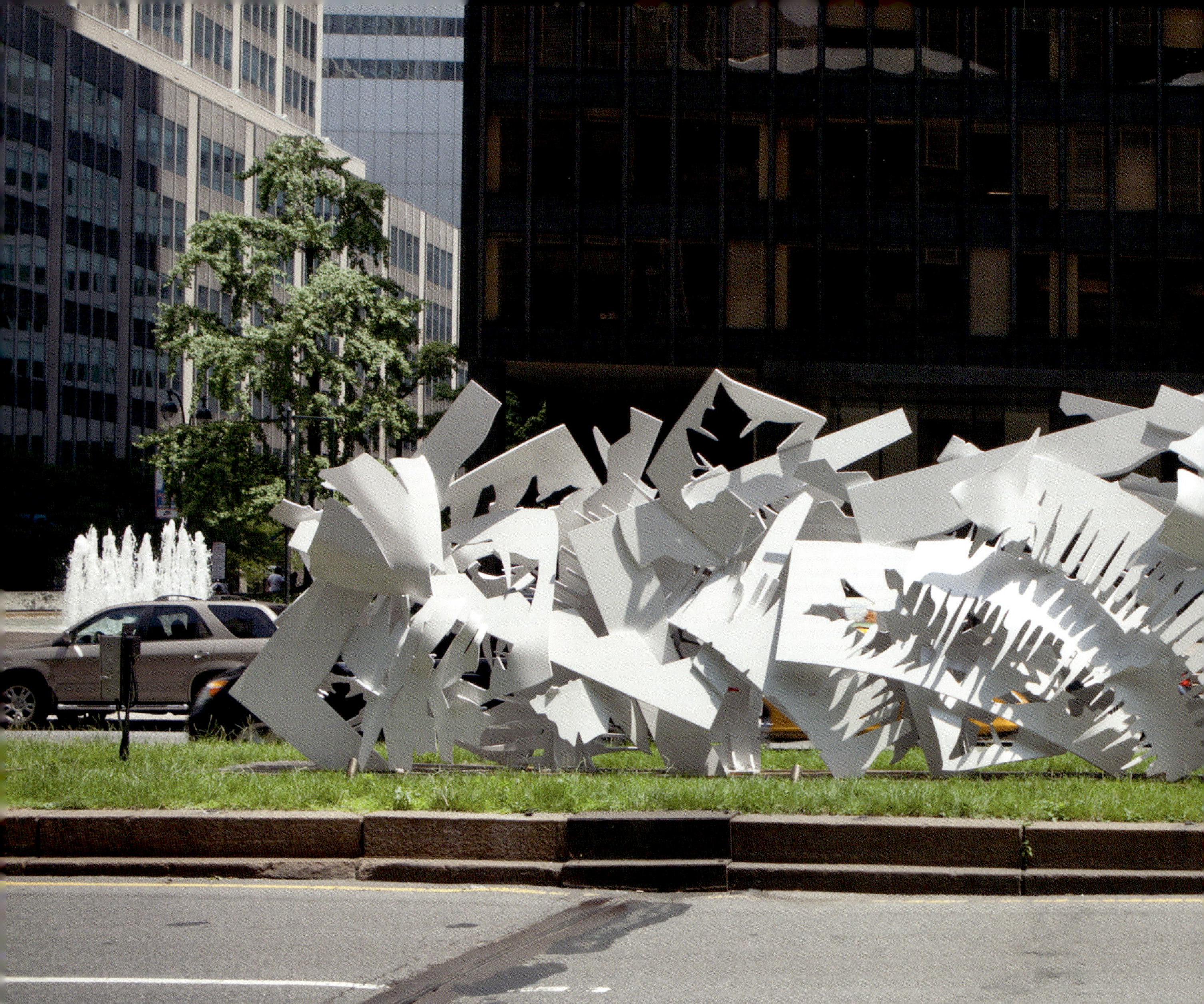

Progression, 2013
Formed and fabricated
painted steel with
weathering steel base
in three sections
9′4″ x 44′4½″ x 4′

pp. 36-37
Progression
Cardboard model
Paley Studios Archive

p. 38
Progression
Maquette
Laser-cut bronze
Paley Studios, Lyell Avenue
Rochester, New York

p. 39
Progression
Fabrication
Paley Studios, Lyell Avenue
Rochester, New York

pp. 40-41
Progression
Installation
52nd Street and Park
Avenue, New York,
June 14, 2013

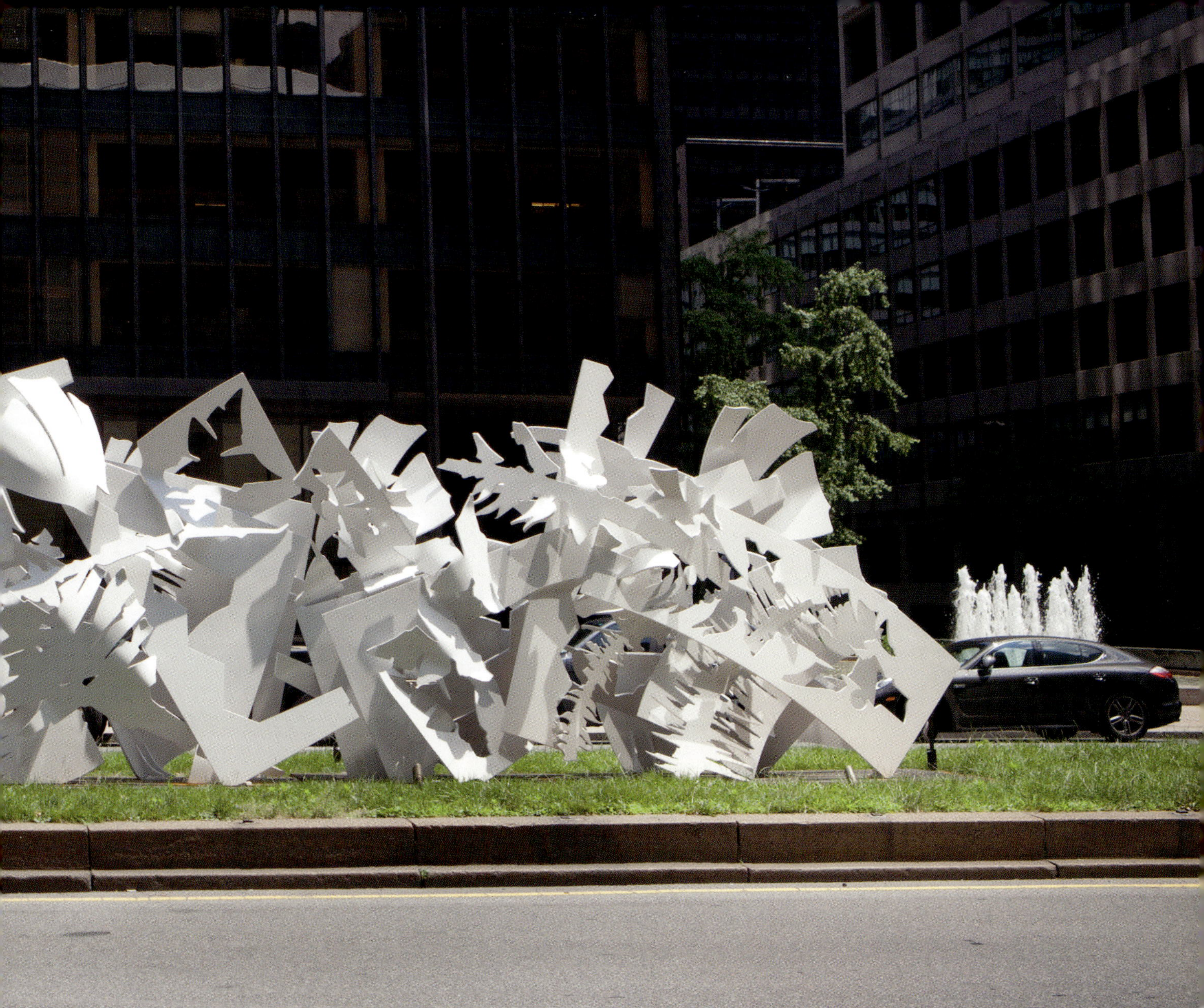

53RD
BETWEEN THE SHADOWS

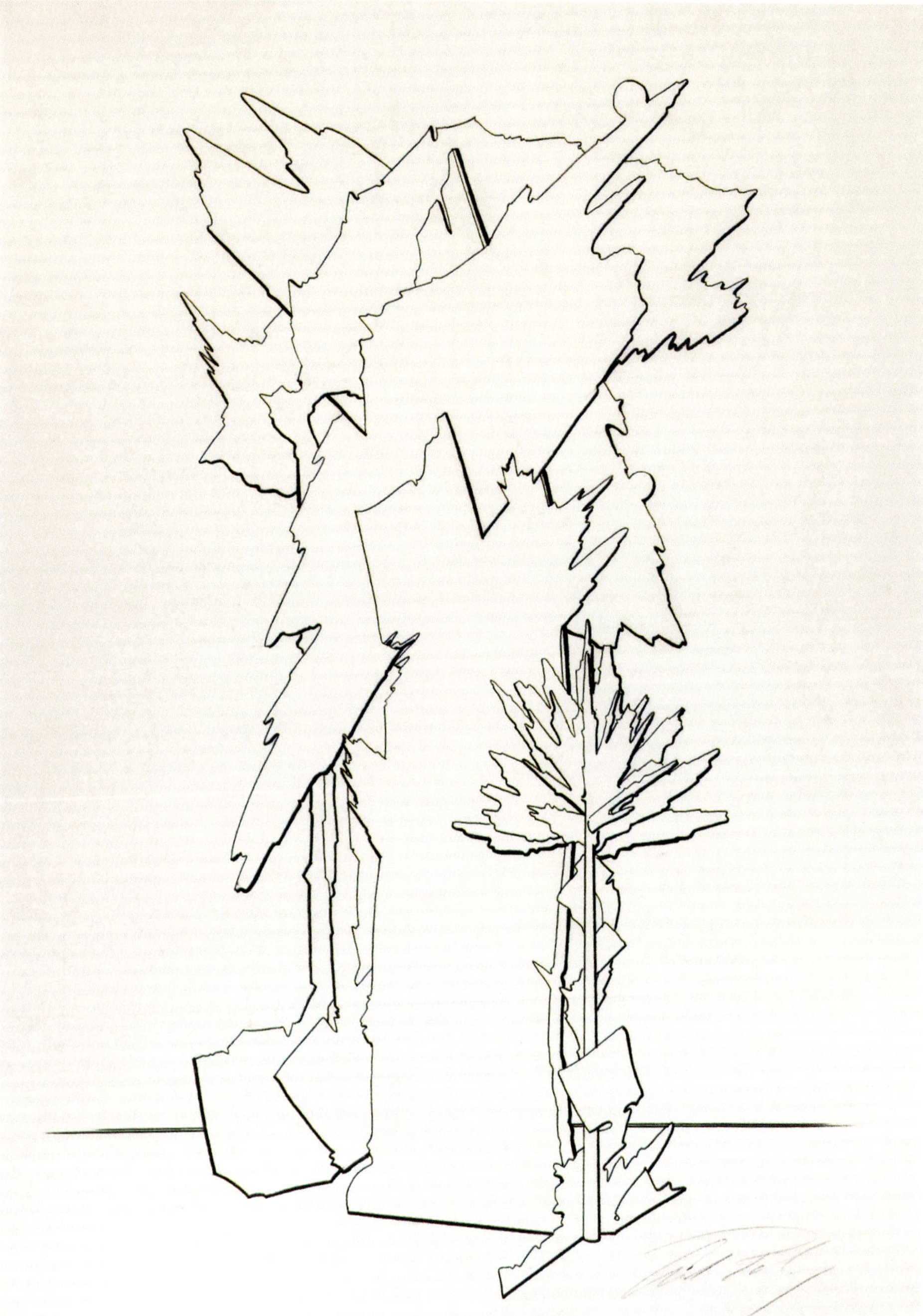

Between the Shadows
Concept drawing
Graphite on paper
30" x 22"
Paley Studios Archive

Between the Shadows
Photomontage
10" x 8"
Paley Studios Archive

Between the Shadows
Maquette
Formed and fabricated
patinated steel
with wood base
38¼" x 15" x 18"
Paley Studios Archive

pp. 46-47
Paley painting
Between the Shadows
Maple Grove Enterprises
Arcade, New York

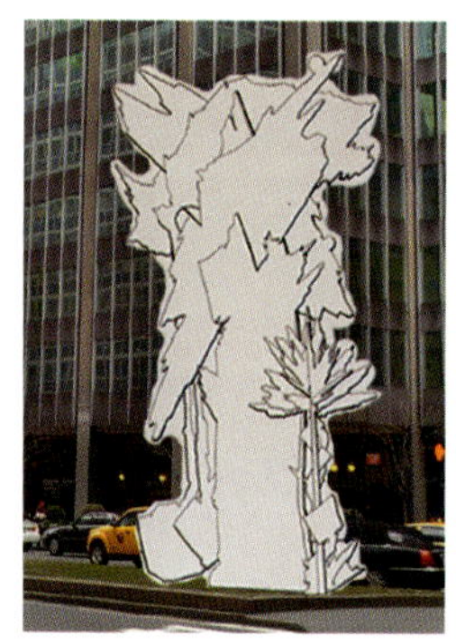

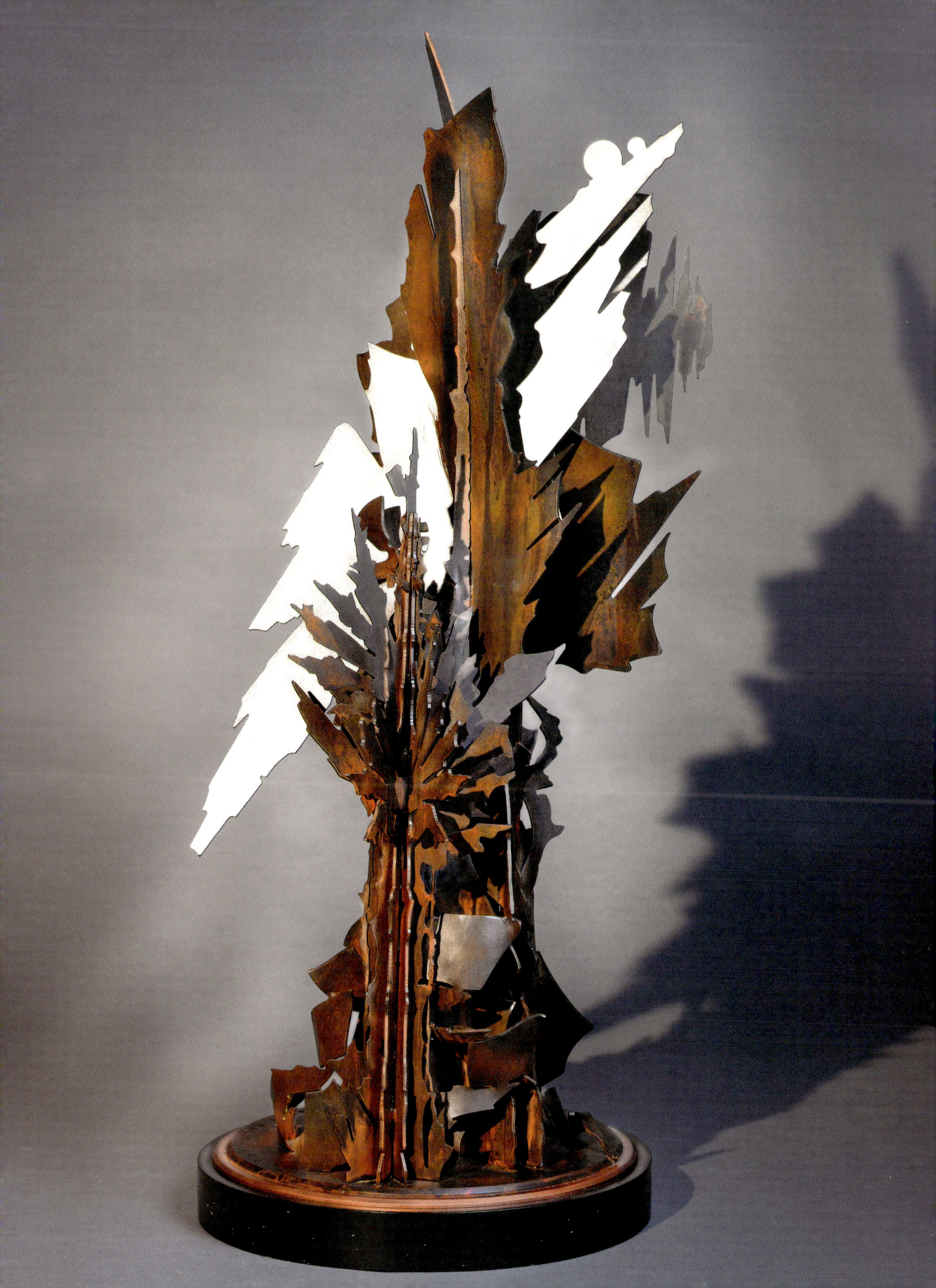

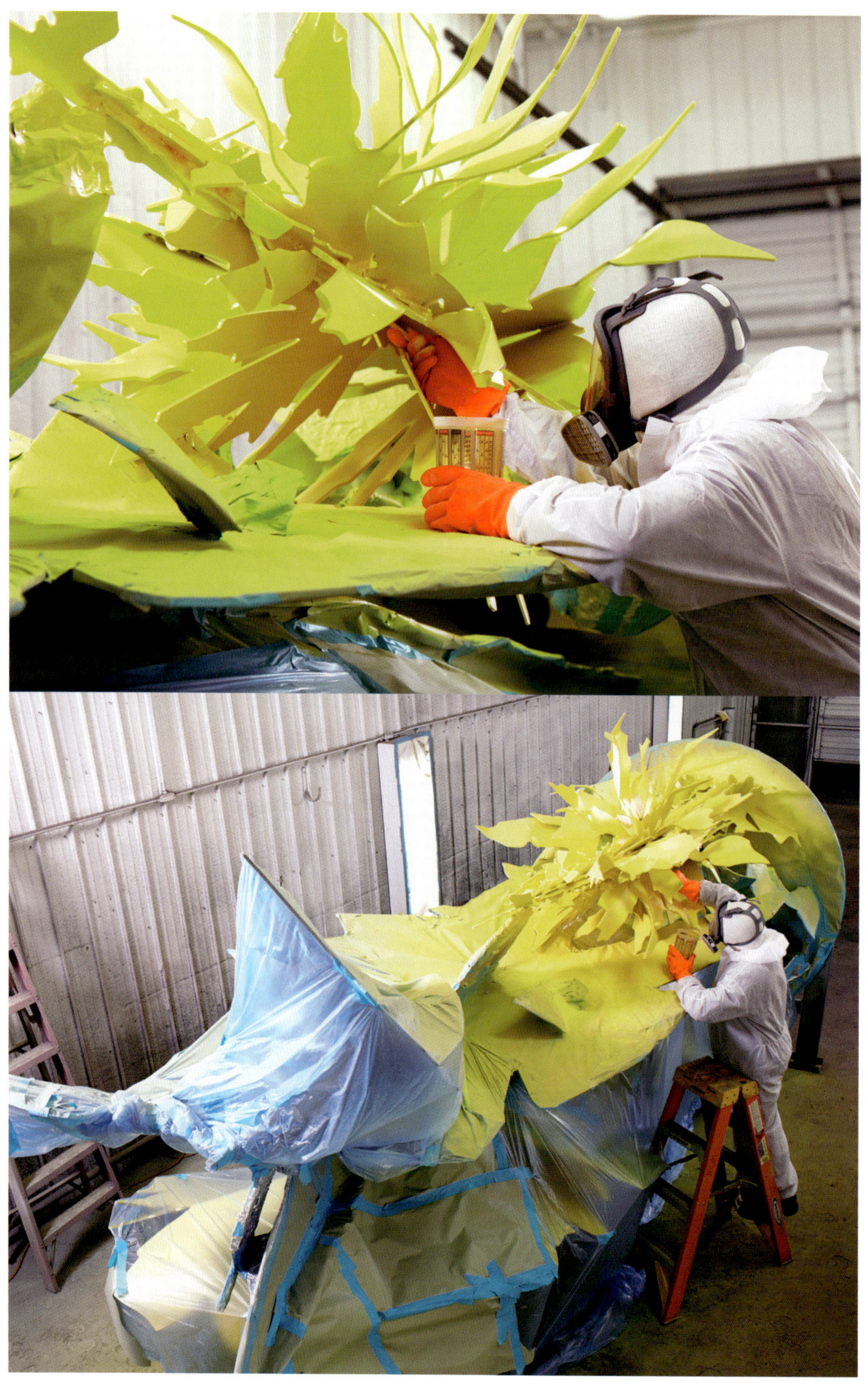

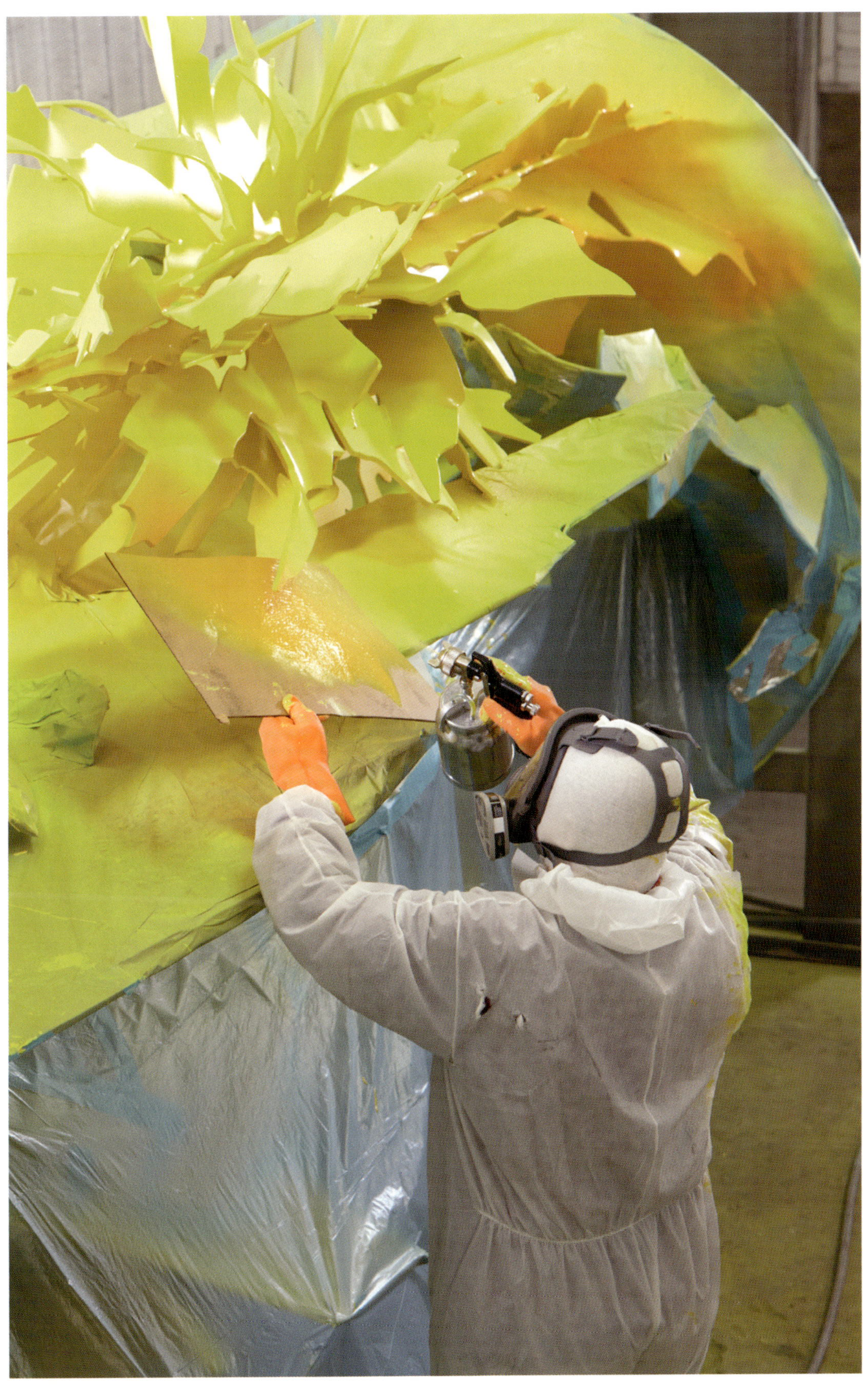

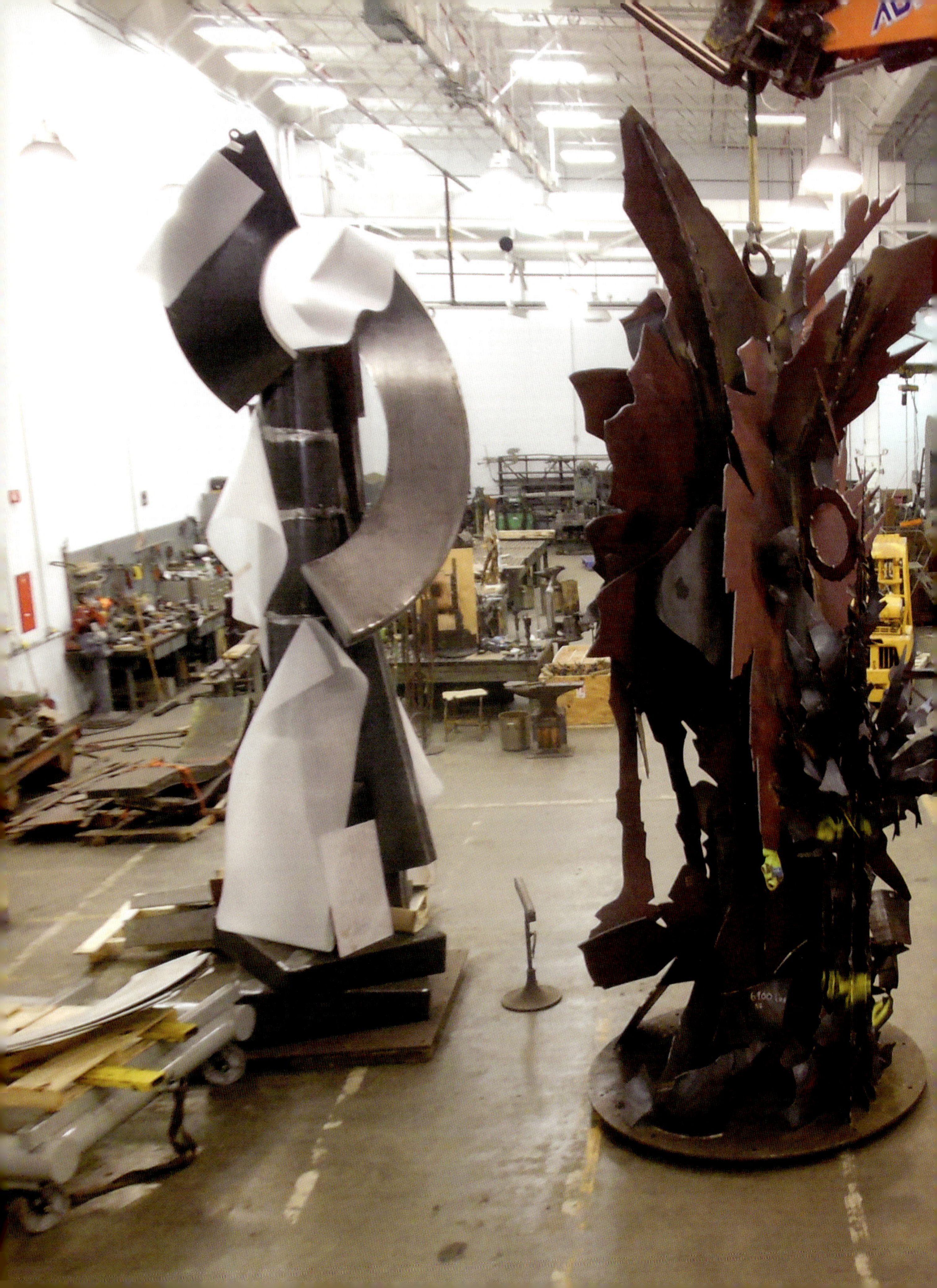

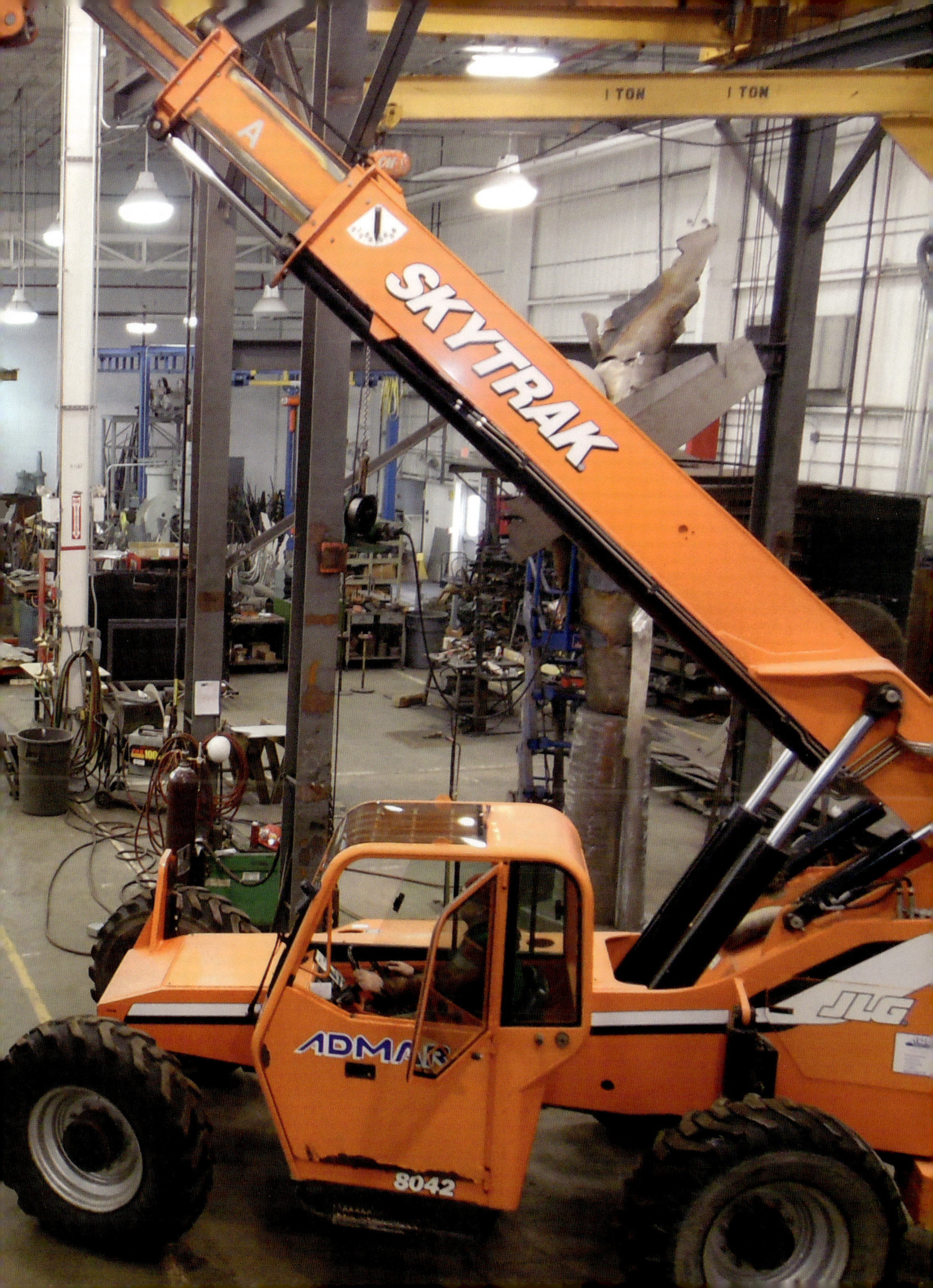
I TON
I TON
A
SKYTRAK
JLG
ADMAR
8042

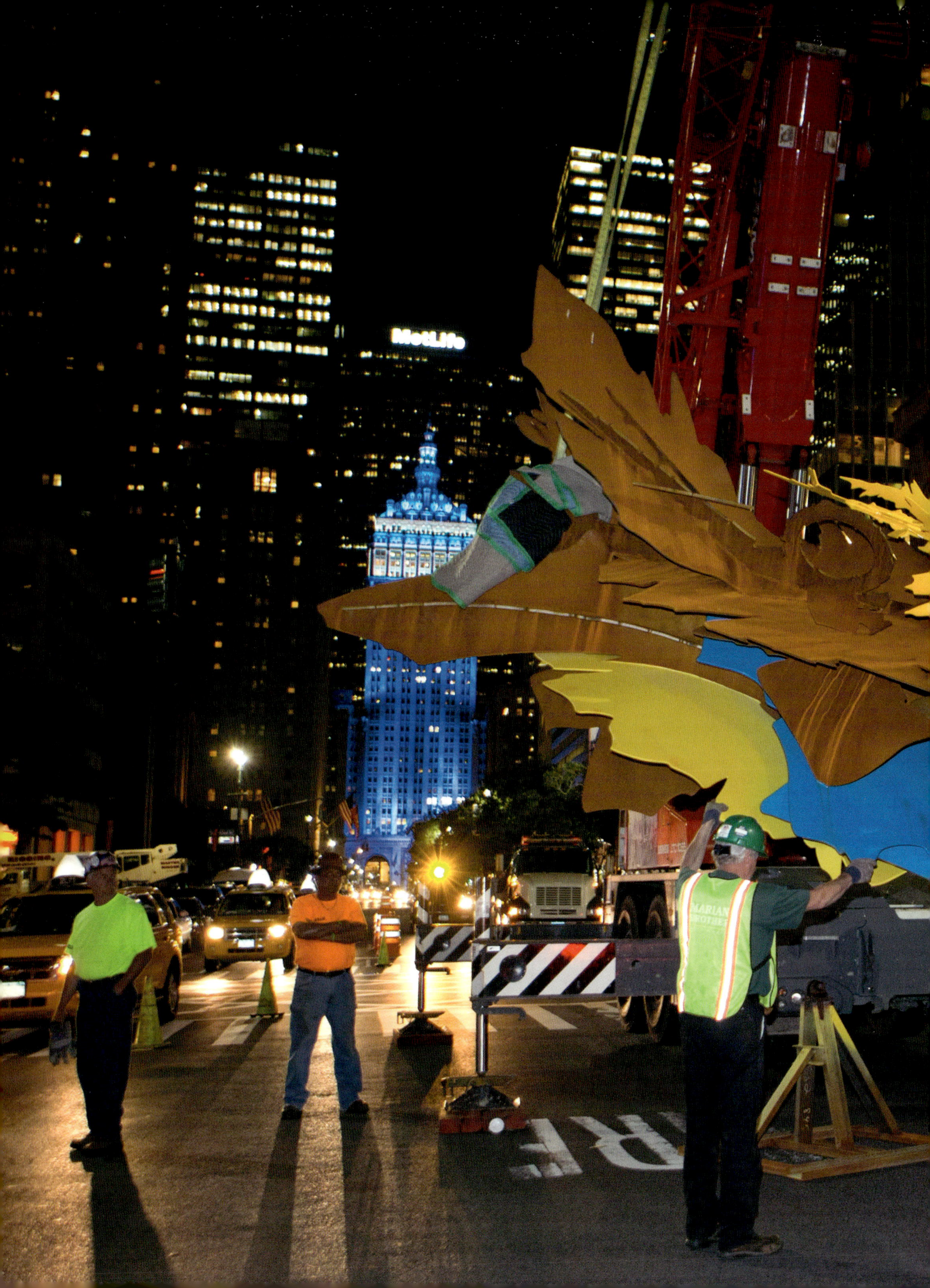
MetLife

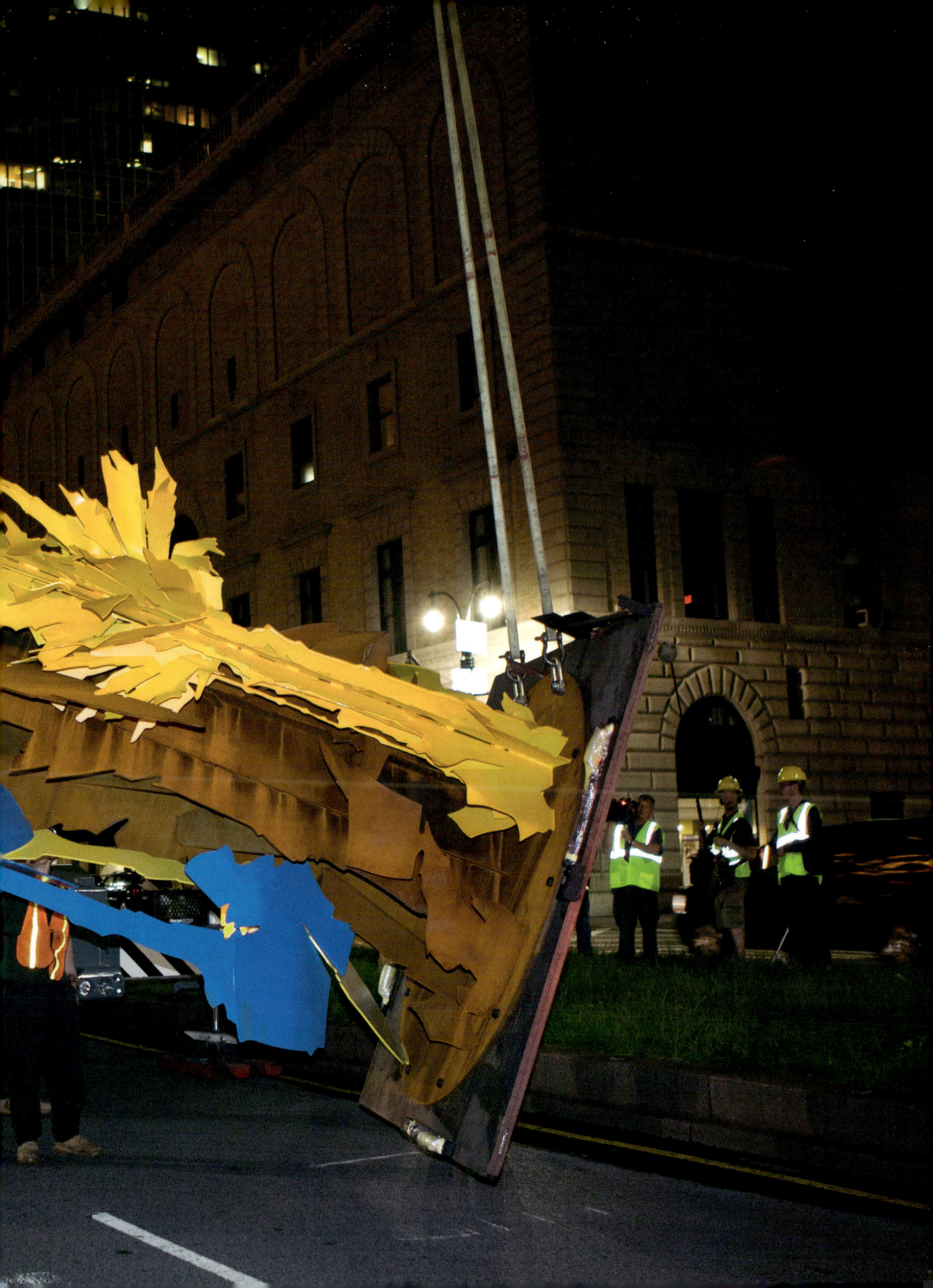

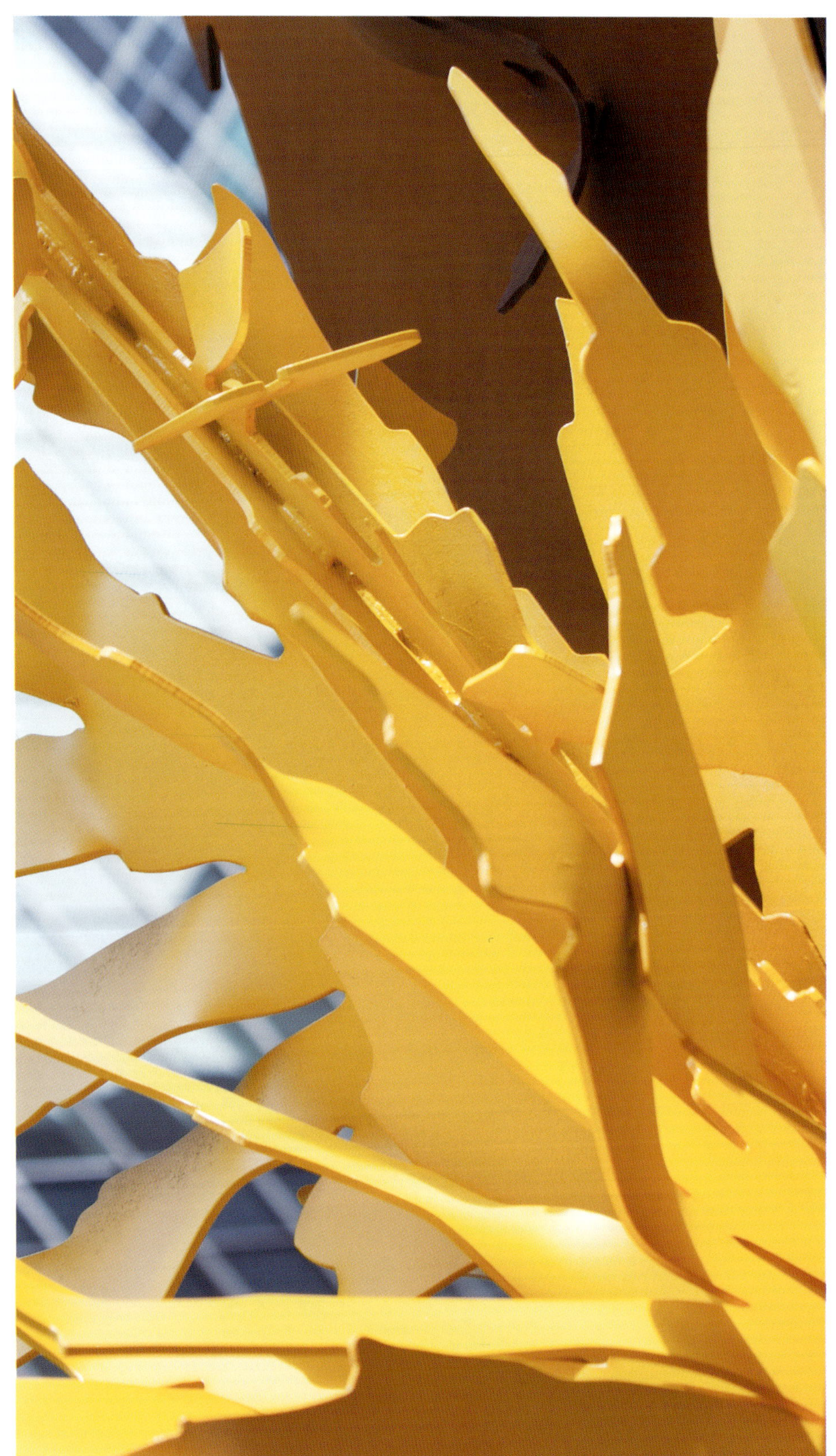

pp. 48-49
Between the Shadows
Fabrication

pp. 50-51
Between the Shadows
Installation
53rd Street and Park
Avenue, New York
June 14, 2013

left
Between the Shadows
Detail

p. 53
Between the Shadows, 2013
Formed and fabricated
painted and weathering
steel
18′5″ x 8′5″ dia.
53rd Street and Park
Avenue, New York

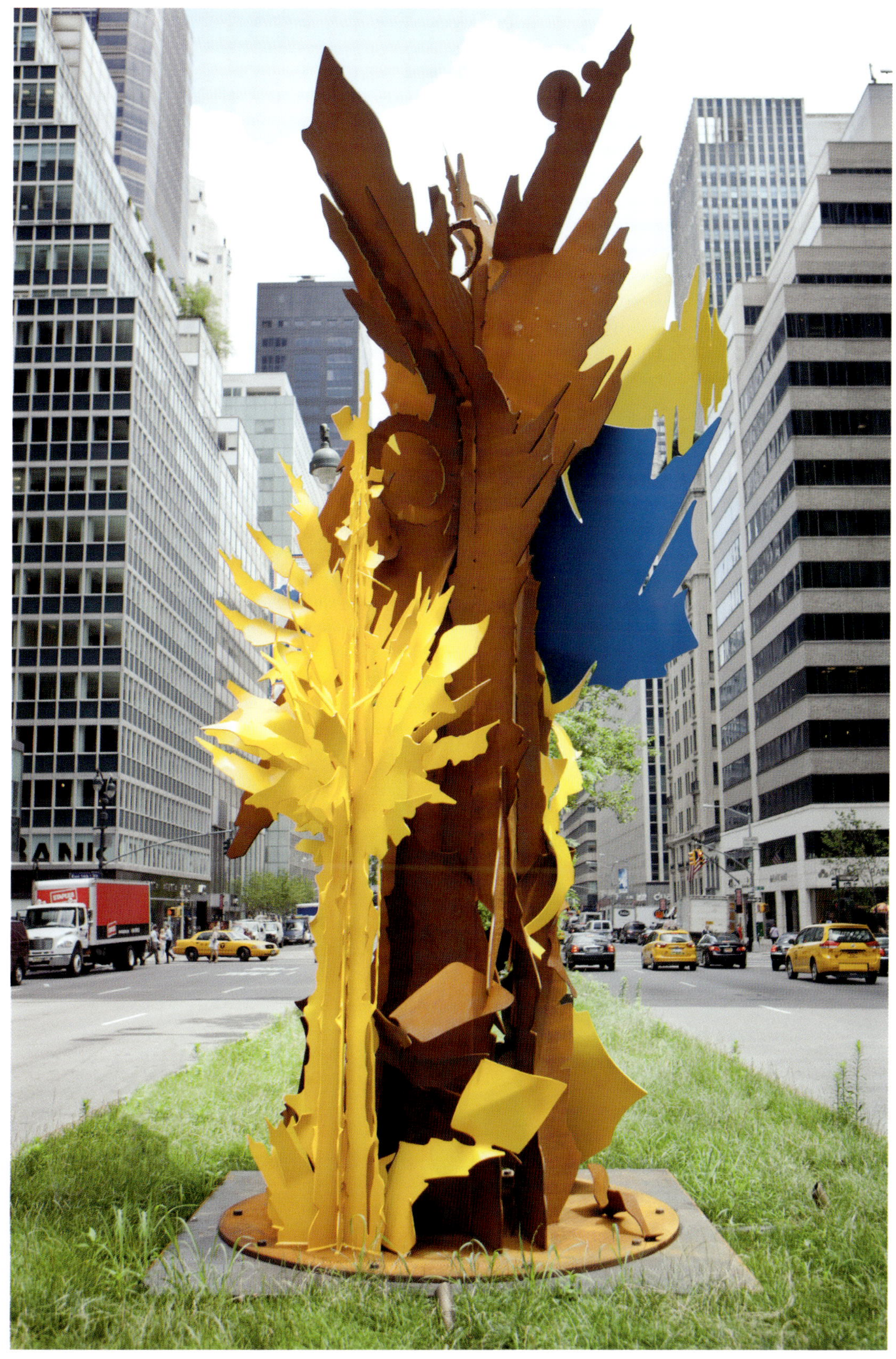

54TH
REFLECTION

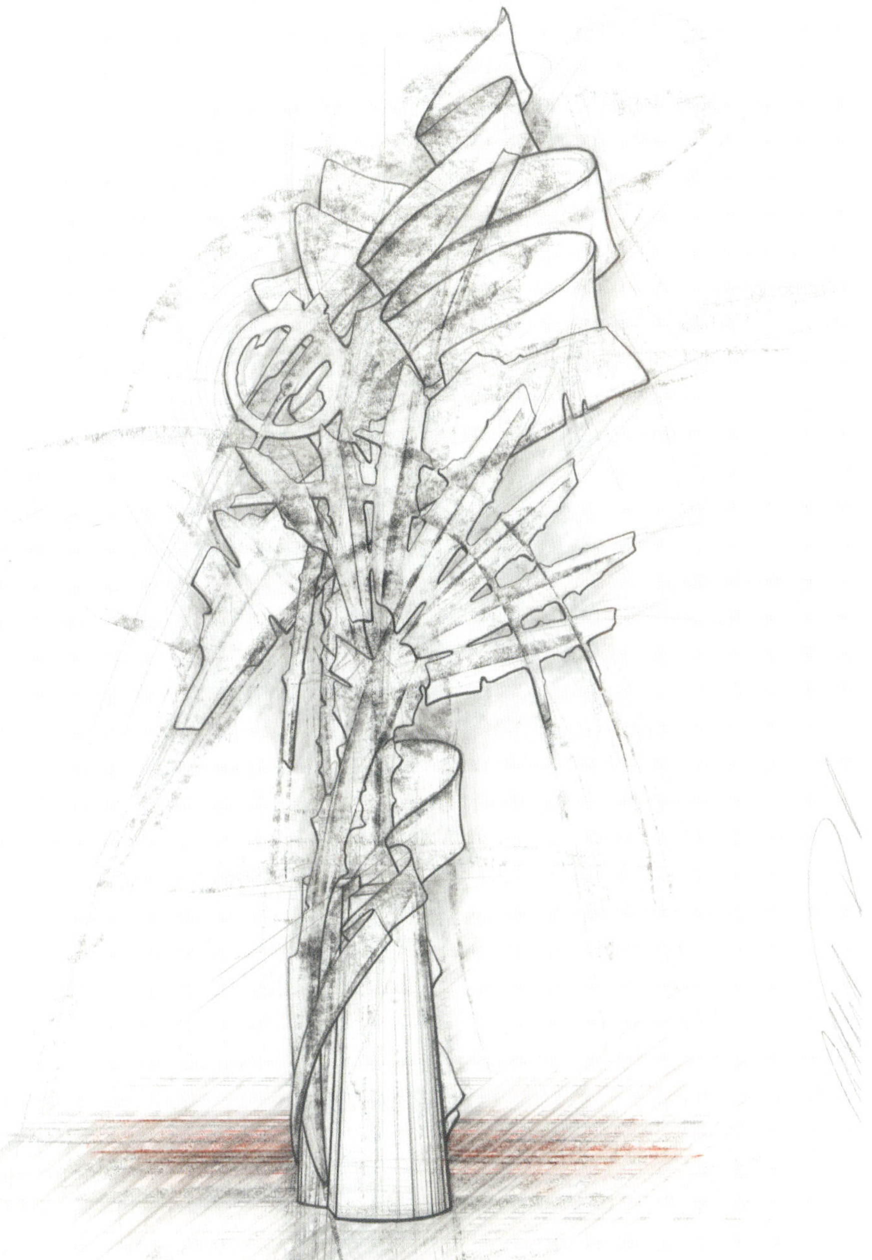

Reflection
Concept drawing
Graphite and red pencil
on paper
30" x 22 1/8"
Paley Studios Archive

Reflection
Photomontage
8" x 10"
Paley Studios Archive

p. 56
Reflection
Maquette fabrication
Paley Studios, Lyell Avenue
Rochester, New York

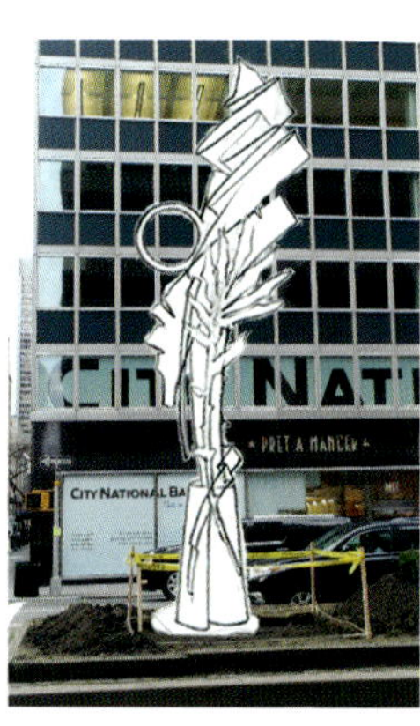

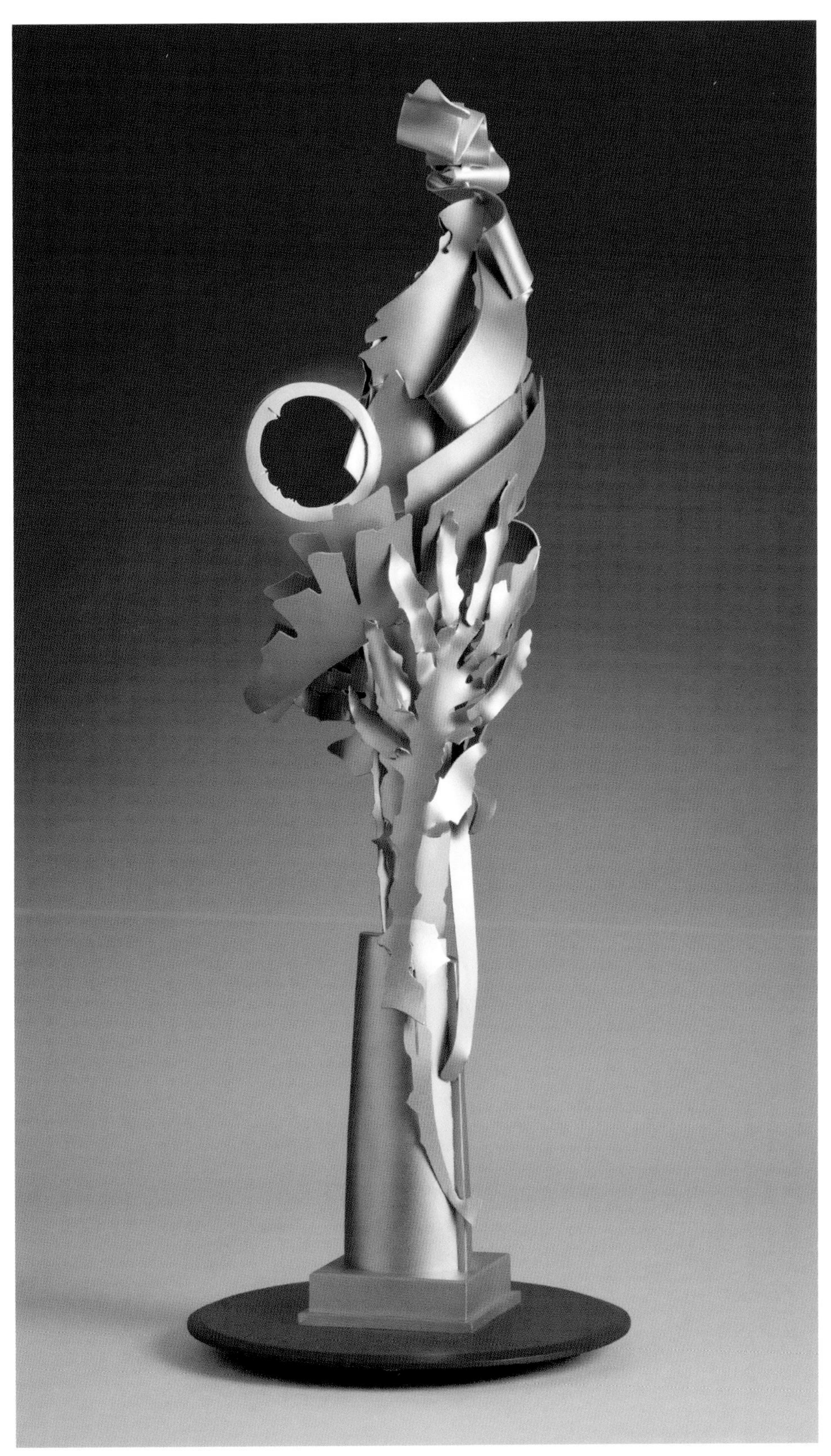

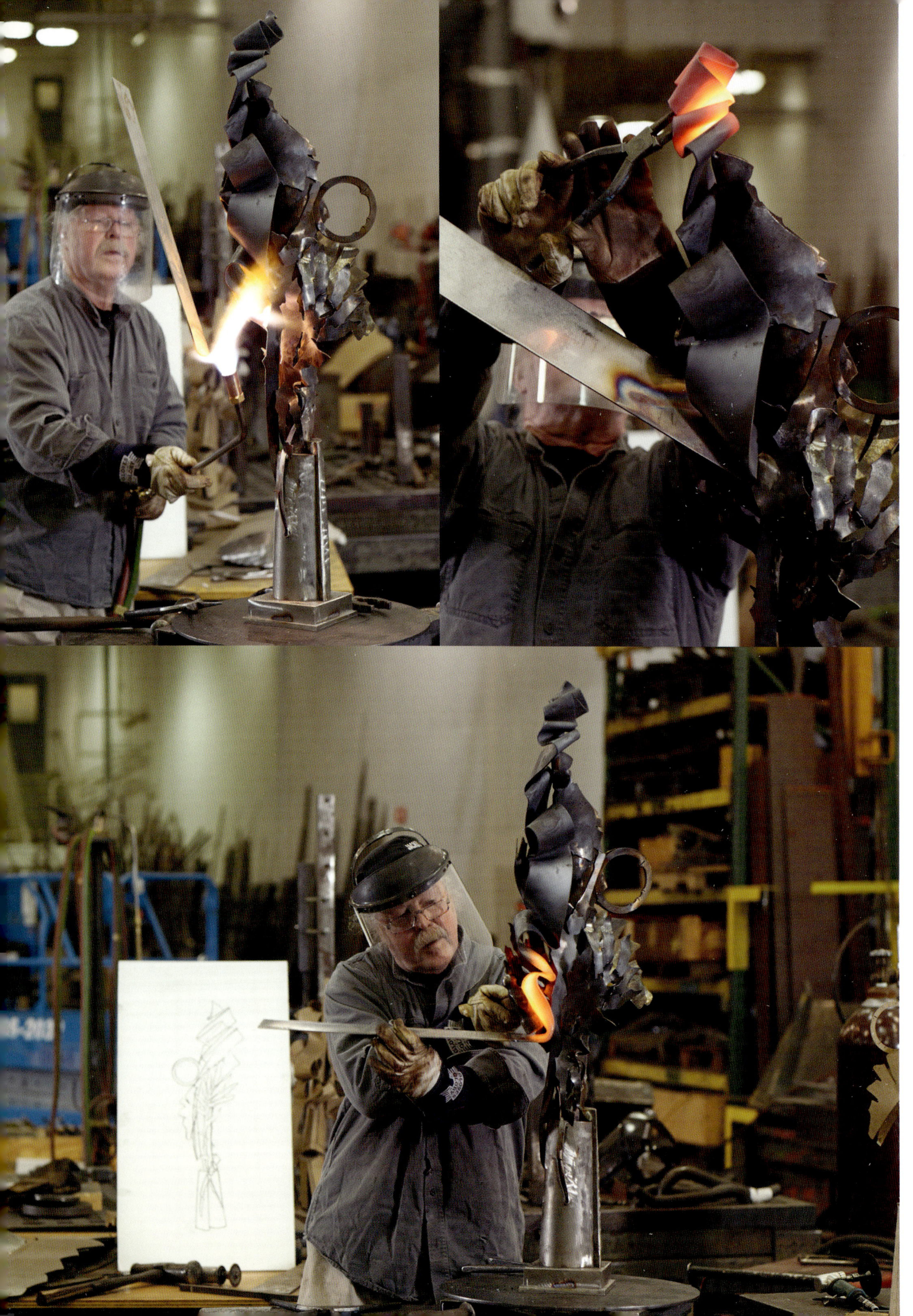

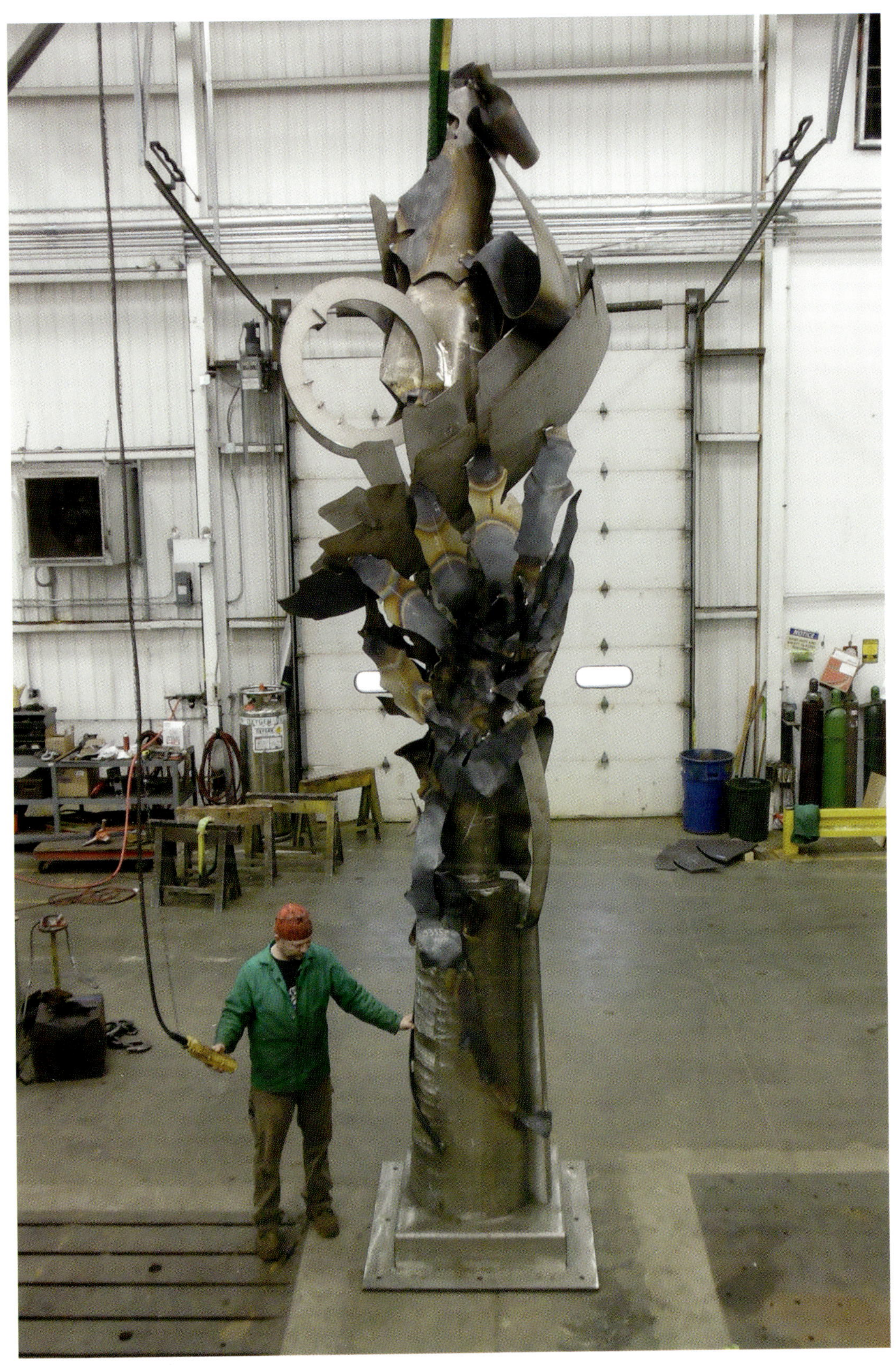

REFLECTION

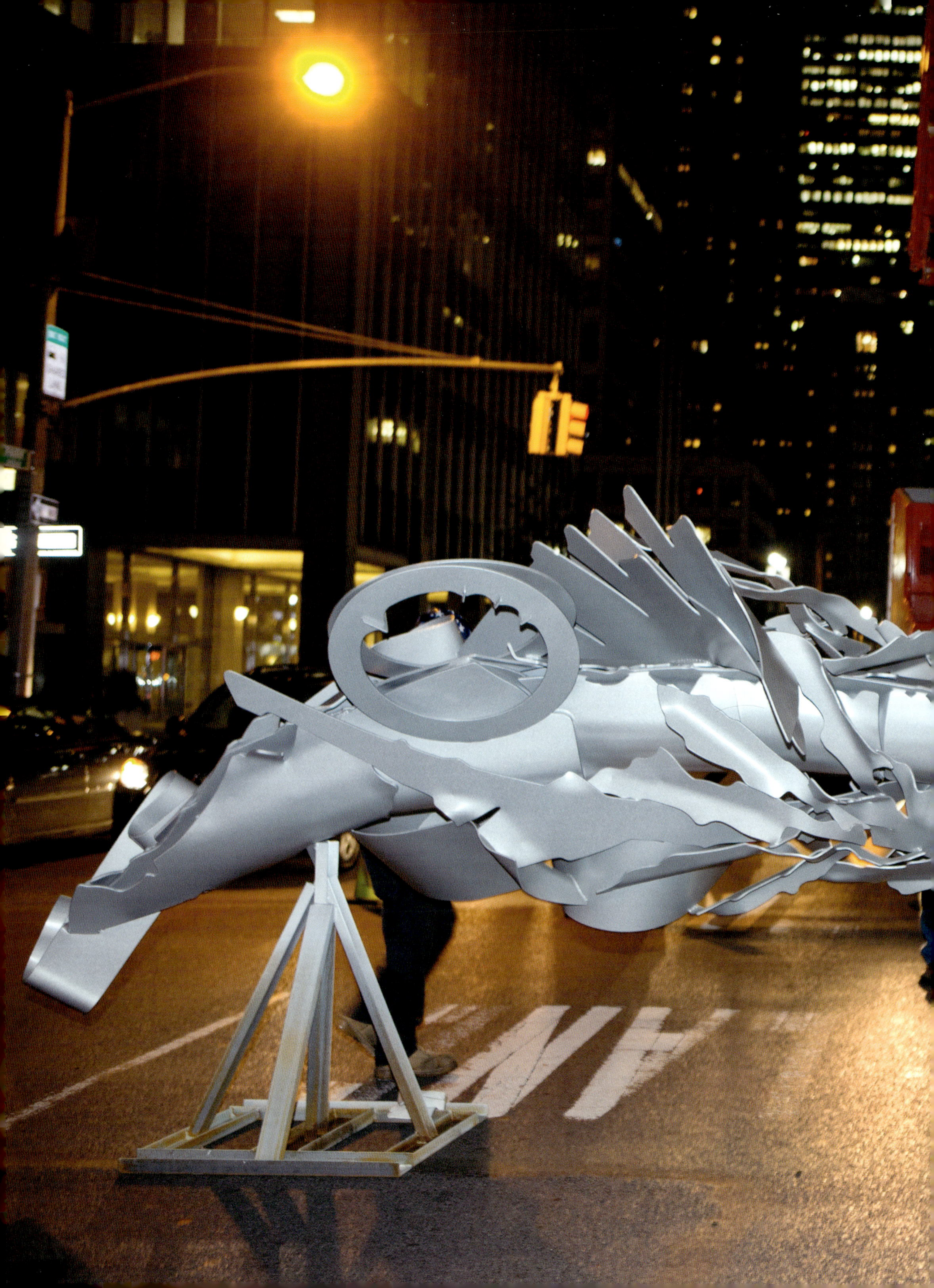

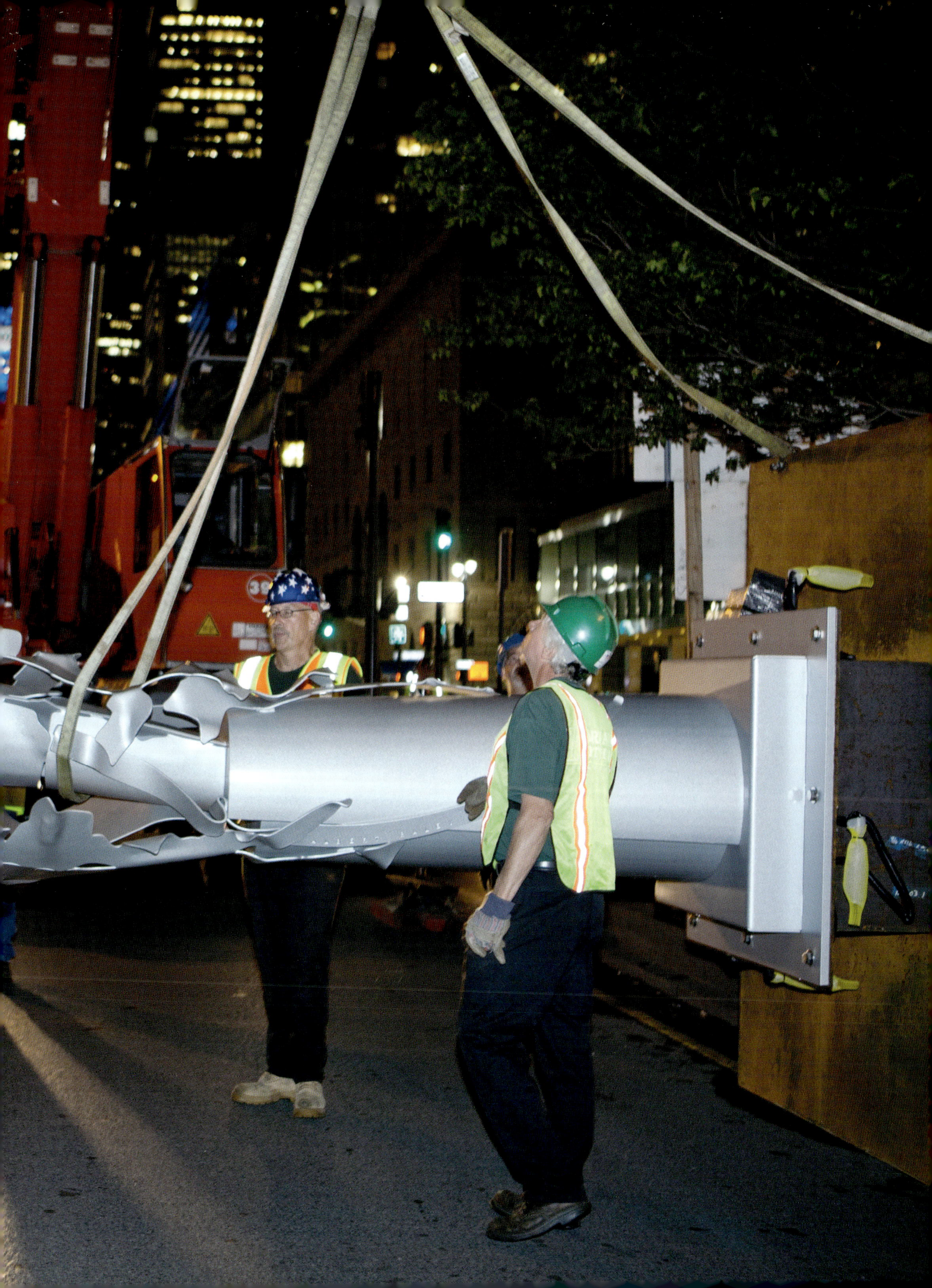

p. 57
Reflection
Fabrication
Paley Studios,
Lyell Avenue
Rochester, New York

pp. 58-59
Reflection
Installation
54th Street and Park
Avenue, New York
June 14, 2013

right
Reflection, 2013
Formed and fabricated
stainless steel
18'9" x 5'5" x 5'2½"
54th Street and Park
Avenue, New York

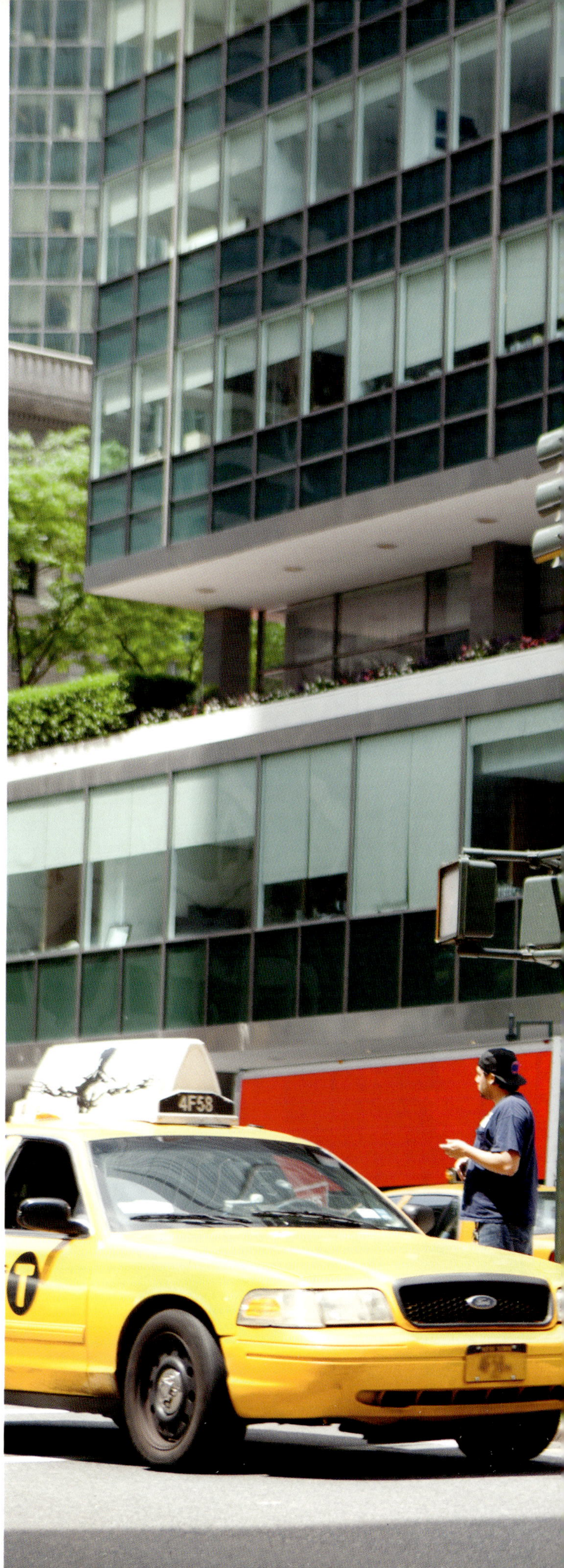

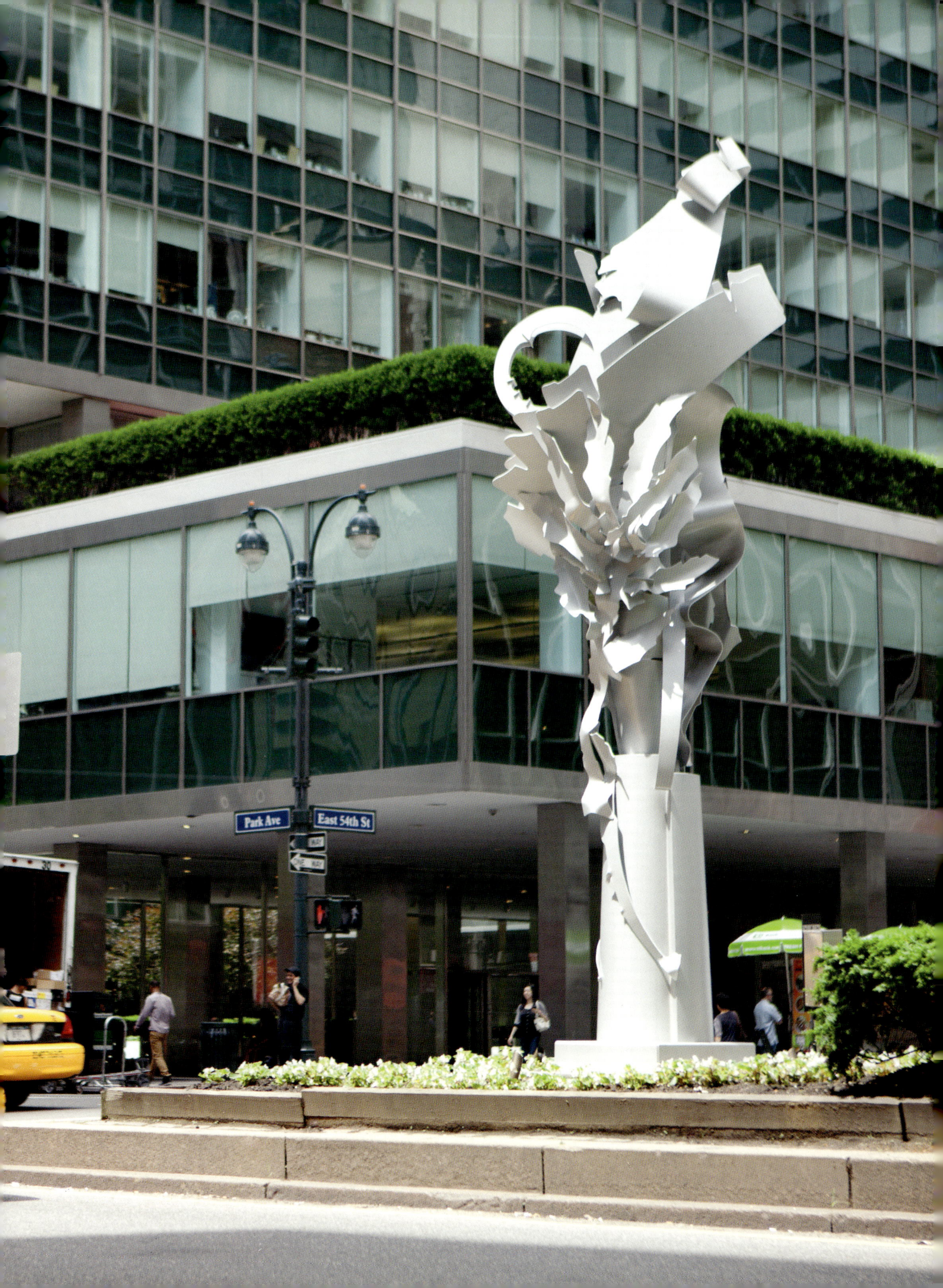
Park Ave
East 54th St

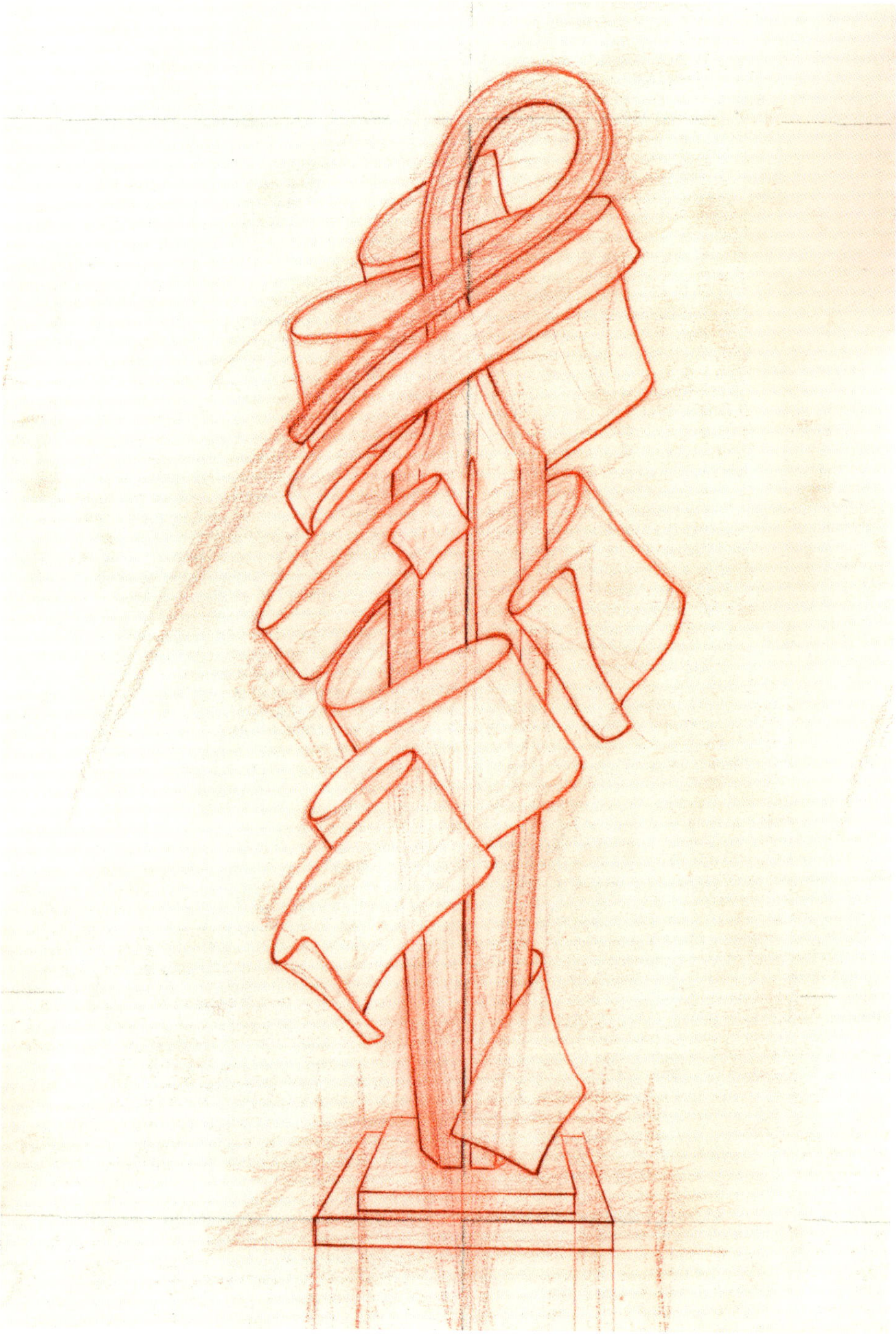

Encore
Concept drawing
Graphite and red pencil
on paper
44" x 30"
Paley Studios Archive

Encore
Photomontage
10" x 8"
Paley Studios Archive

Encore
Maquette
Formed and fabricated
painted steel
40½" x 12" x 12"
Paley Studios Archive

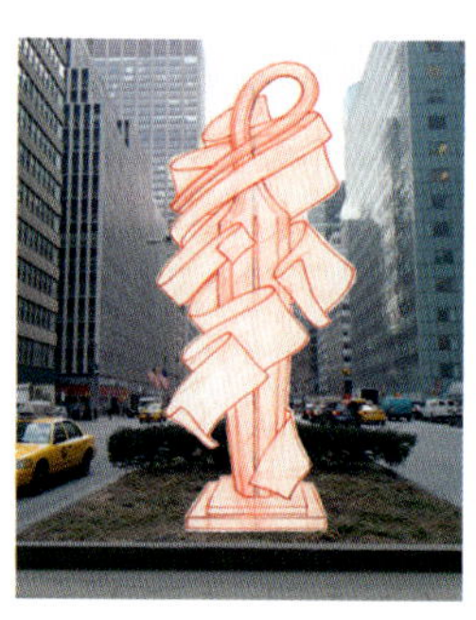

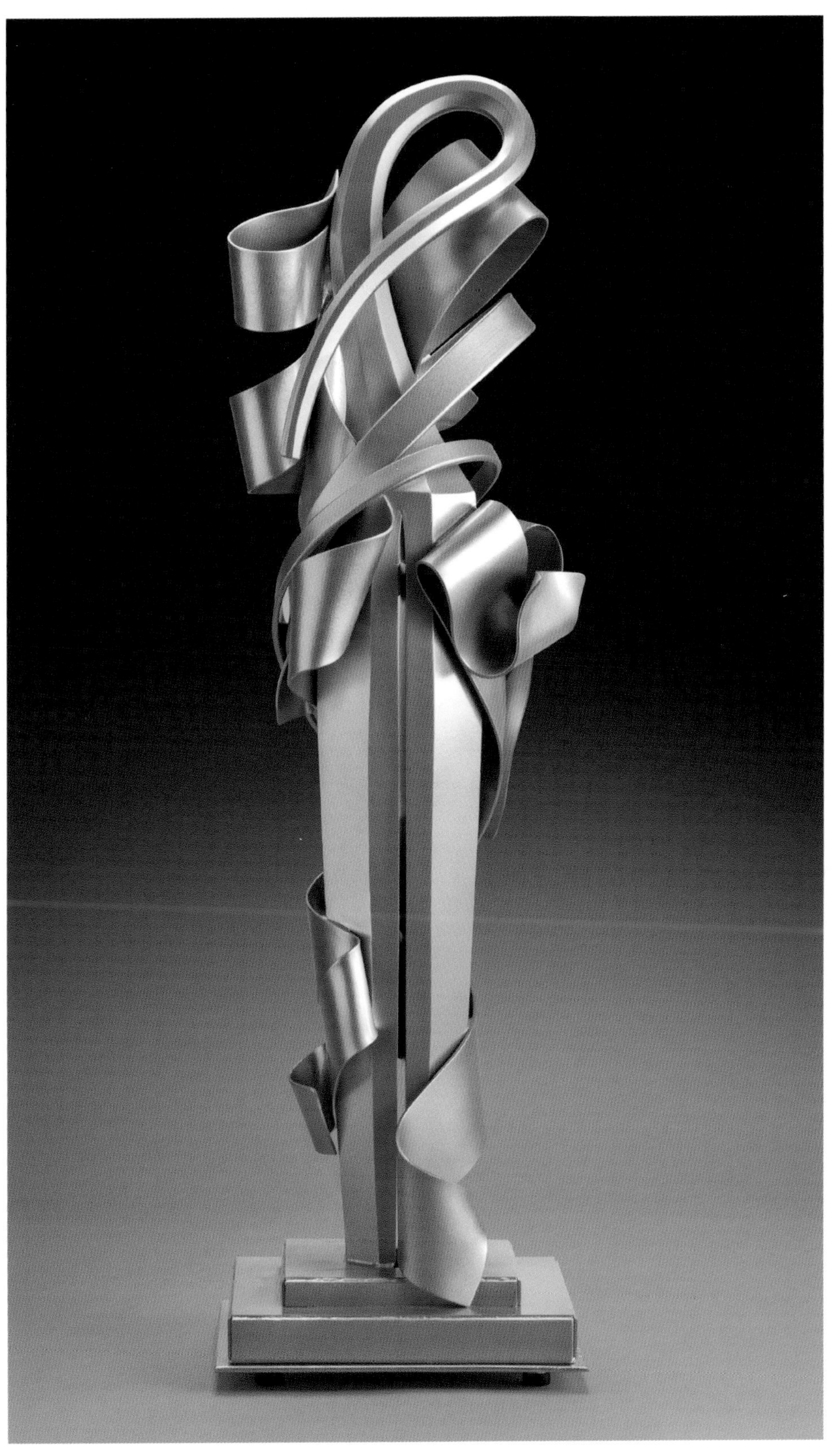

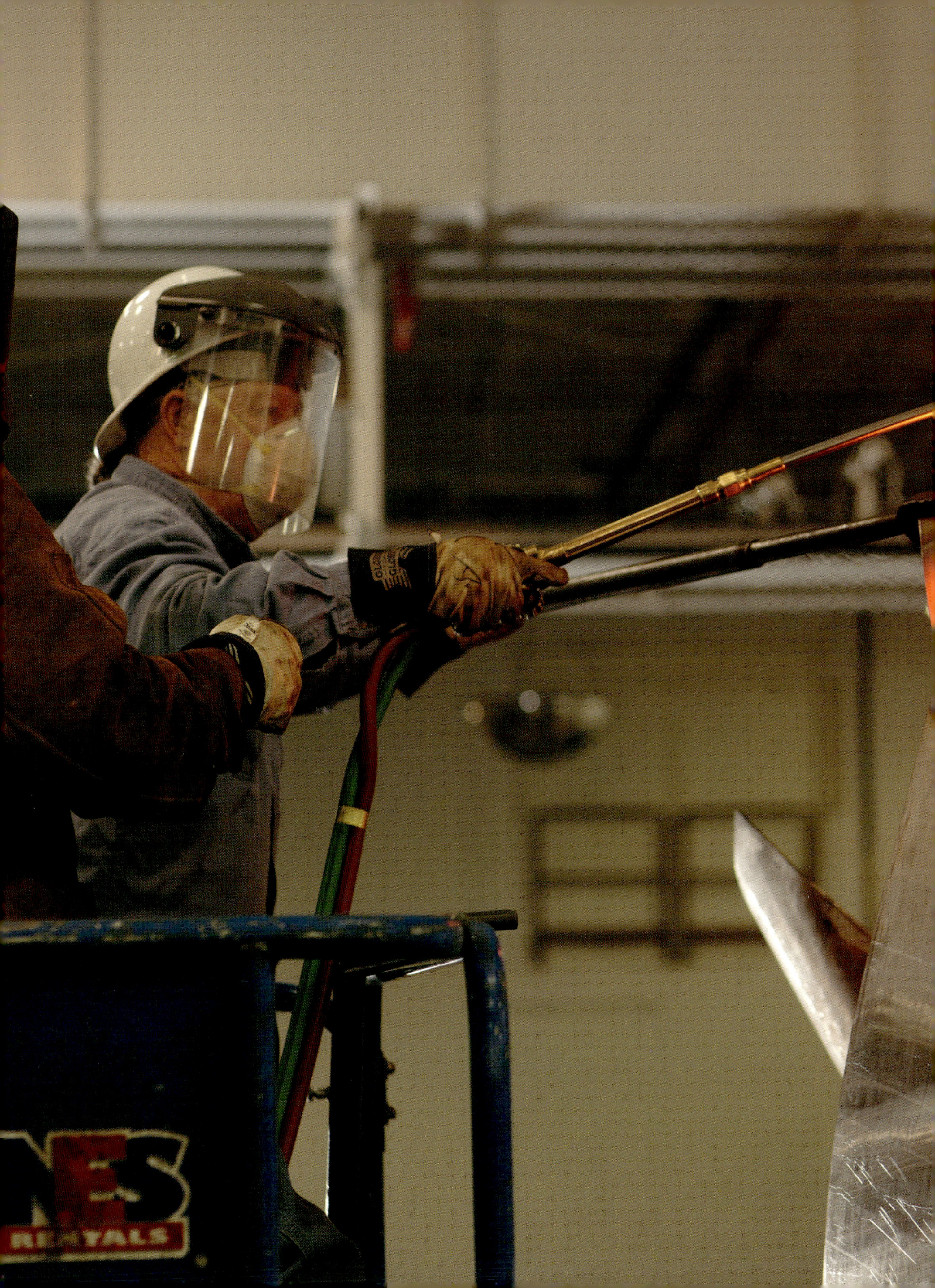

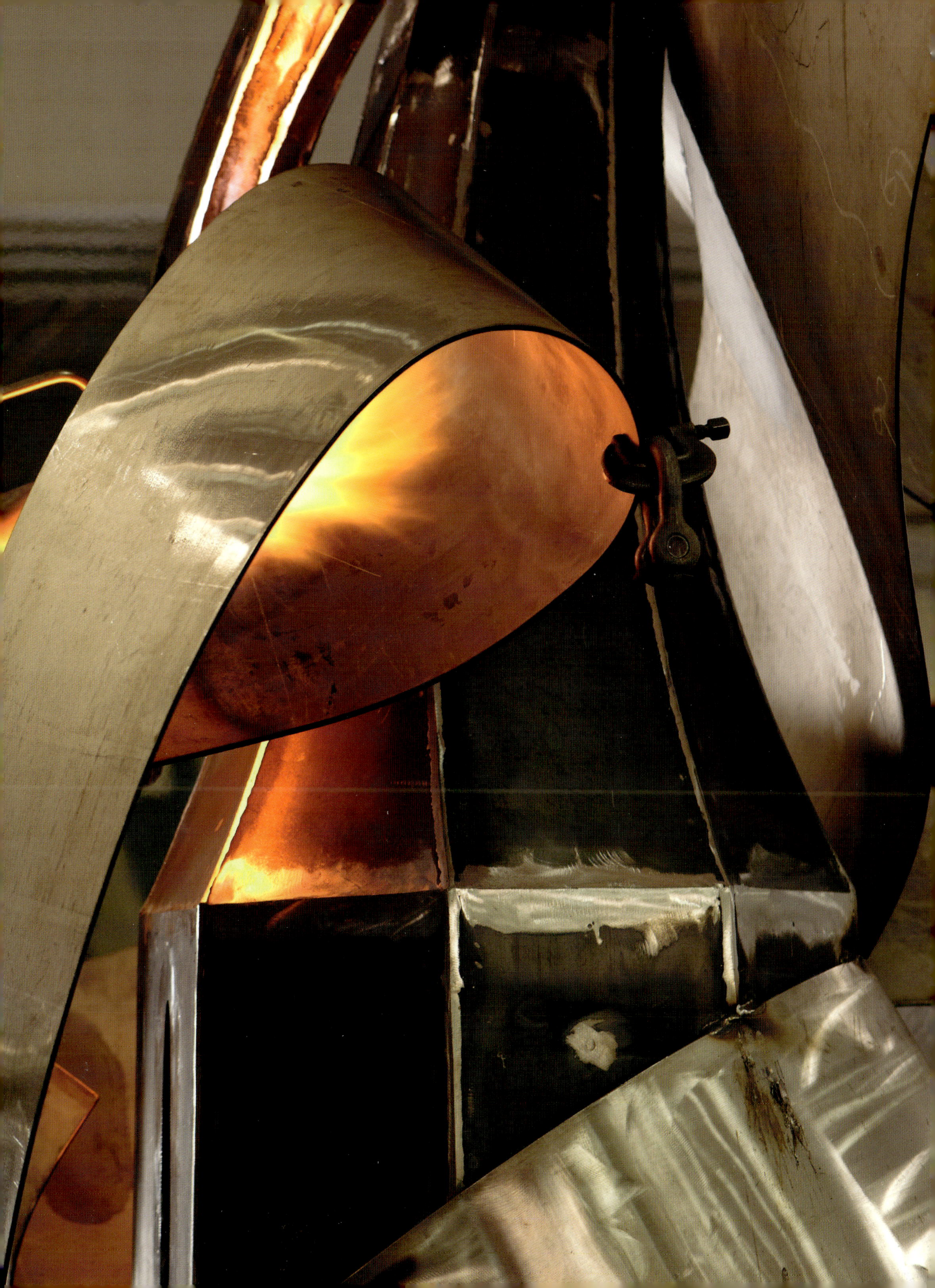

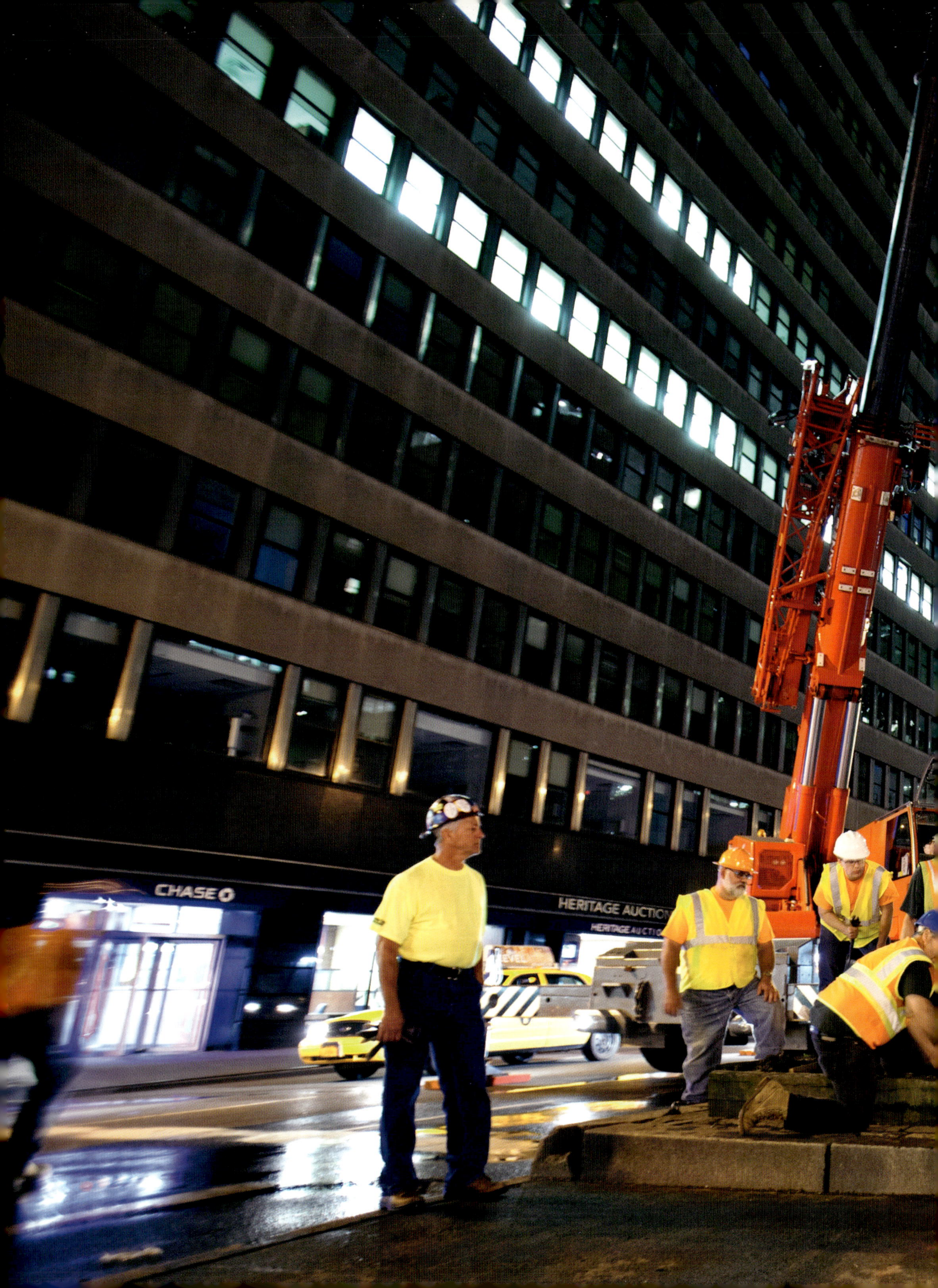

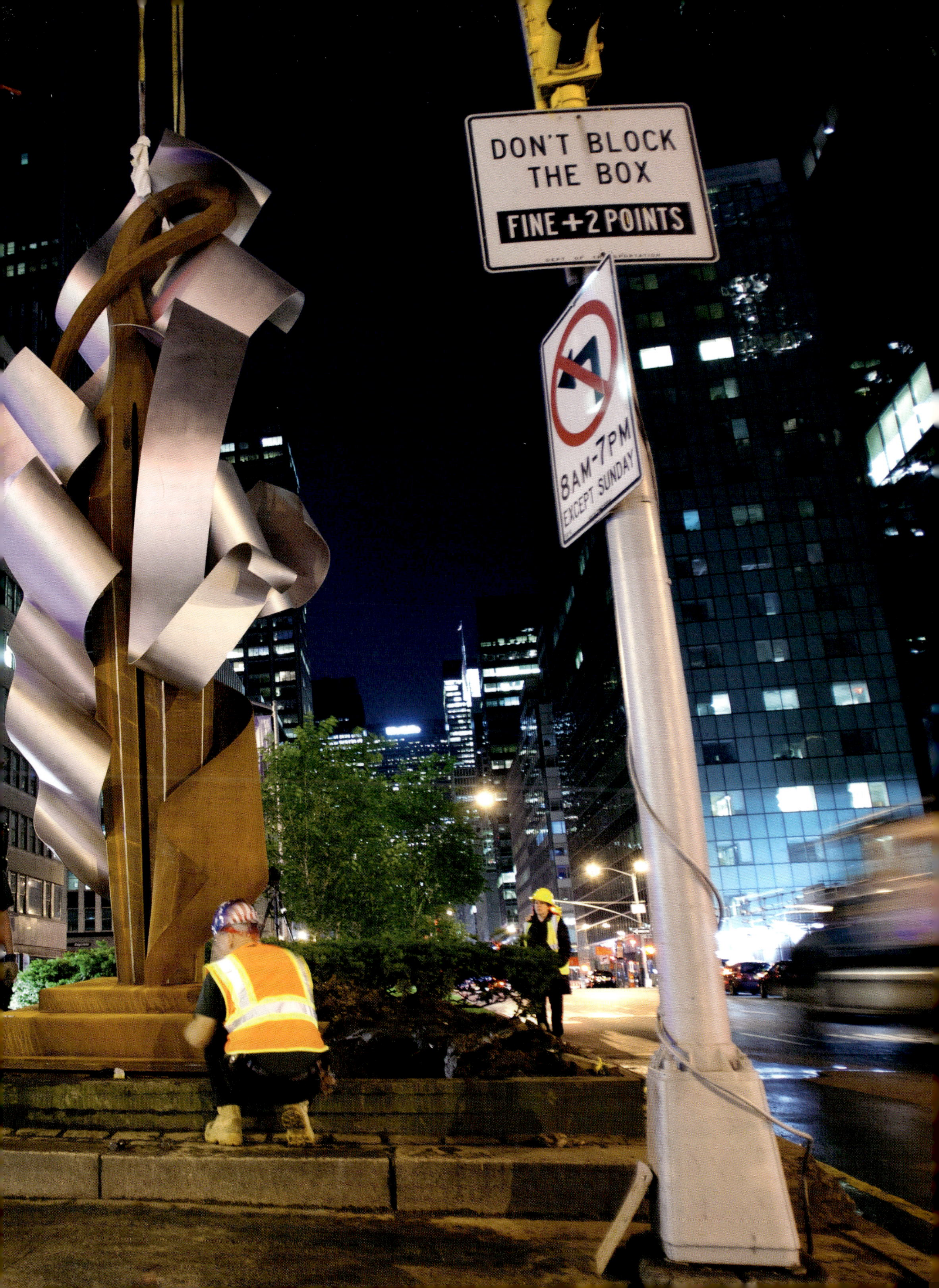

DON'T BLOCK
THE BOX
FINE + 2 POINTS
8AM-7PM
EXCEPT SUNDAY

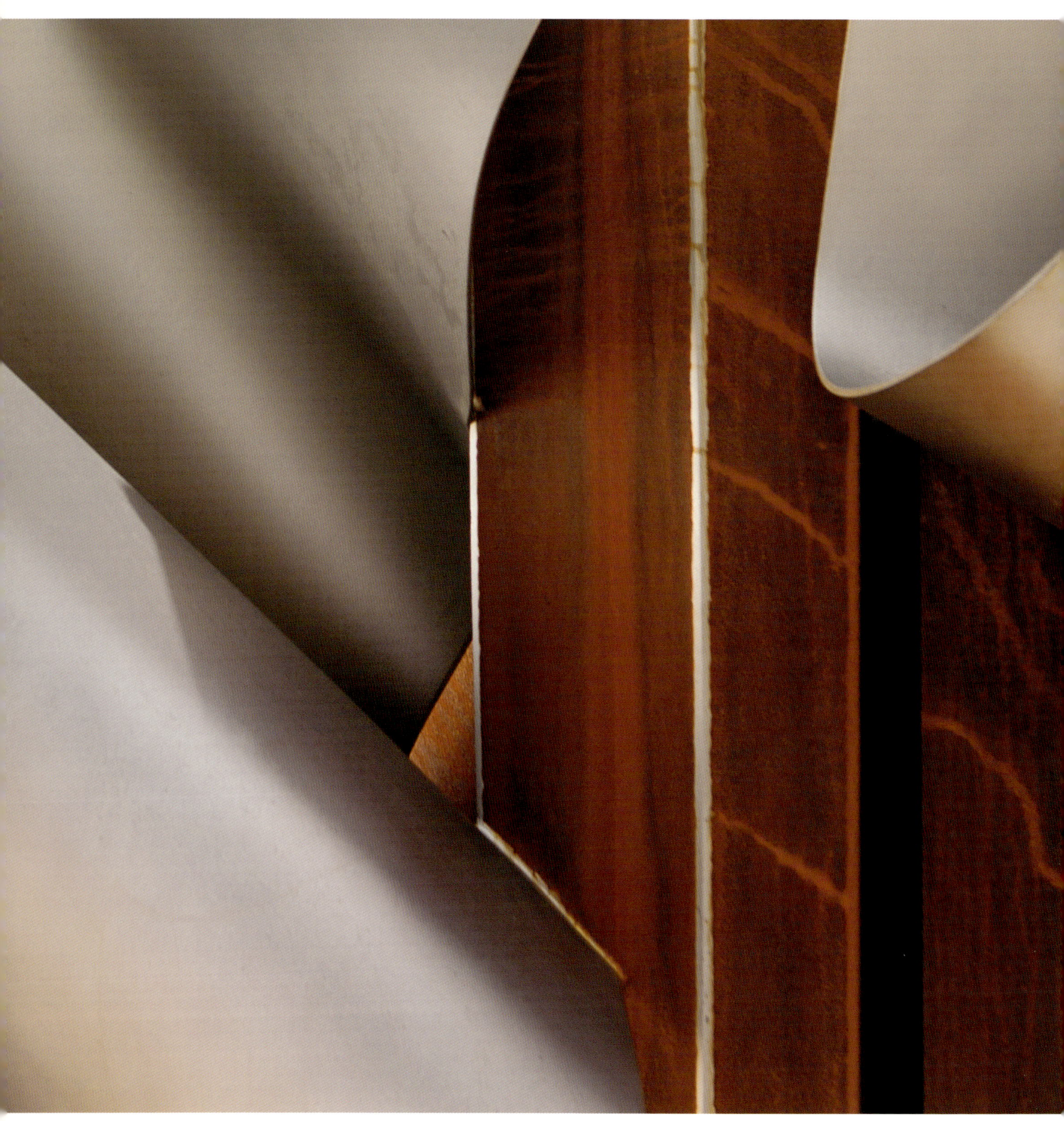

pp. 64-65
Encore
Fabrication
Paley Studios,
Lyell Avenue
Rochester, New York

pp. 66-67
Encore
Installation
57th Street and Park
Avenue
New York, New York
June 14, 2013

above
Encore
Detail

p. 69
Encore, 2013
Formed and fabricated
stainless steel and
weathering steel
20′11″ x 8′2″ x 6′2½″

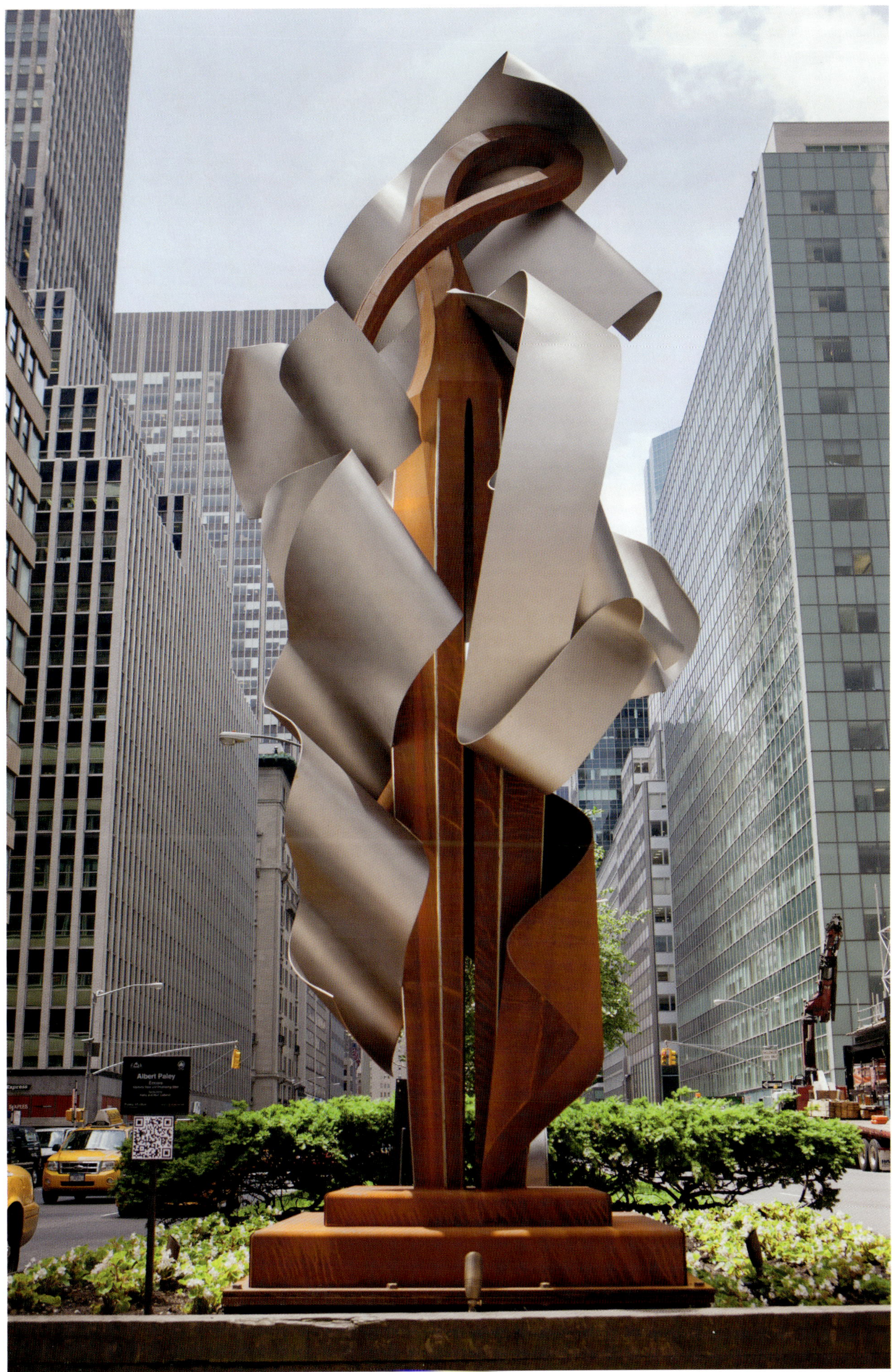

Albert Paley
Encore

57TH NORTH
JESTER

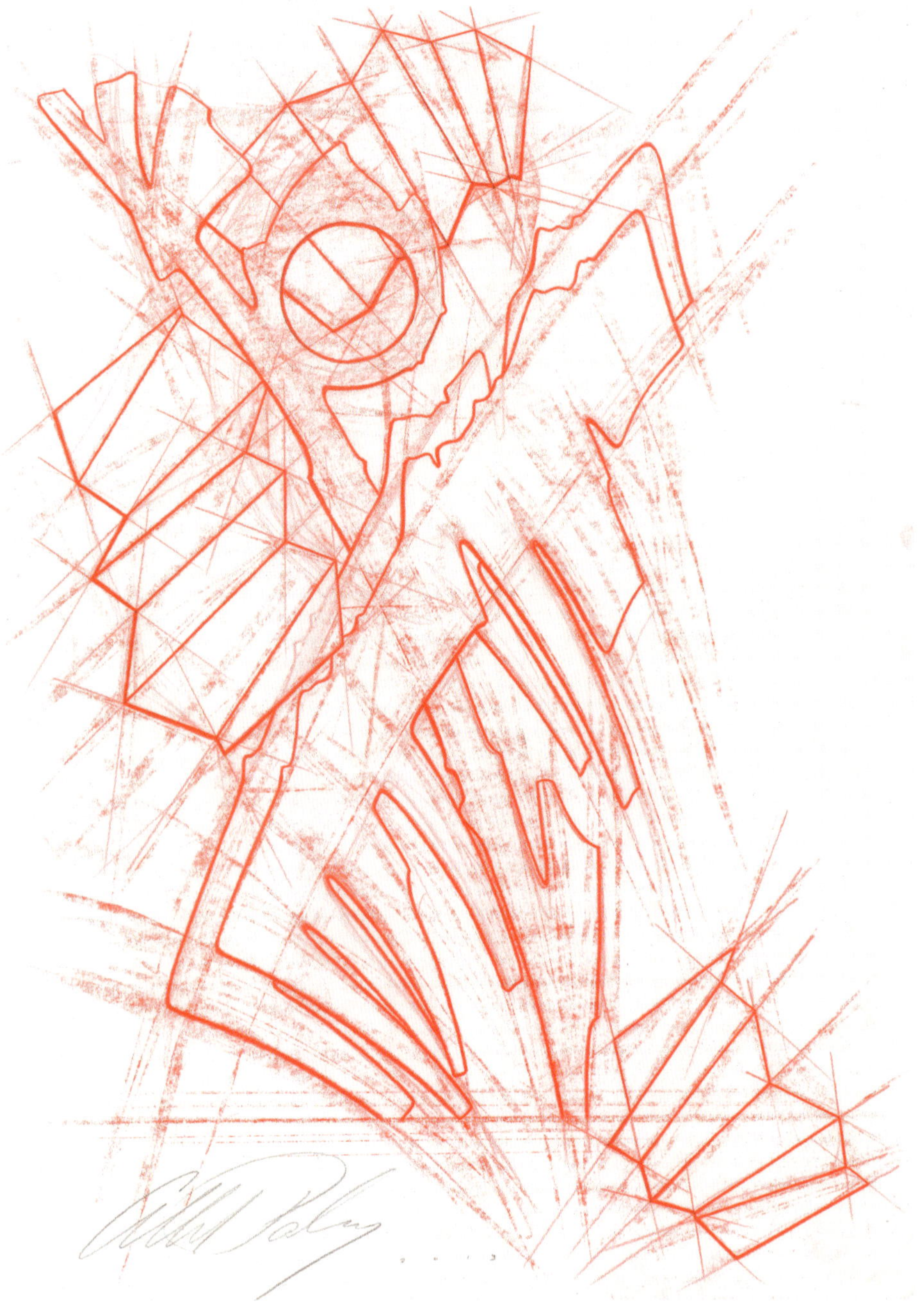

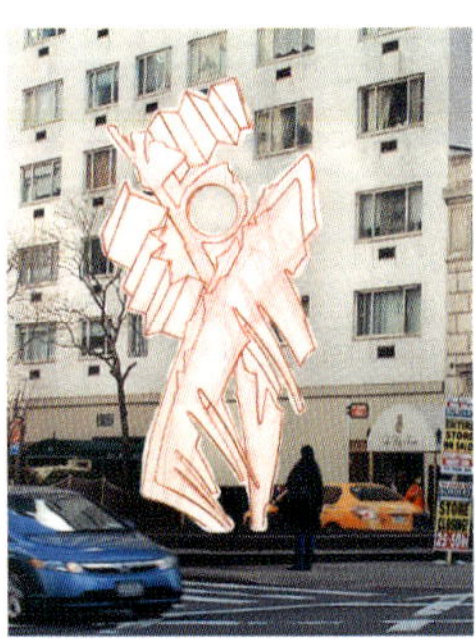

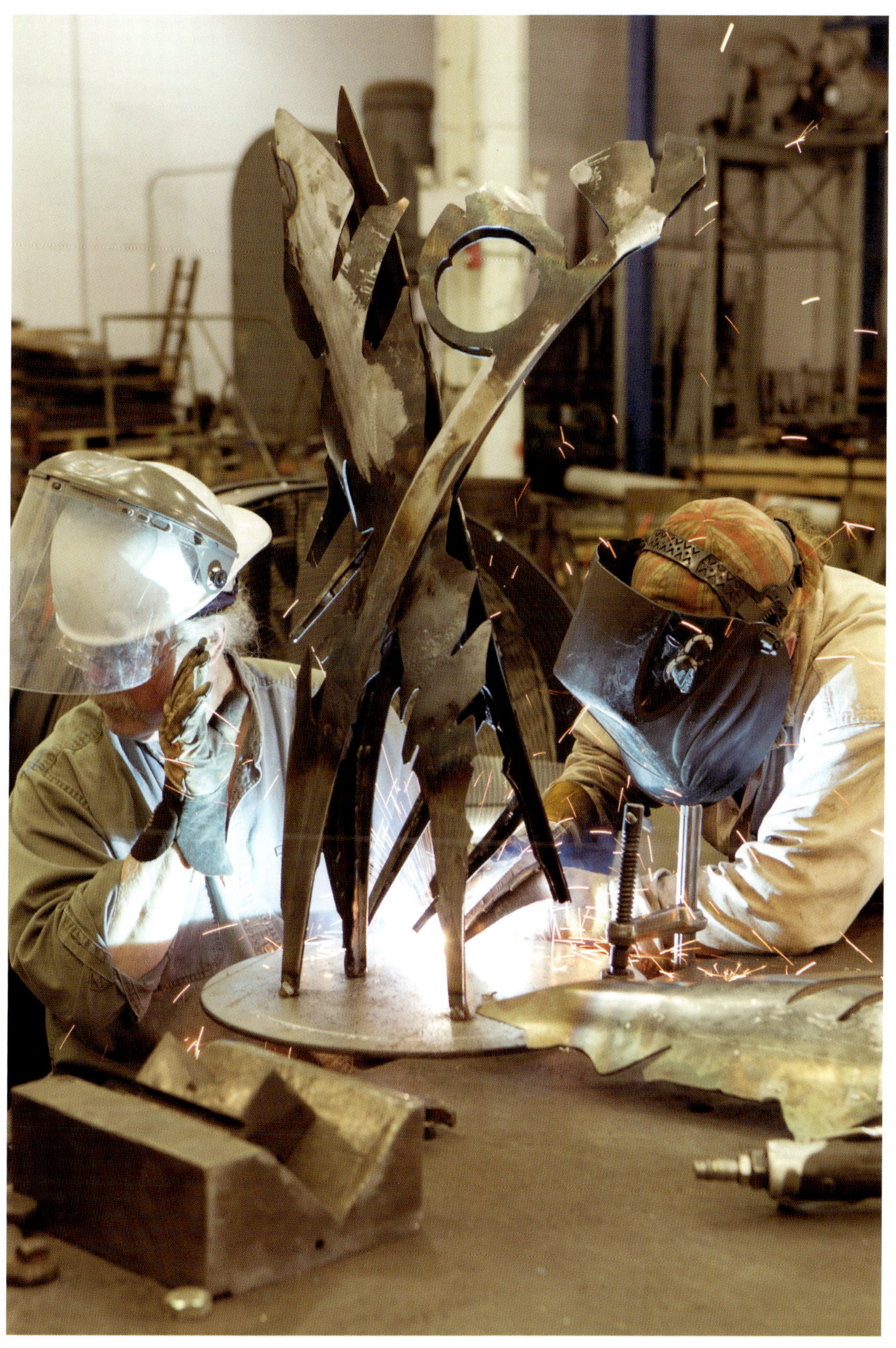

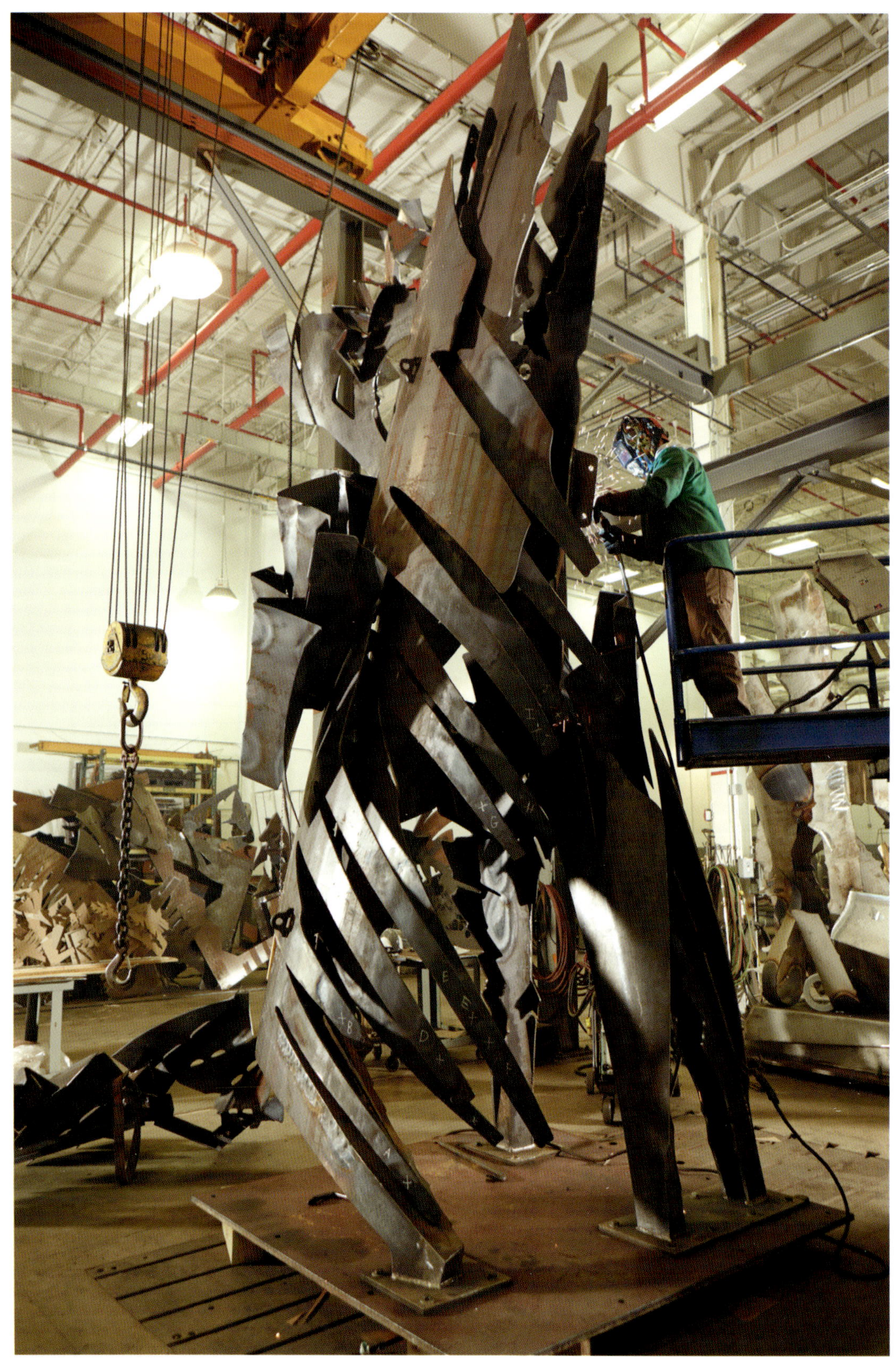

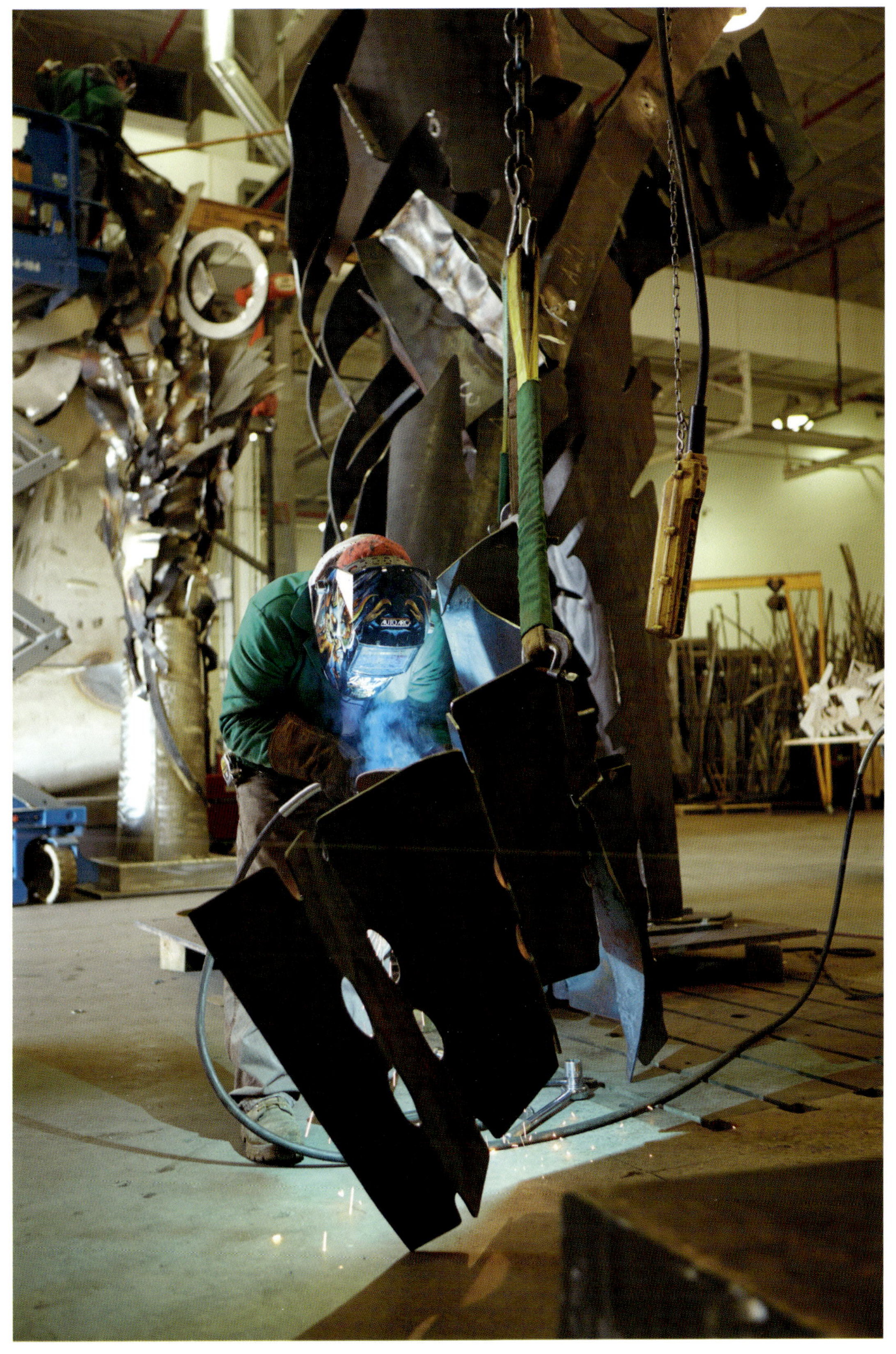

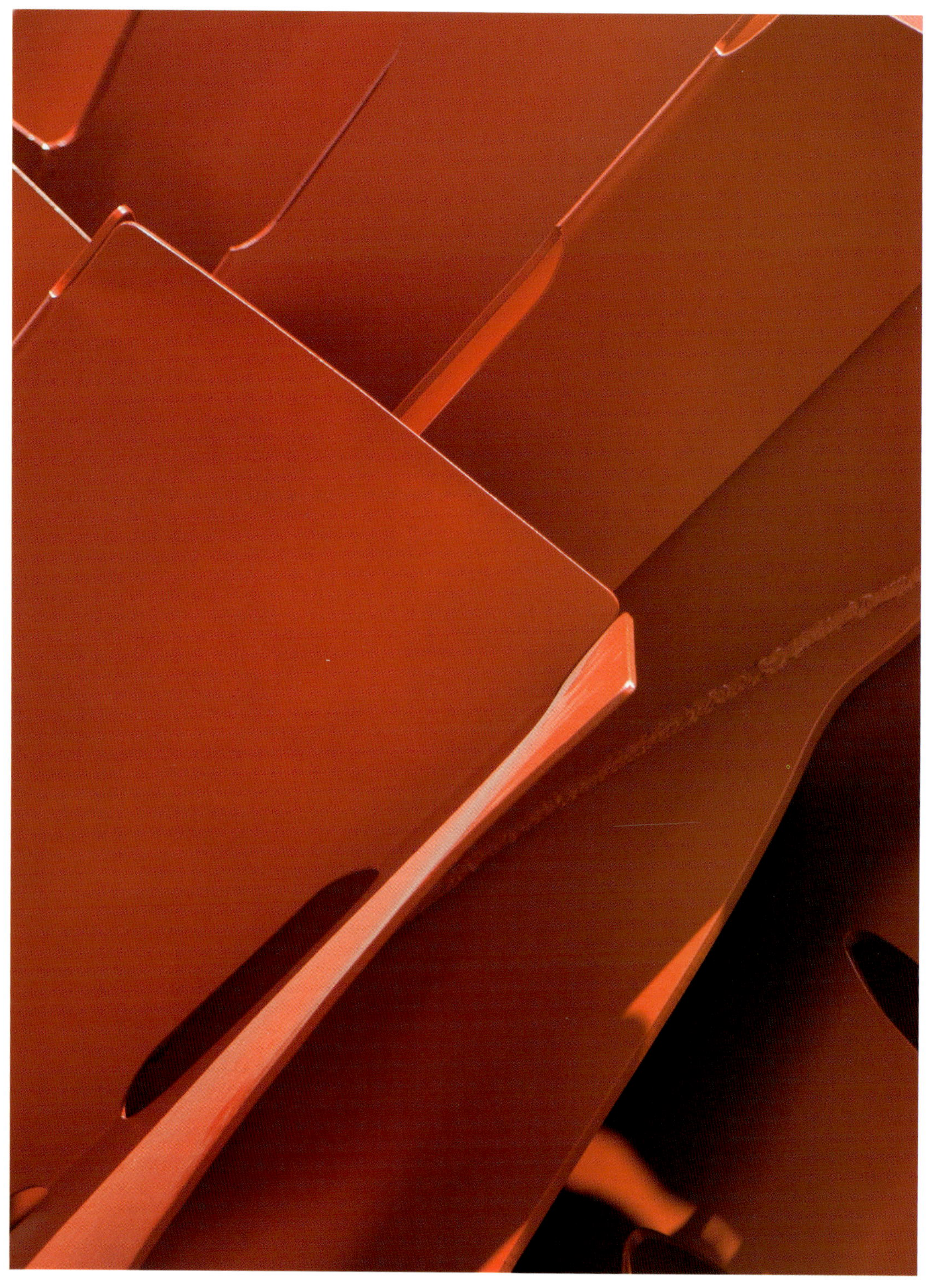

pp. 72-73
Jester
Fabrication
Paley Studios, Lyell Avenue
Rochester, New York

above
Jester
Detail

p. 75
Jester, 2013
Formed and fabricated
painted steel
18'9" x 9' x 7'

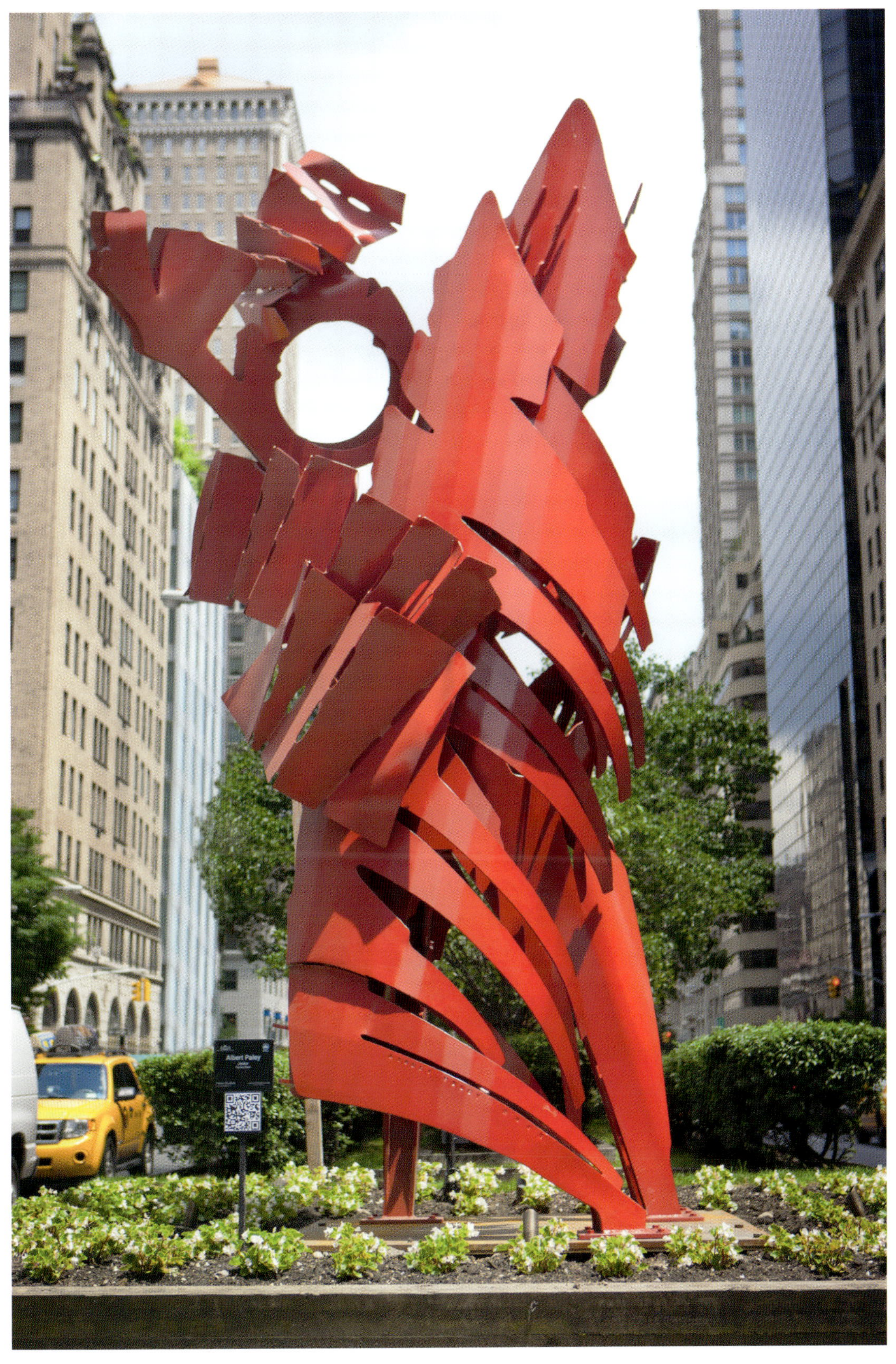

Albert Paley

COUNTER BALANCE

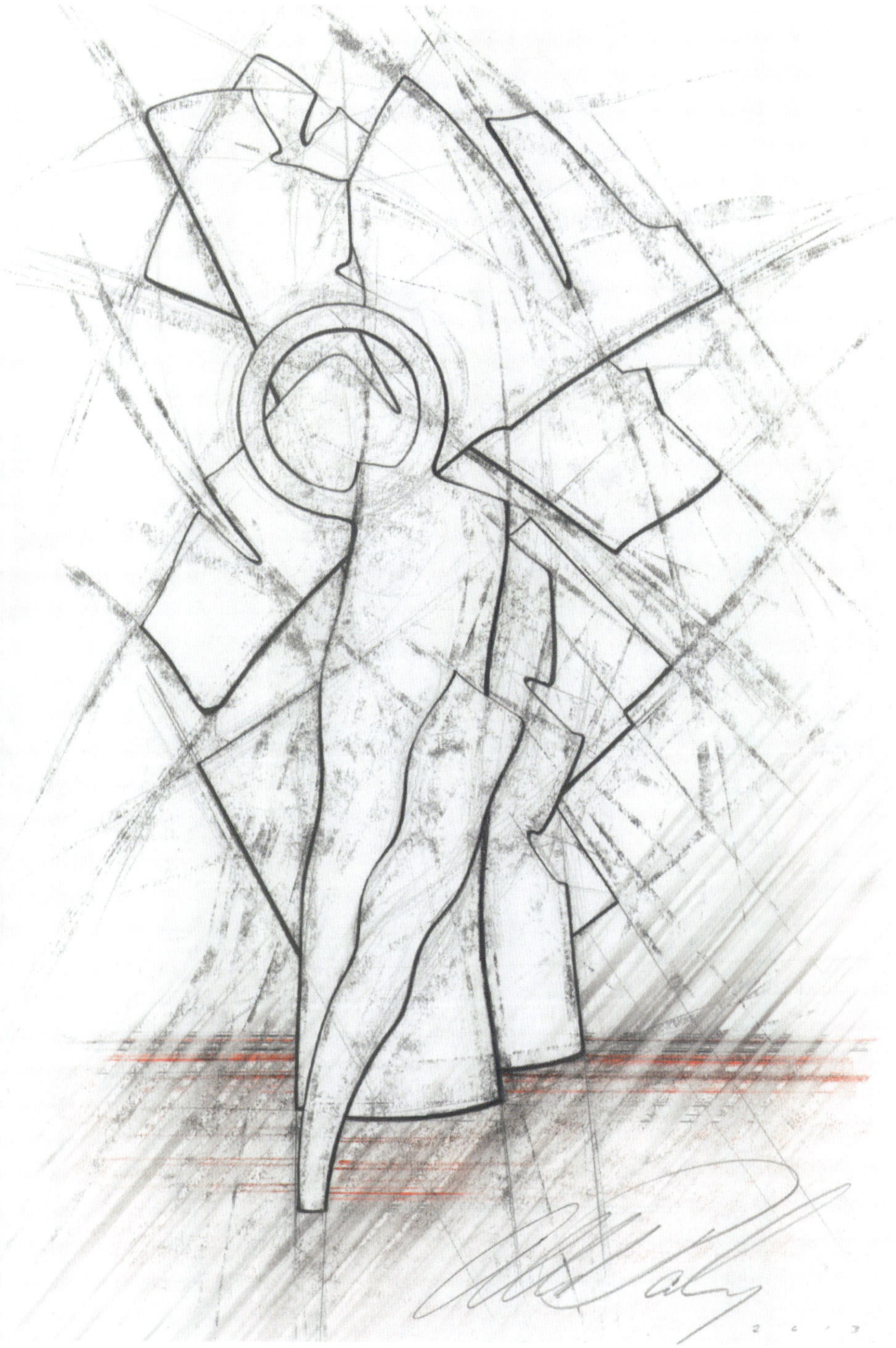

Counter Balance
Concept drawing
Graphite and red pencil
on paper
22 1/8″ x 15¼″
Paley Studios Archive

Counter Balance
Cardboard model
25″ x 12″ x 9½″
Paley Studios Archive

Counter Balance
Maquette
Formed and fabricated
patinated steel with
stainless steel base
37½″ x 21½″ dia.
Paley Studios Archive

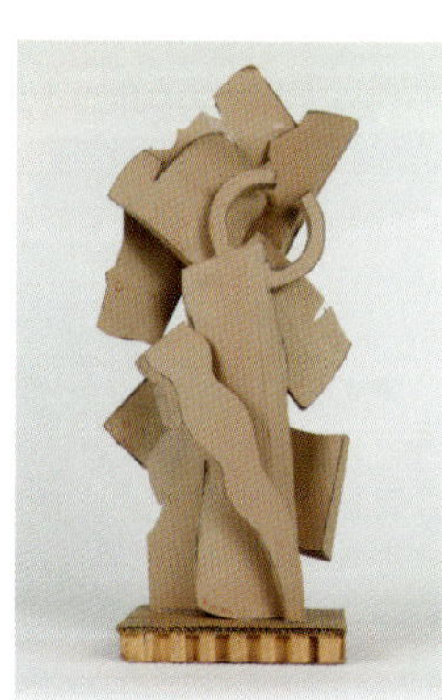

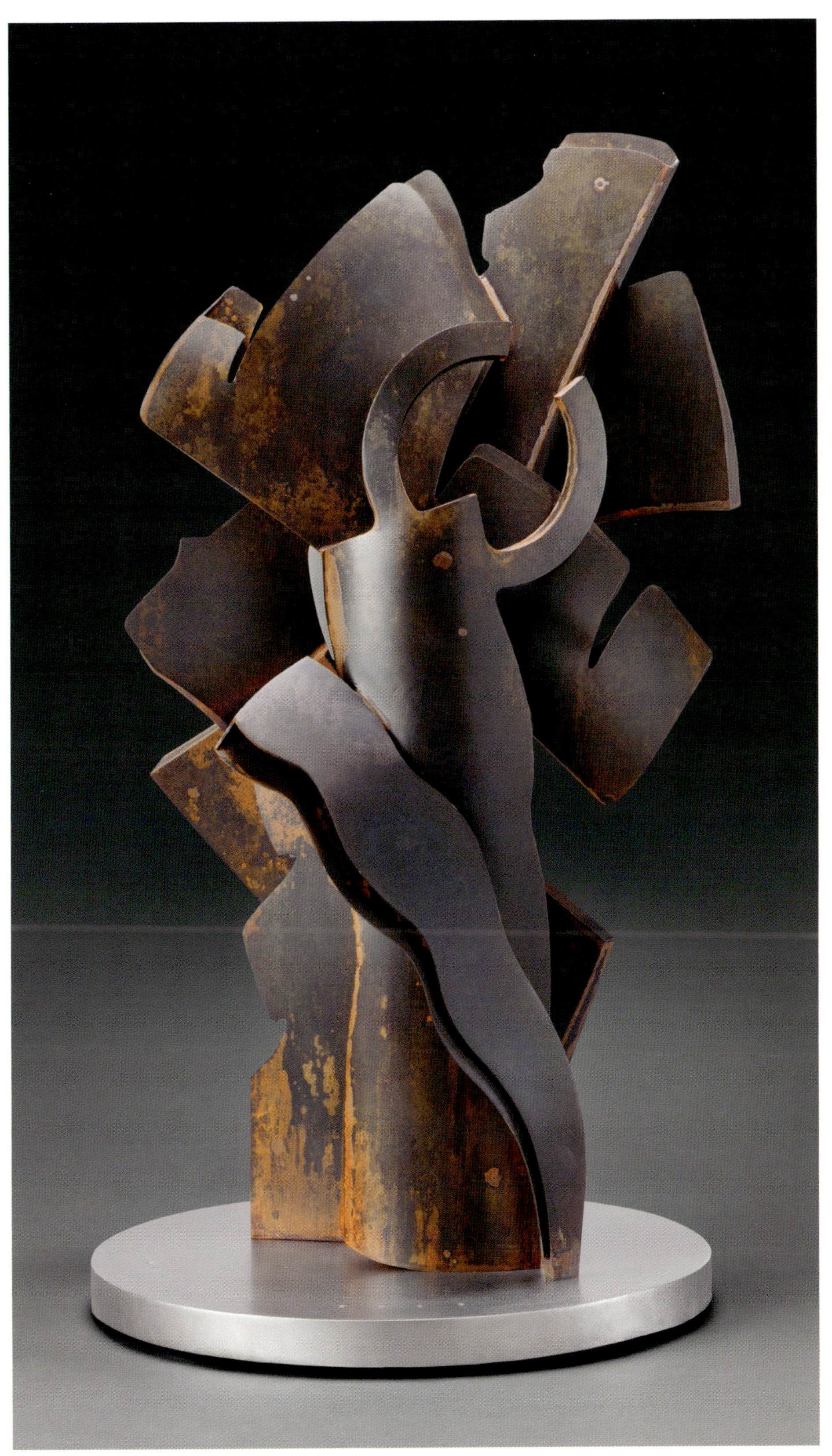

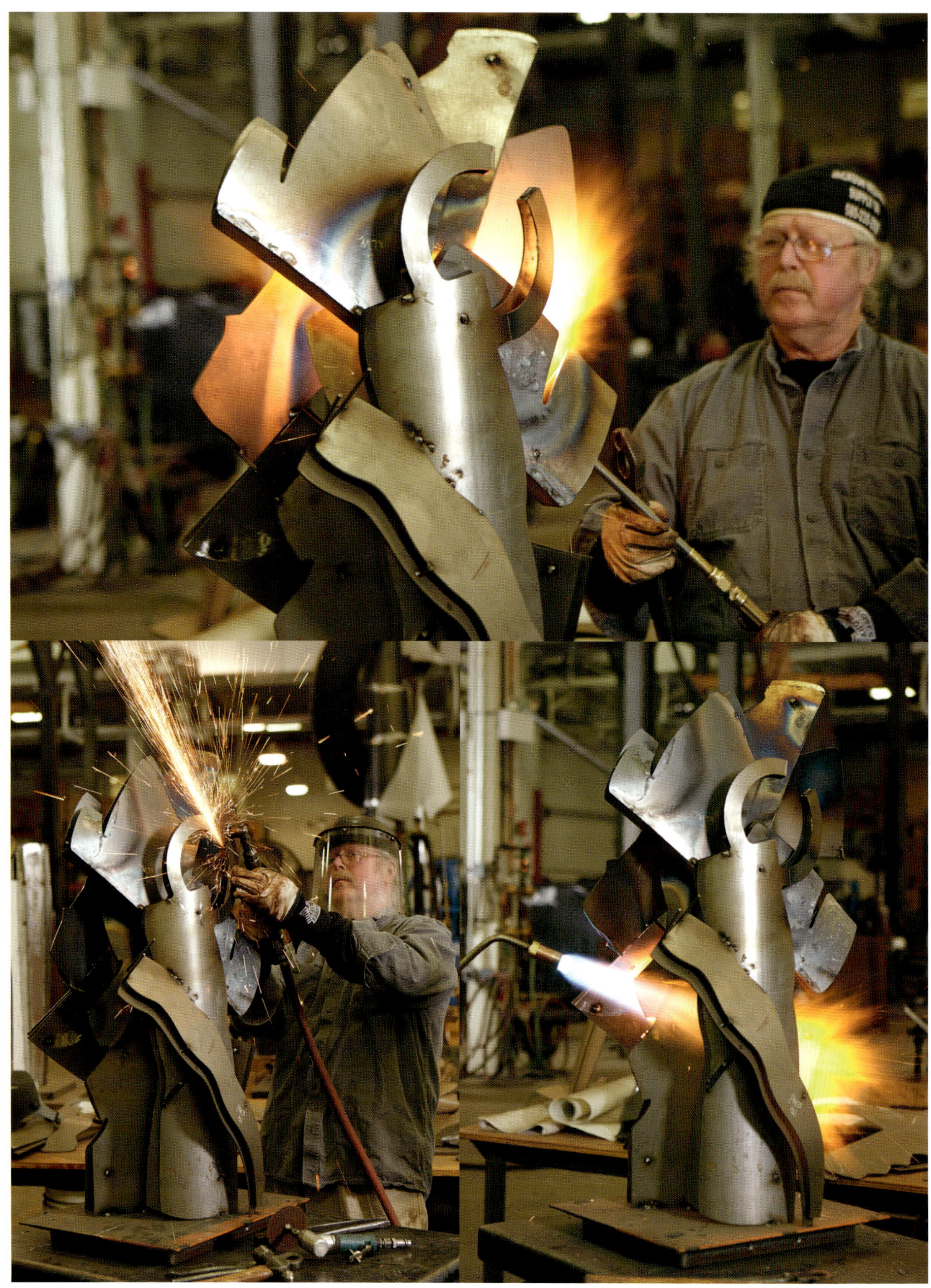

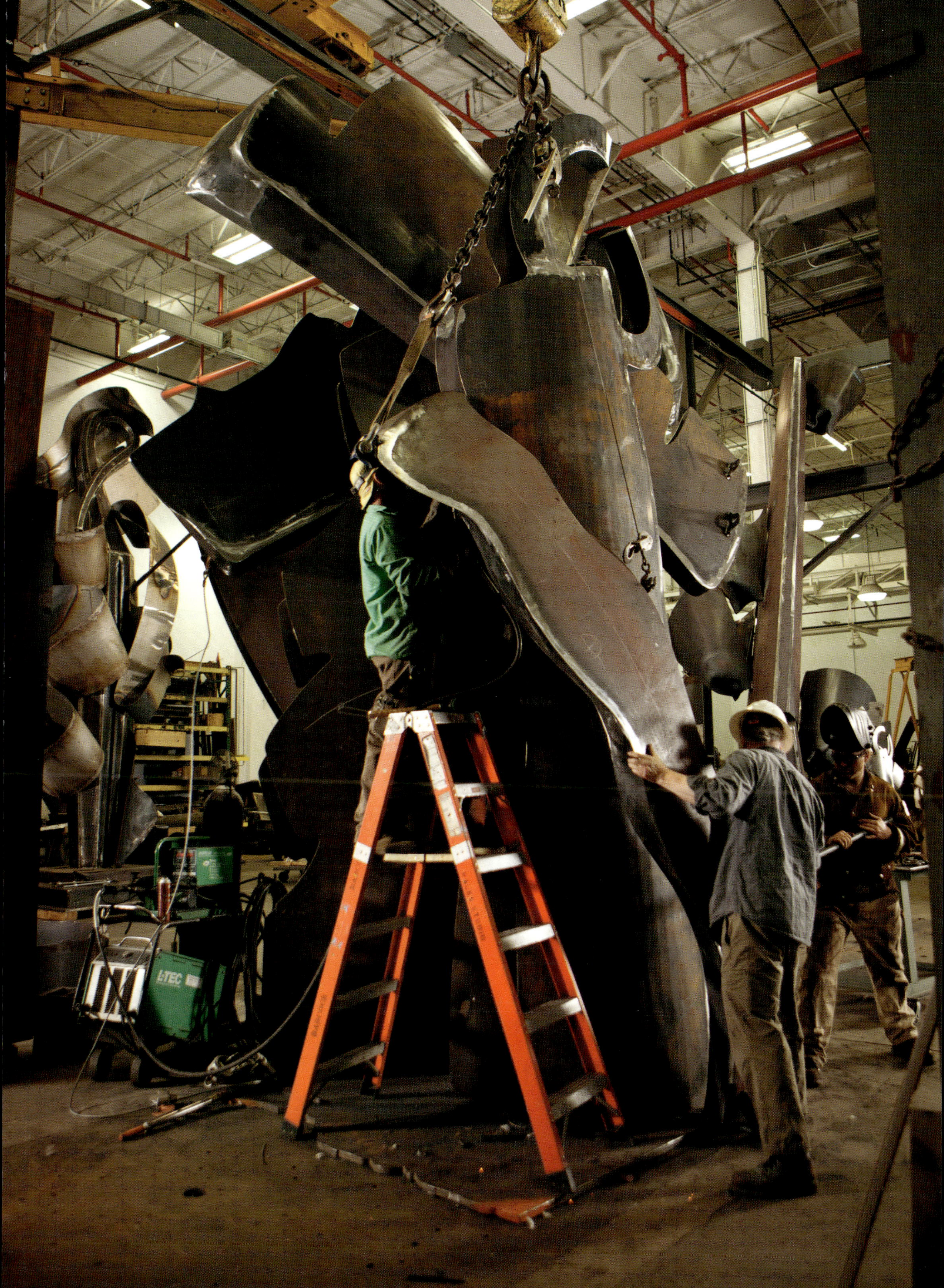

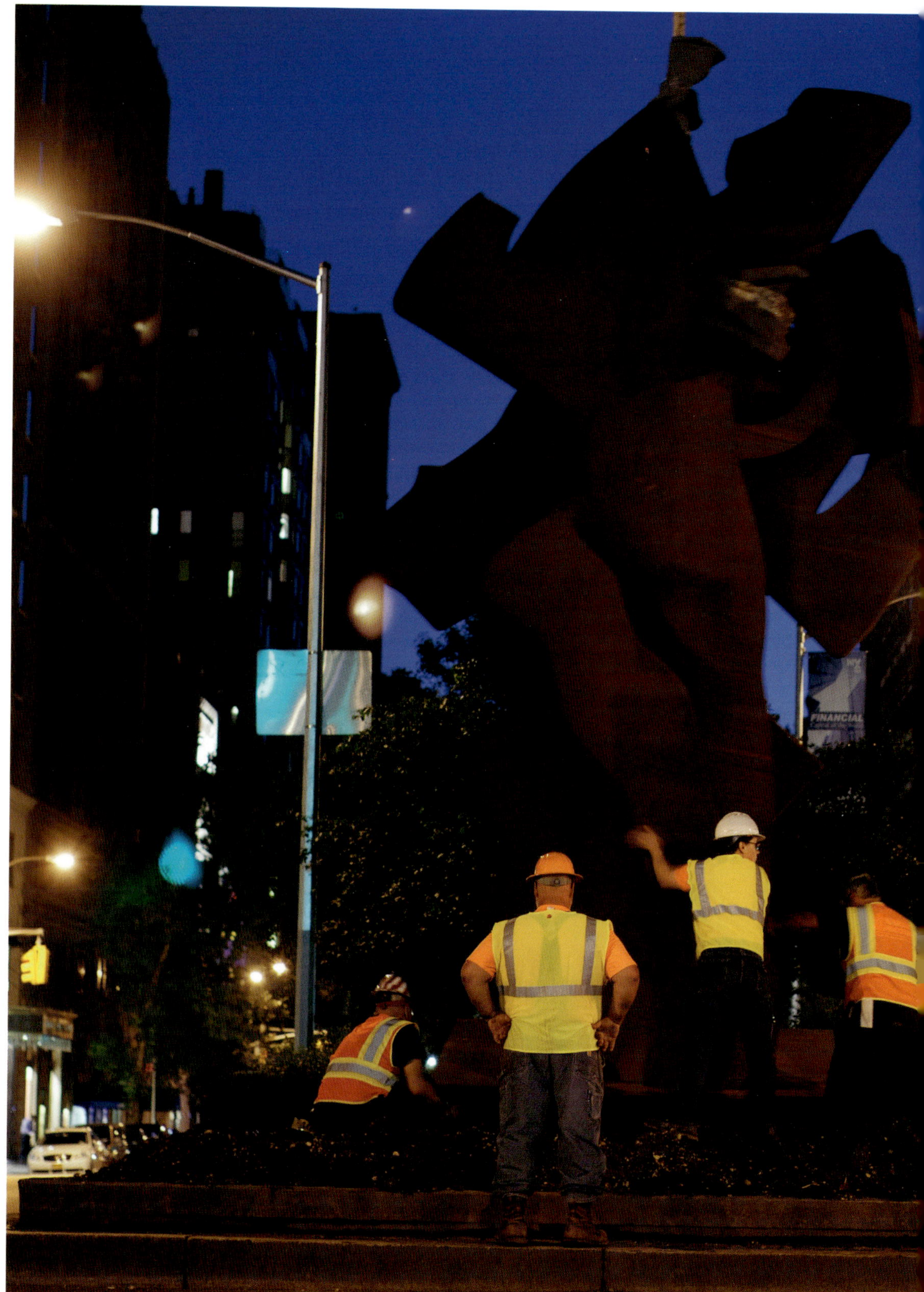

p. 78
Counter Balance
Maquette fabrication
Paley Studios,
Lyell Avenue
Rochester, New York

p. 79
Counter Balance
Fabrication
Paley Studios,
Lyell Avenue
Rochester, New York

right
Counter Balance
Installation

p. 82
Counter Balance
Detail

p. 83
Counter Balance, 2013
Formed and fabricated
weathering steel
58th Street and Park
Avenue, New York
June 14, 2013

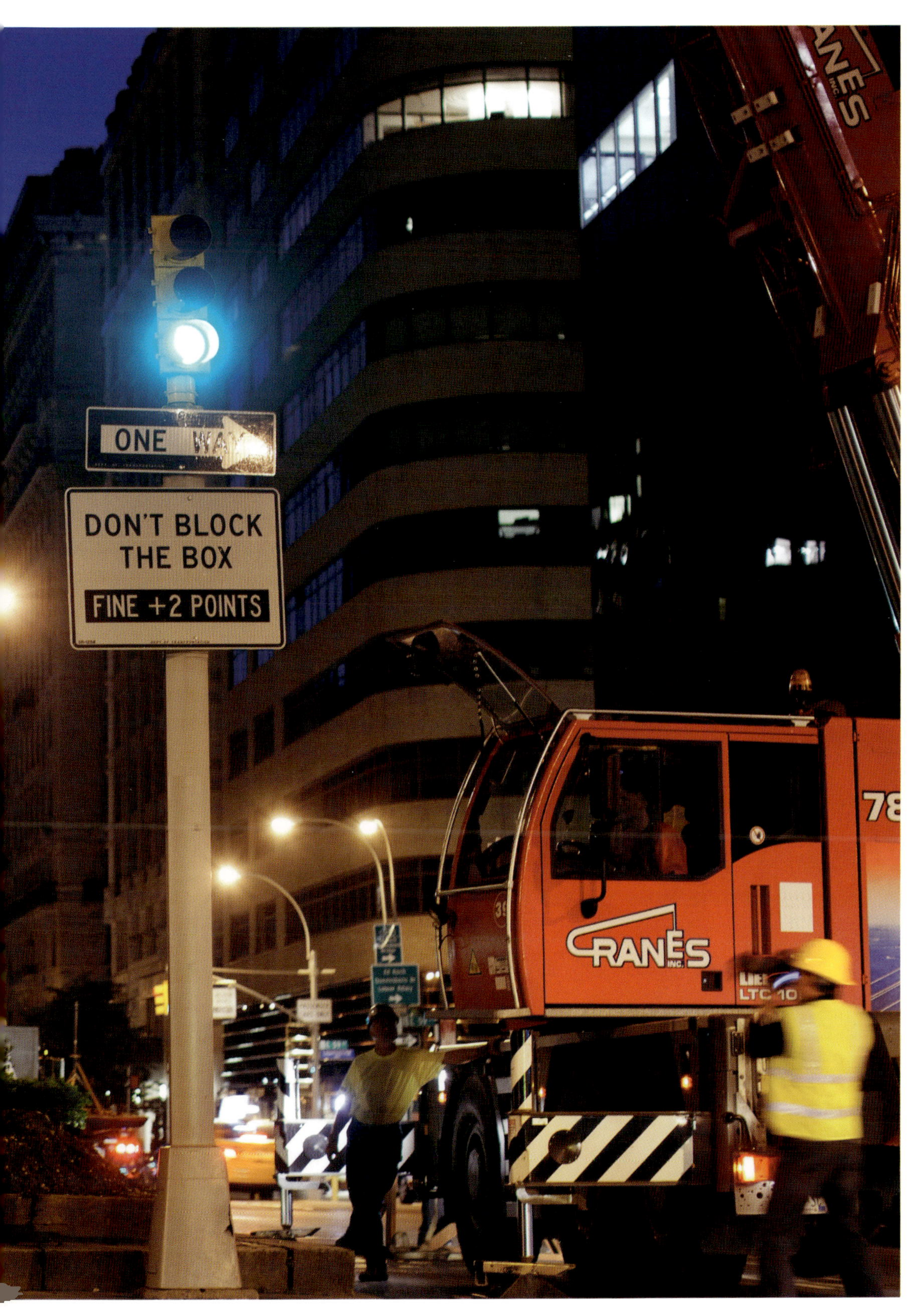ONE WAY
DON'T BLOCK
THE BOX
FINE +2 POINTS
CRANES
INC.

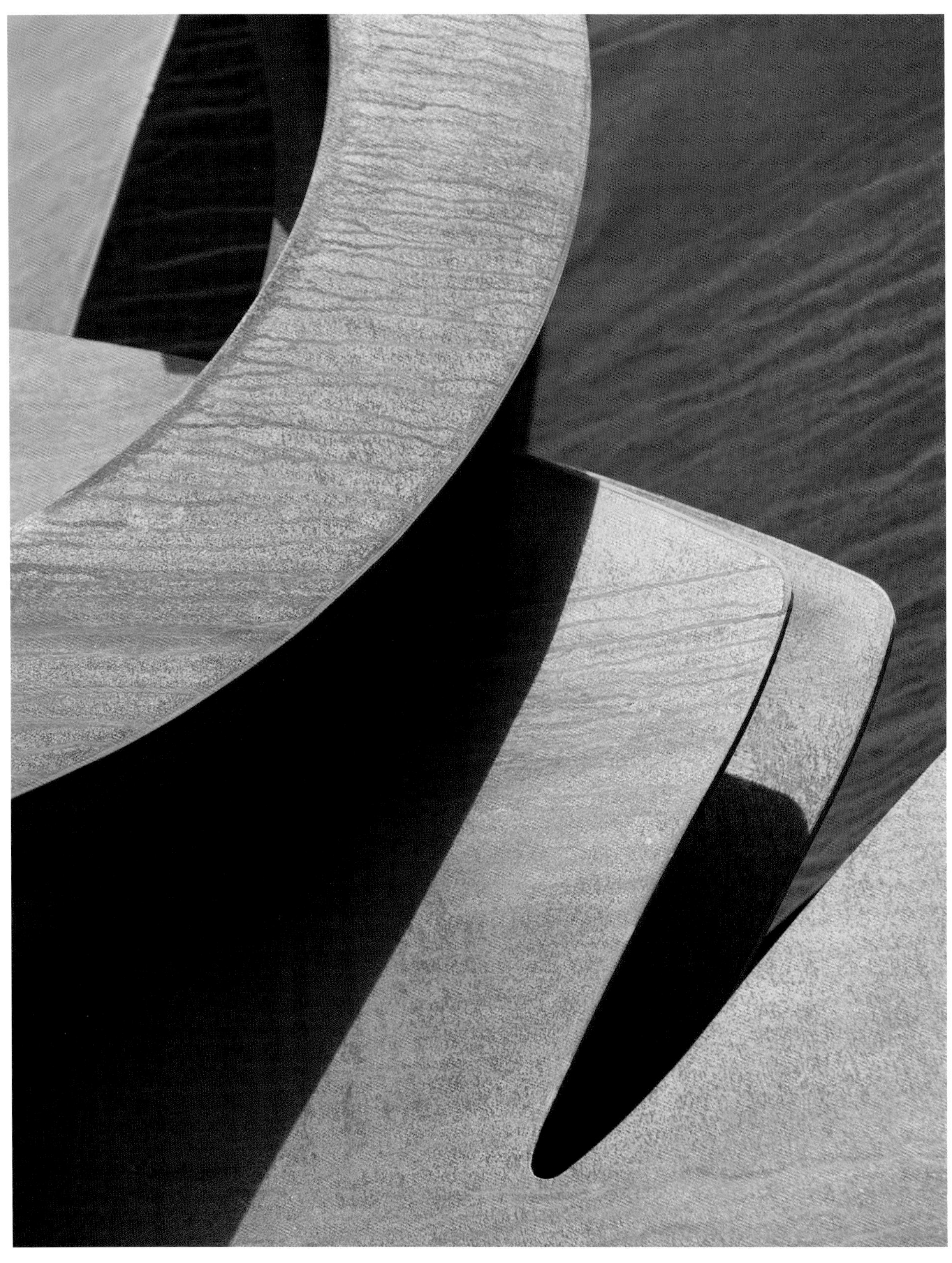

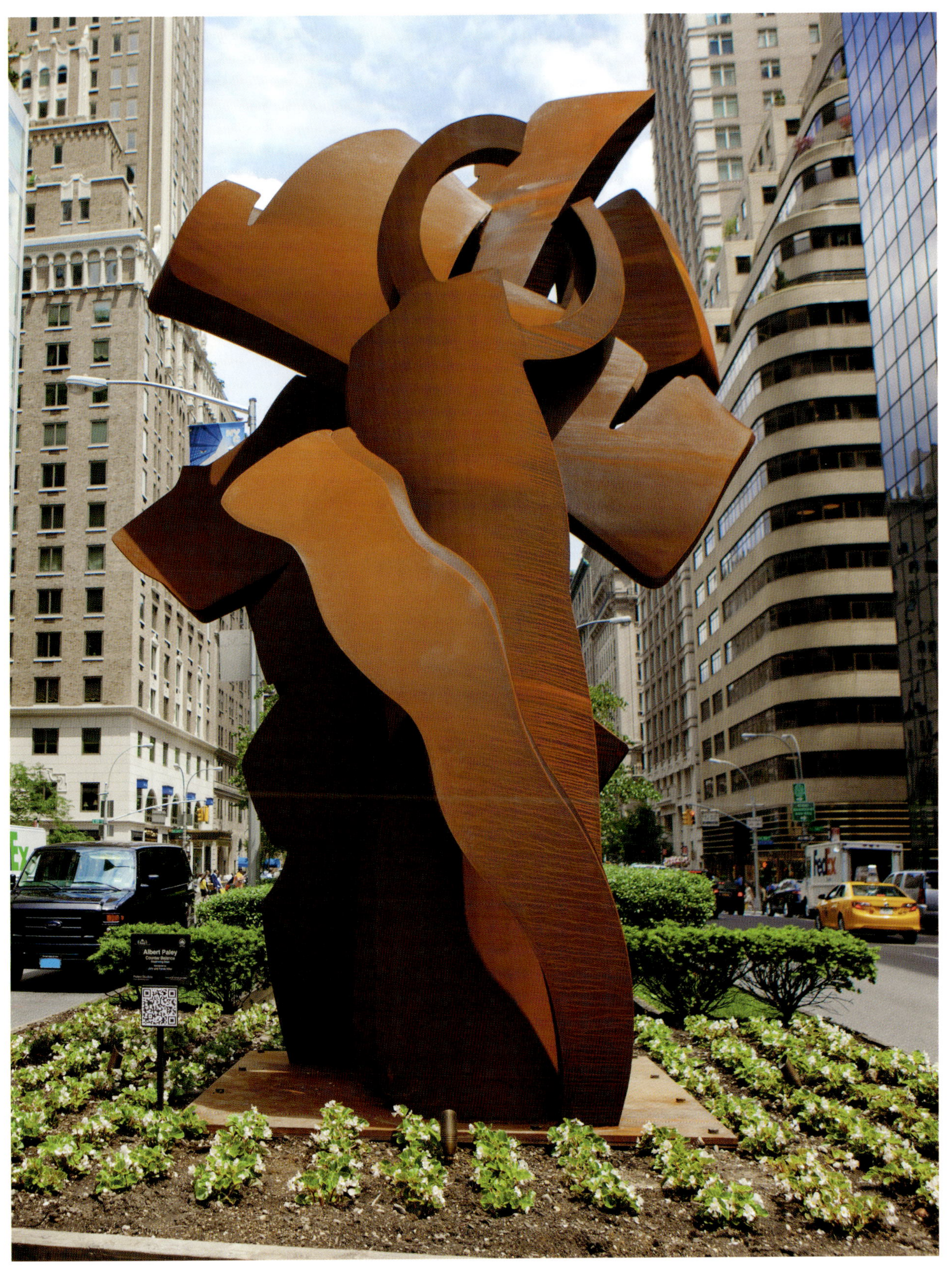

COUNTER BALANCE

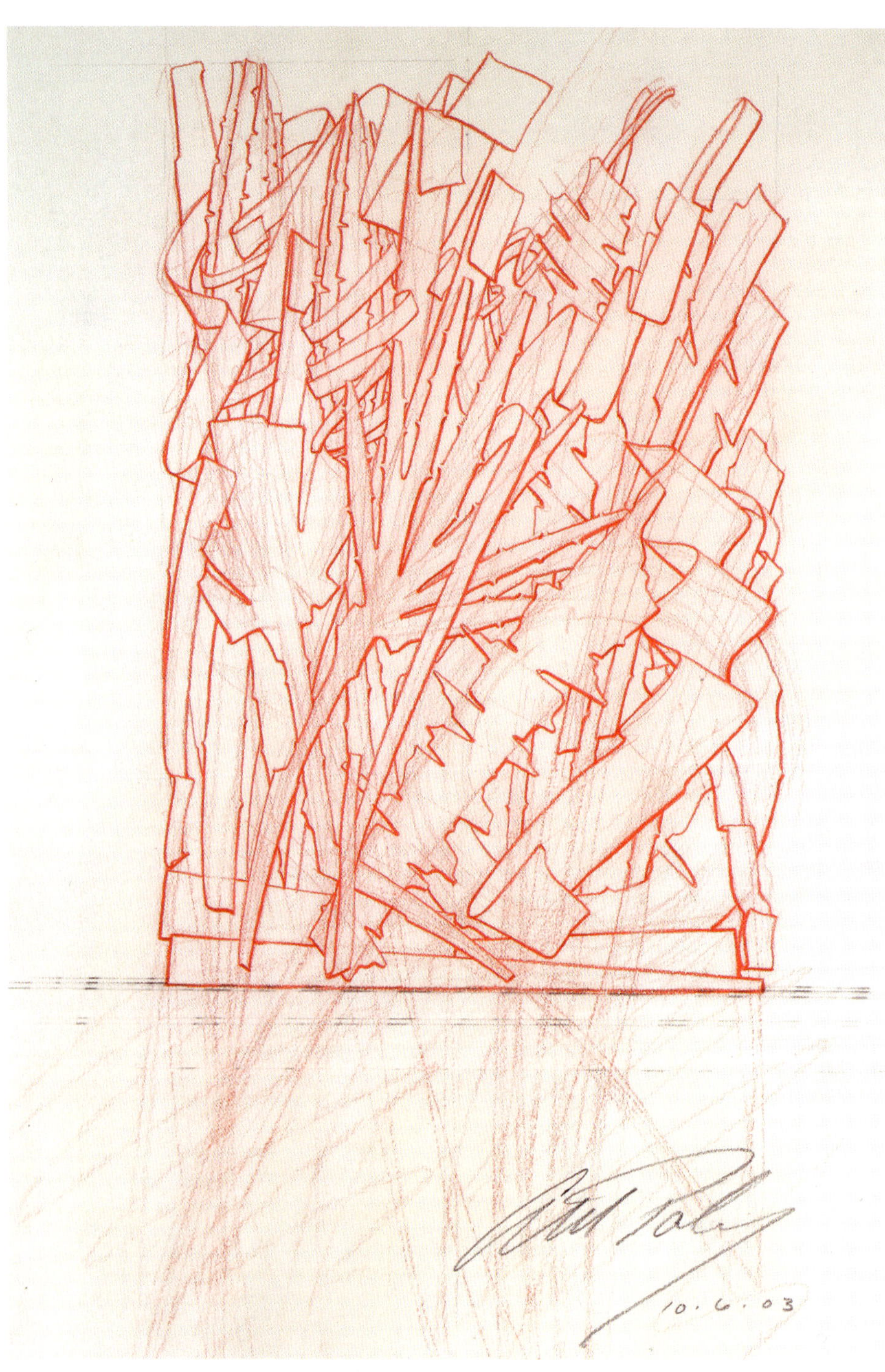

Variance
Concept drawing
Graphite and red pencil
on paper
18" x 12"
Paley Studios Archive

Variance
Maquette
Formed and fabricated
patinated bronze, wood
base
53½" x 39¼" x 15"
Paley Studios Archive

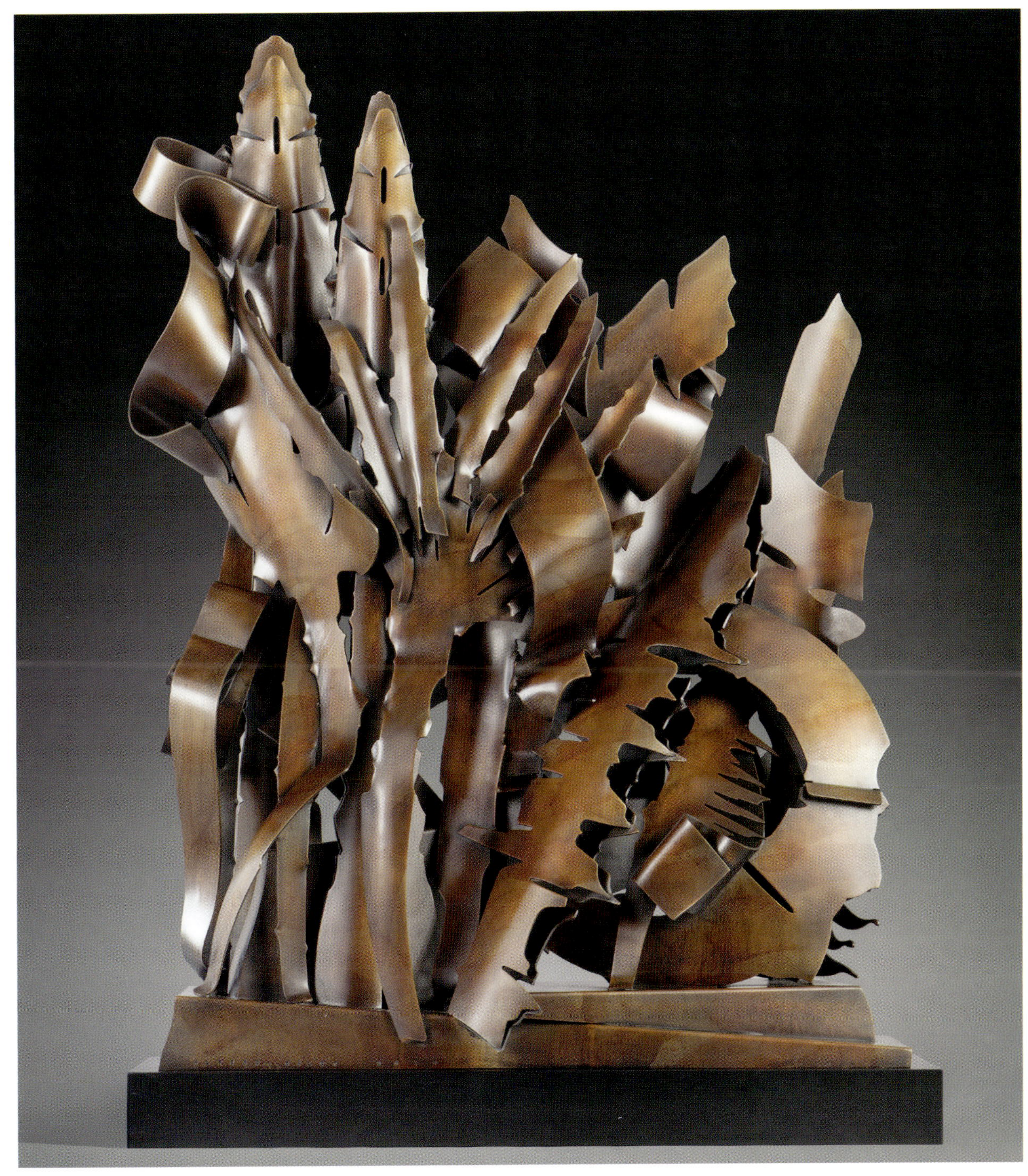

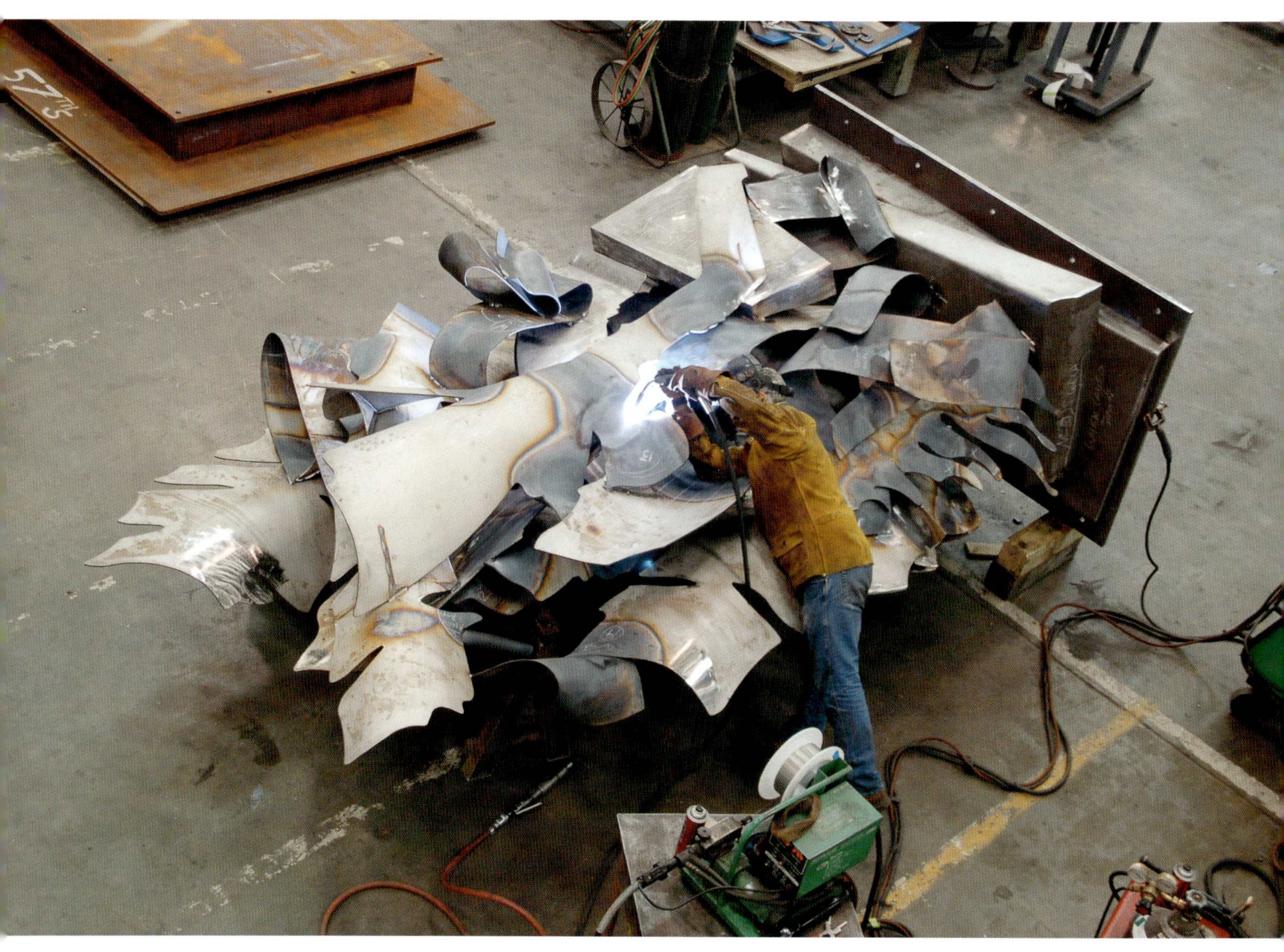

above
Variance
Fabrication
Paley Studios, Lyell Avenue
Rochester, New York

pp. 84-85
Variance
Installation
59th Street and Park
Avenue, New York
June 14, 2013

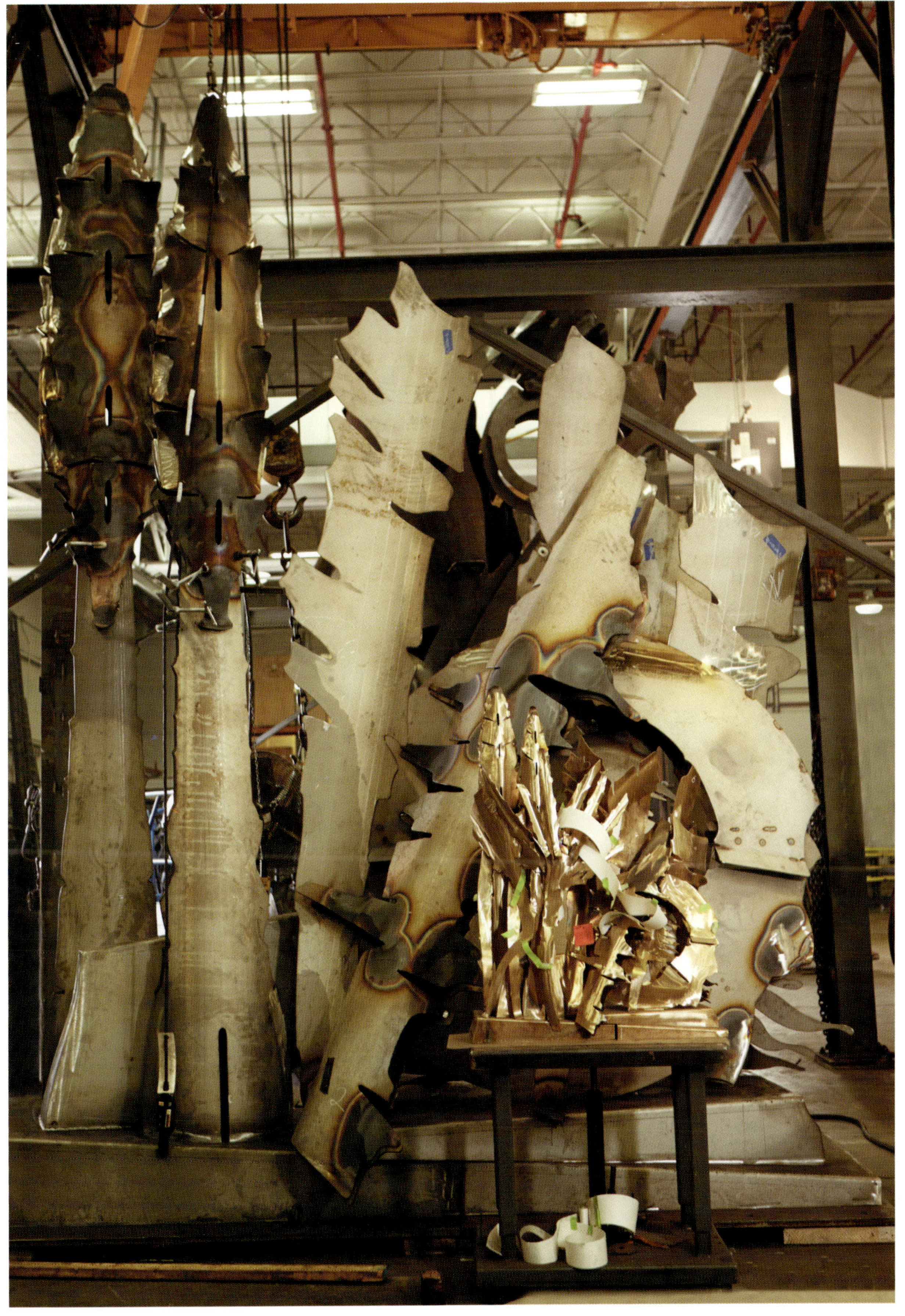

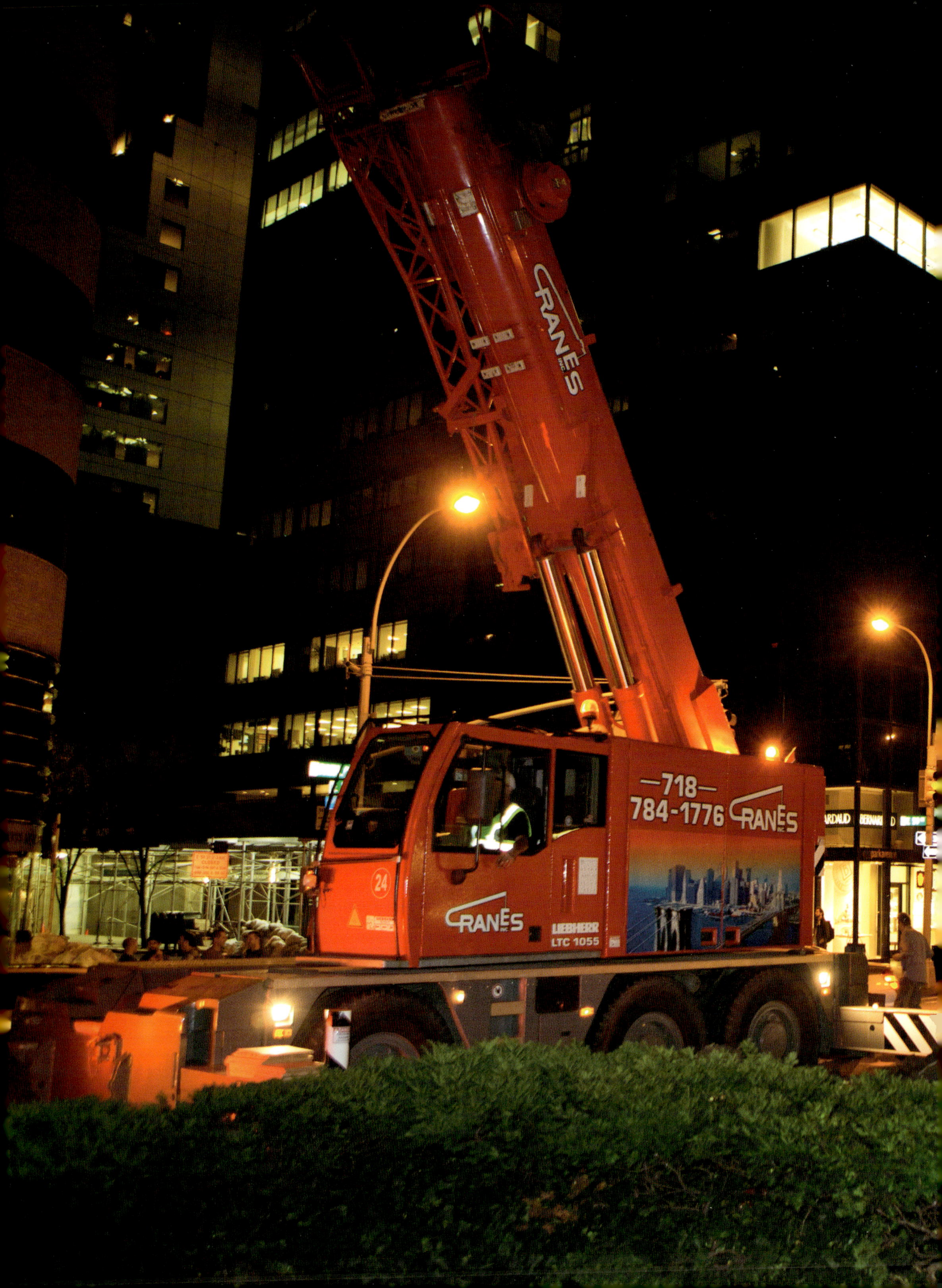
CRANES
INC
—718—
784-1776 RANES
INC
CRANES
INC
LIEBHERR
LTC 1055
24

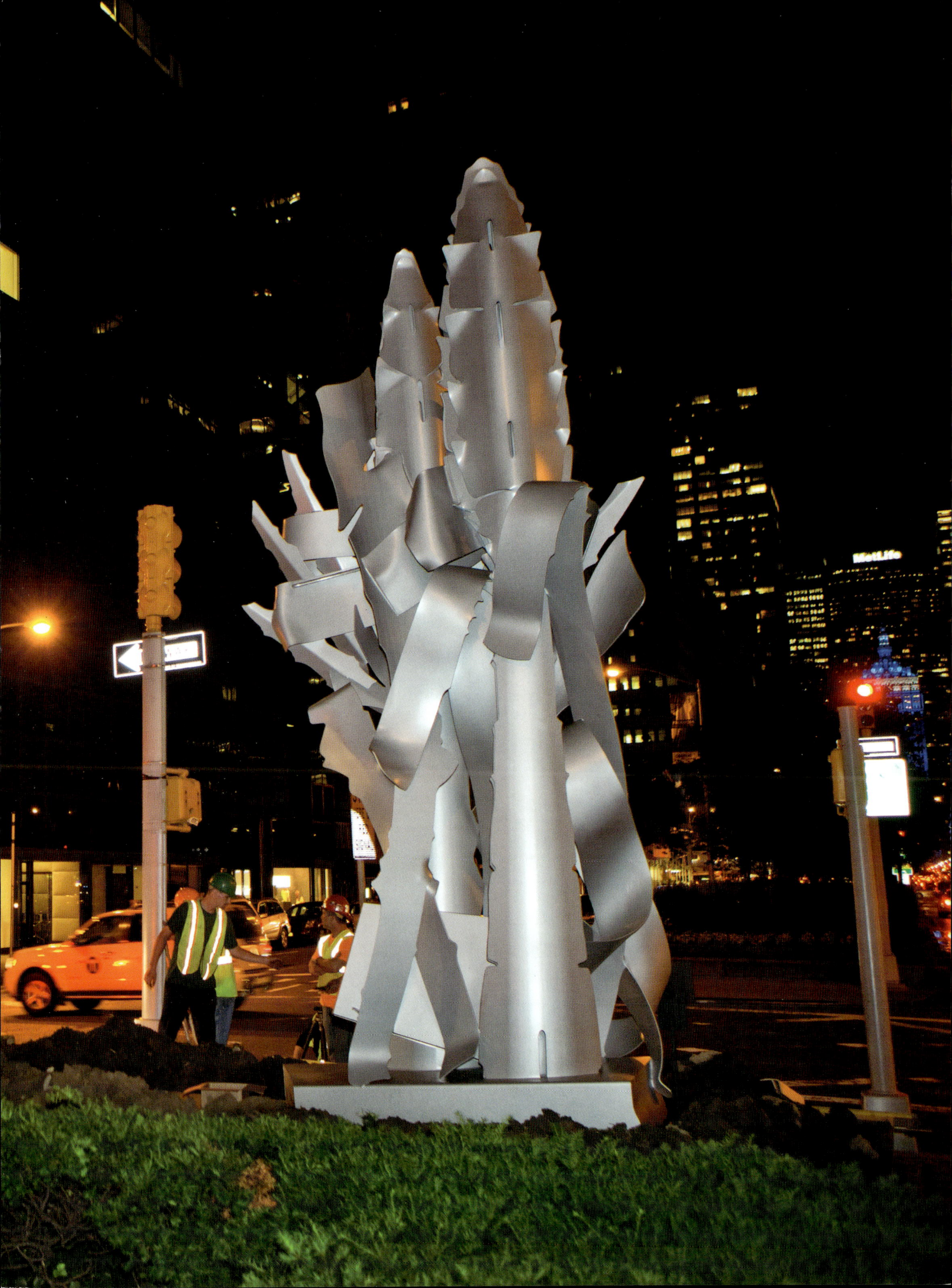

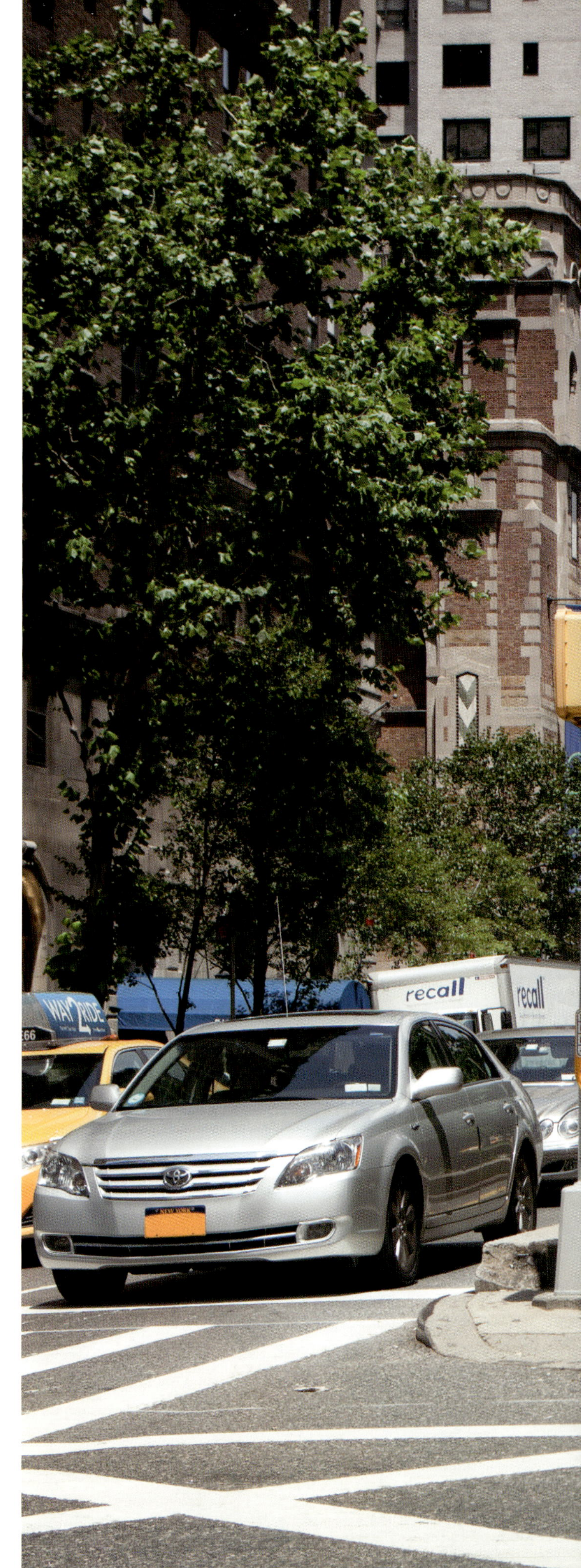

Variance, 2013
Formed and fabricated
stainless steel in two
sections
16′11″ x 12′10½″ x 5′2″
59th Street and Park
Avenue, New York

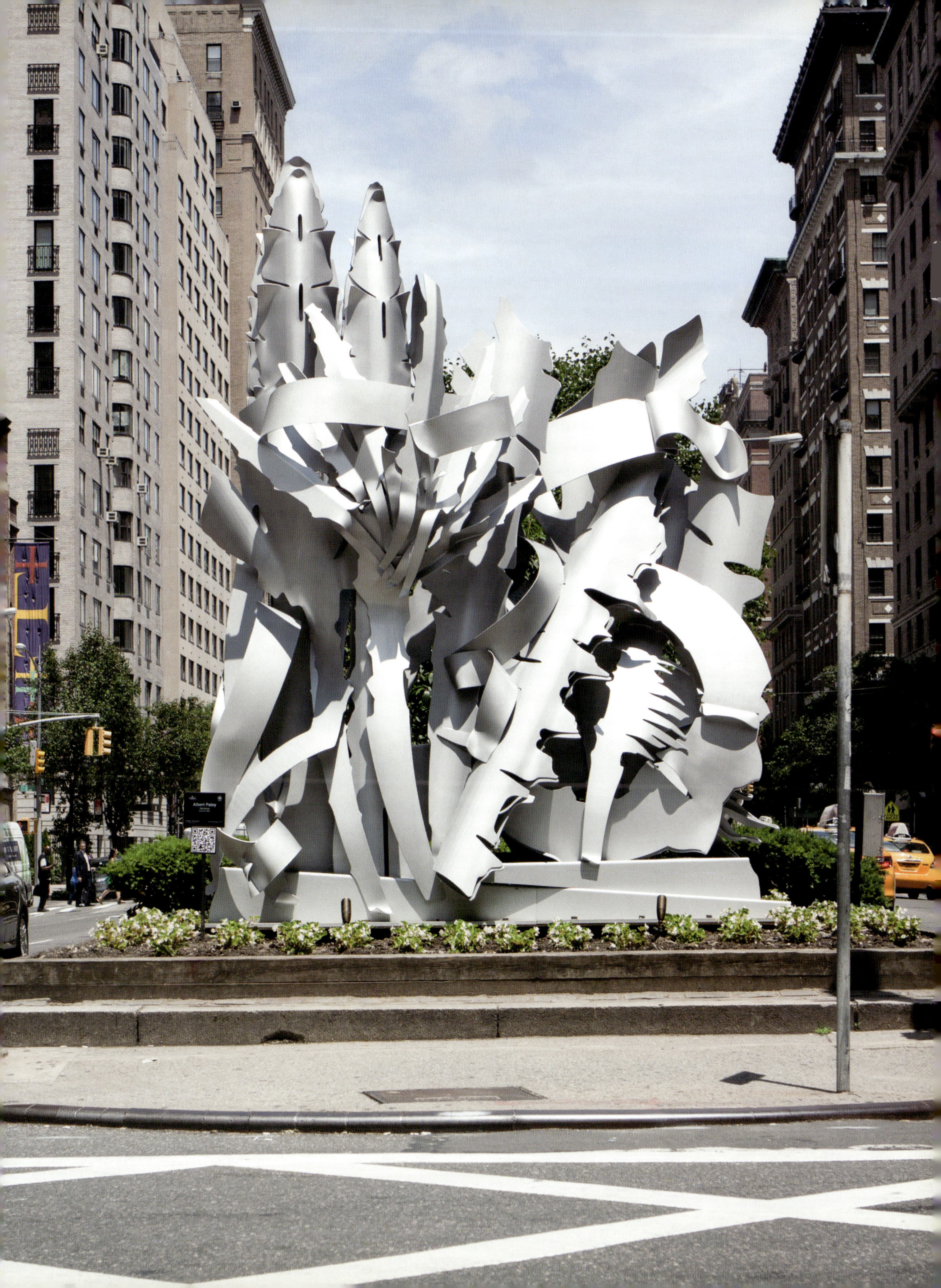

TILTED COLUMN

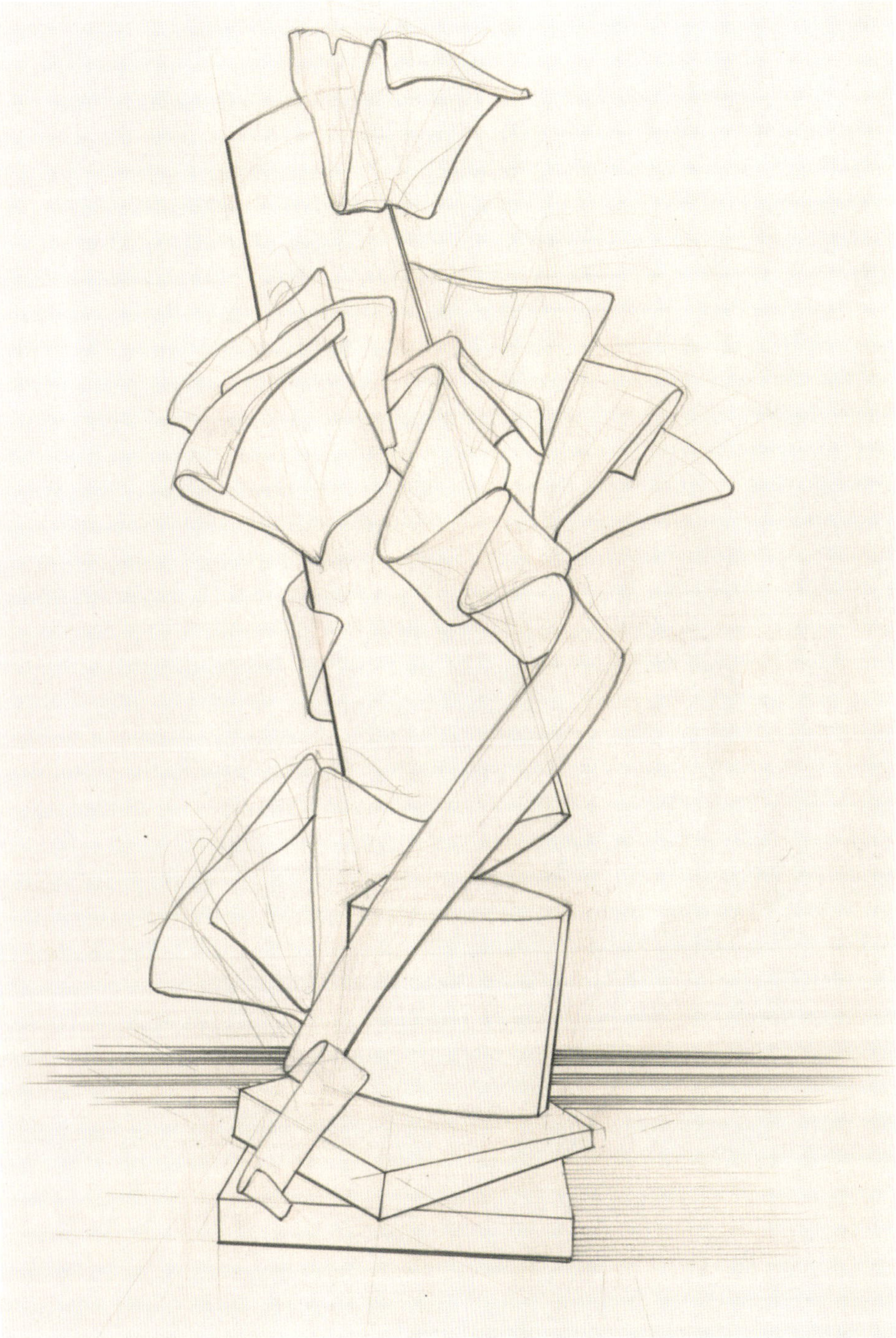

Tilted Column
Concept drawing
Graphite and red pencil
on paper
24″ x 19″
Paley Studios Archive

Tilted Column
Cardboard model
27″ x 12″ x 8″
Paley Studios Archive

Tilted Column
Maquette
Formed and fabricated
patinated steel, wood base
40″ x 17″ x 15″
Paley Studios Archive

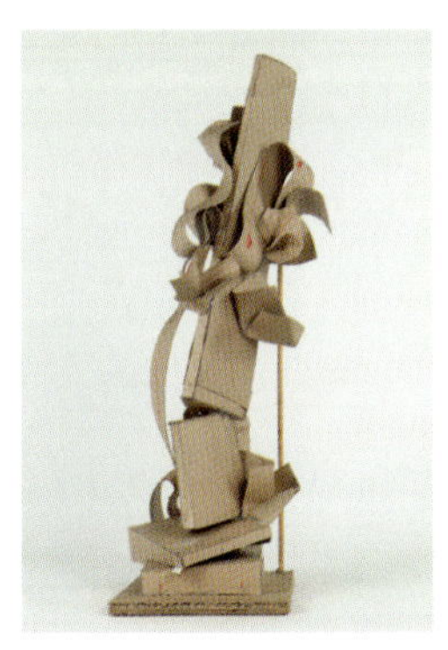

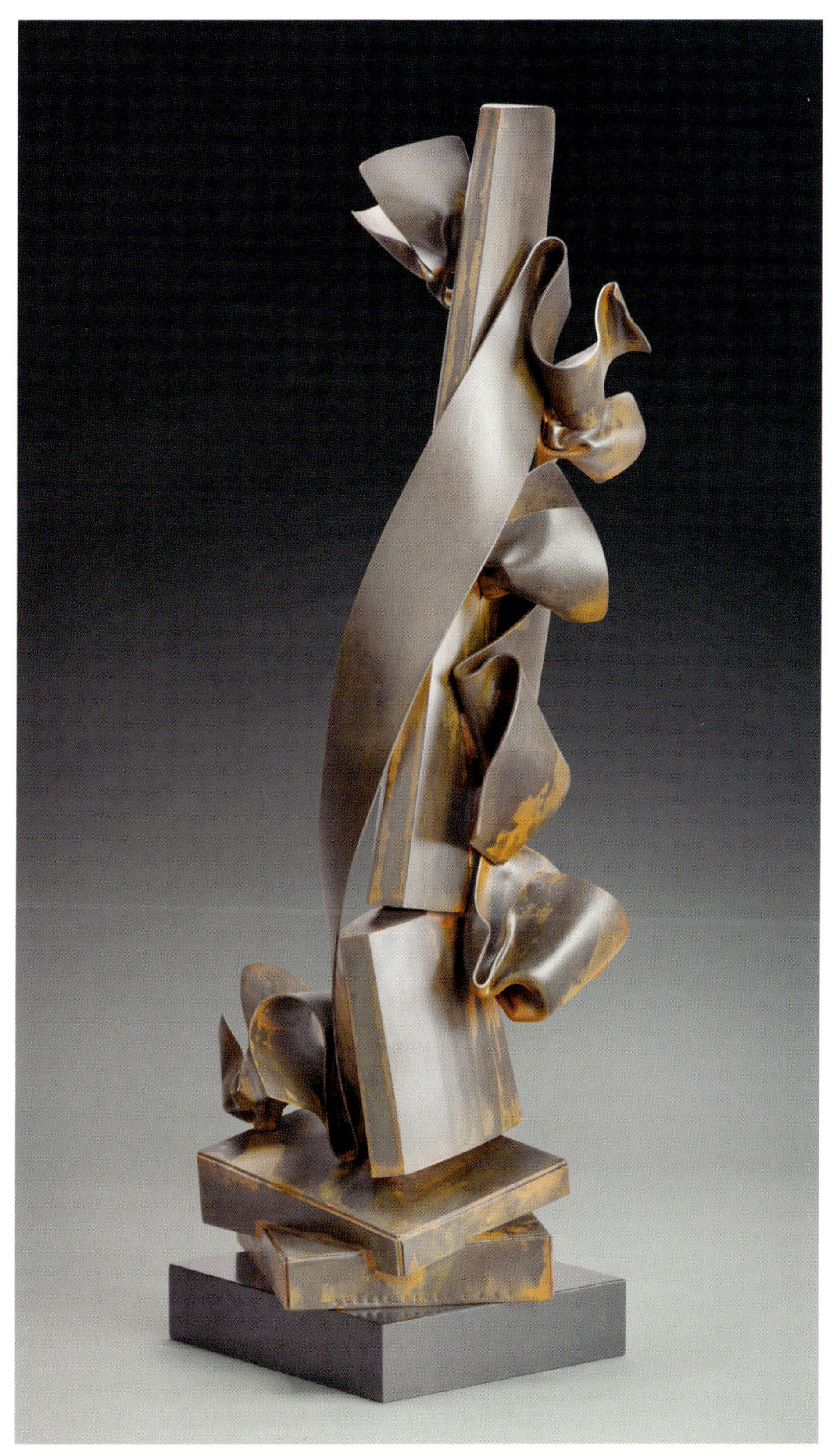

TILTED COLUMN

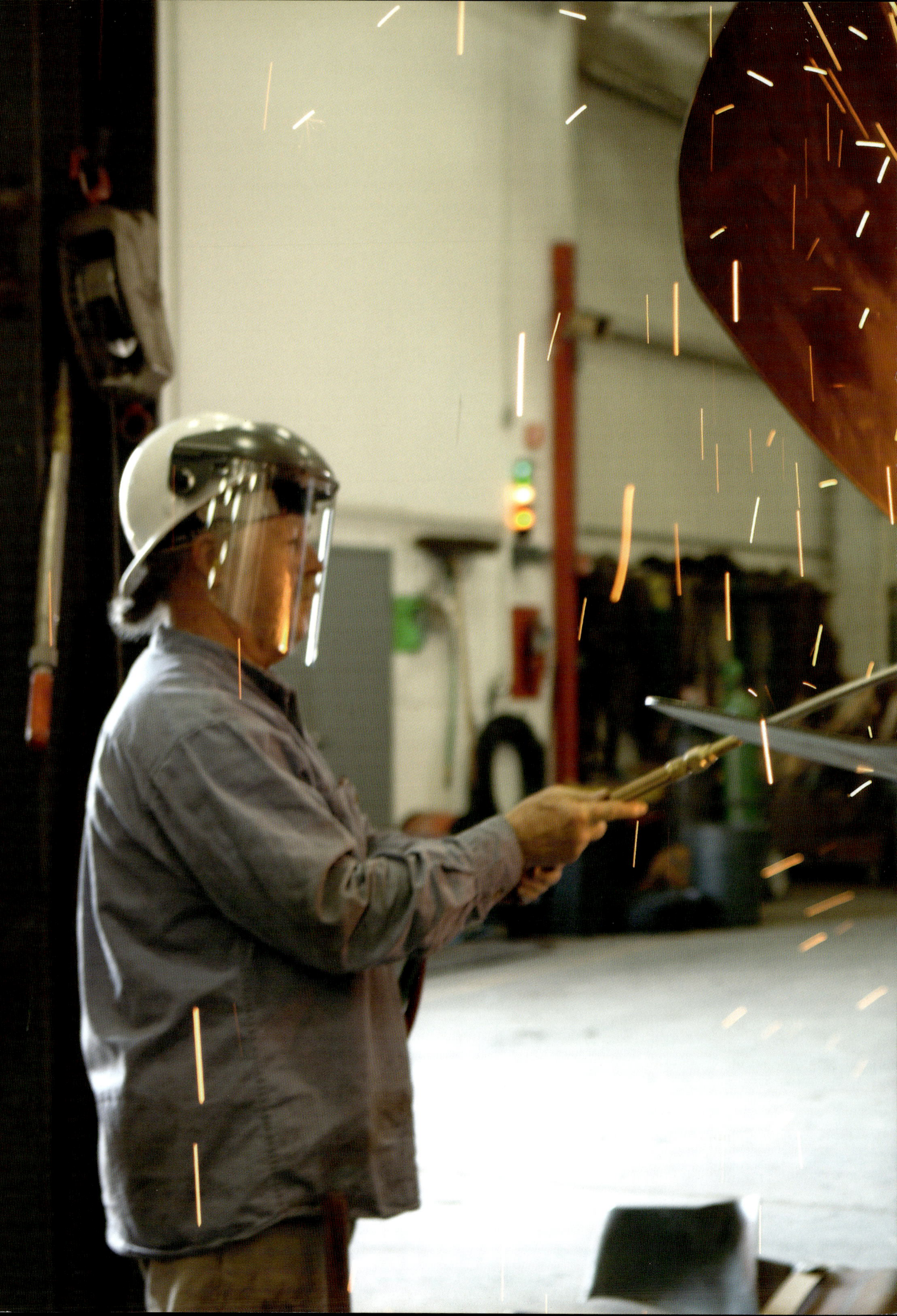

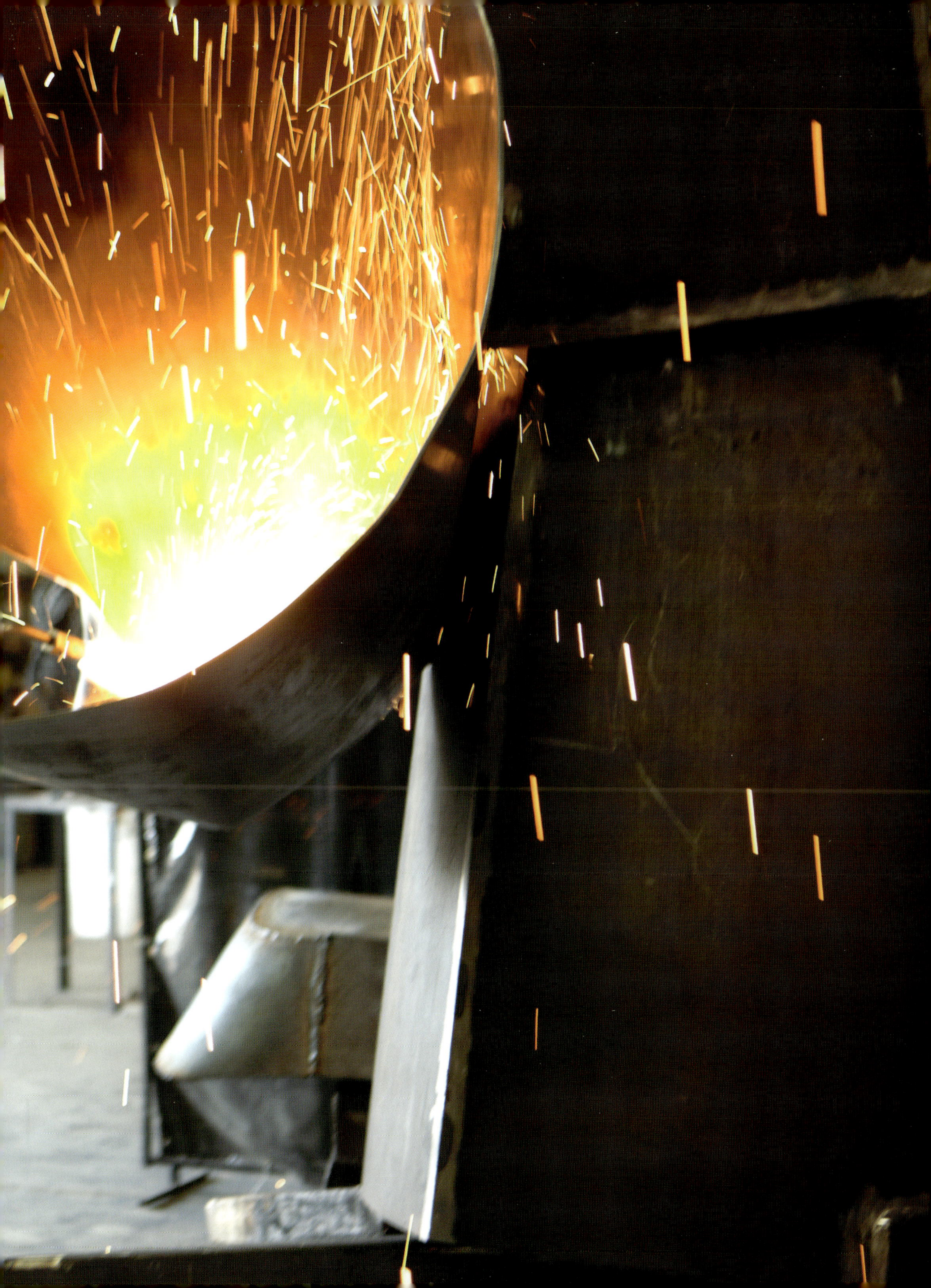

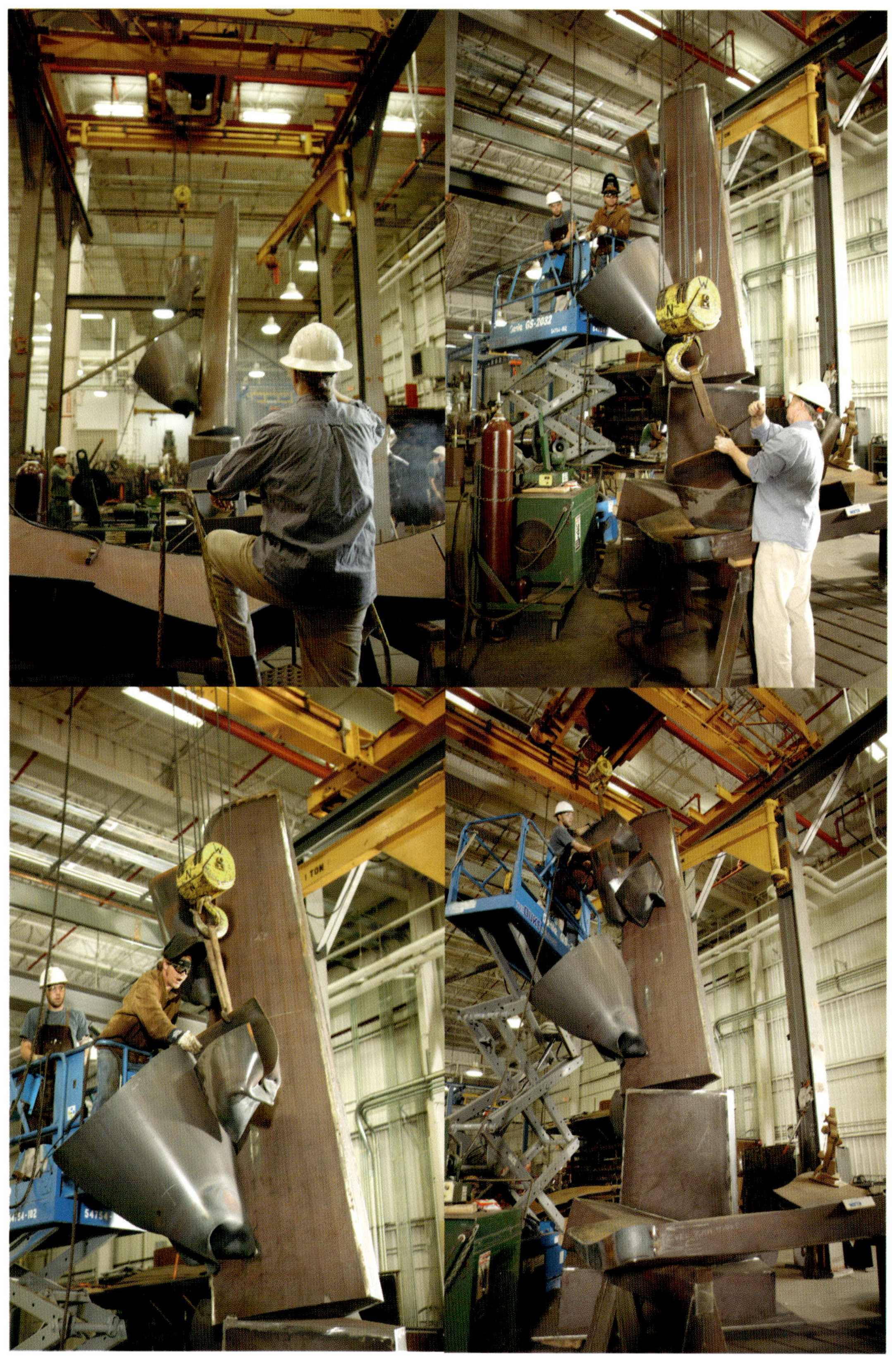

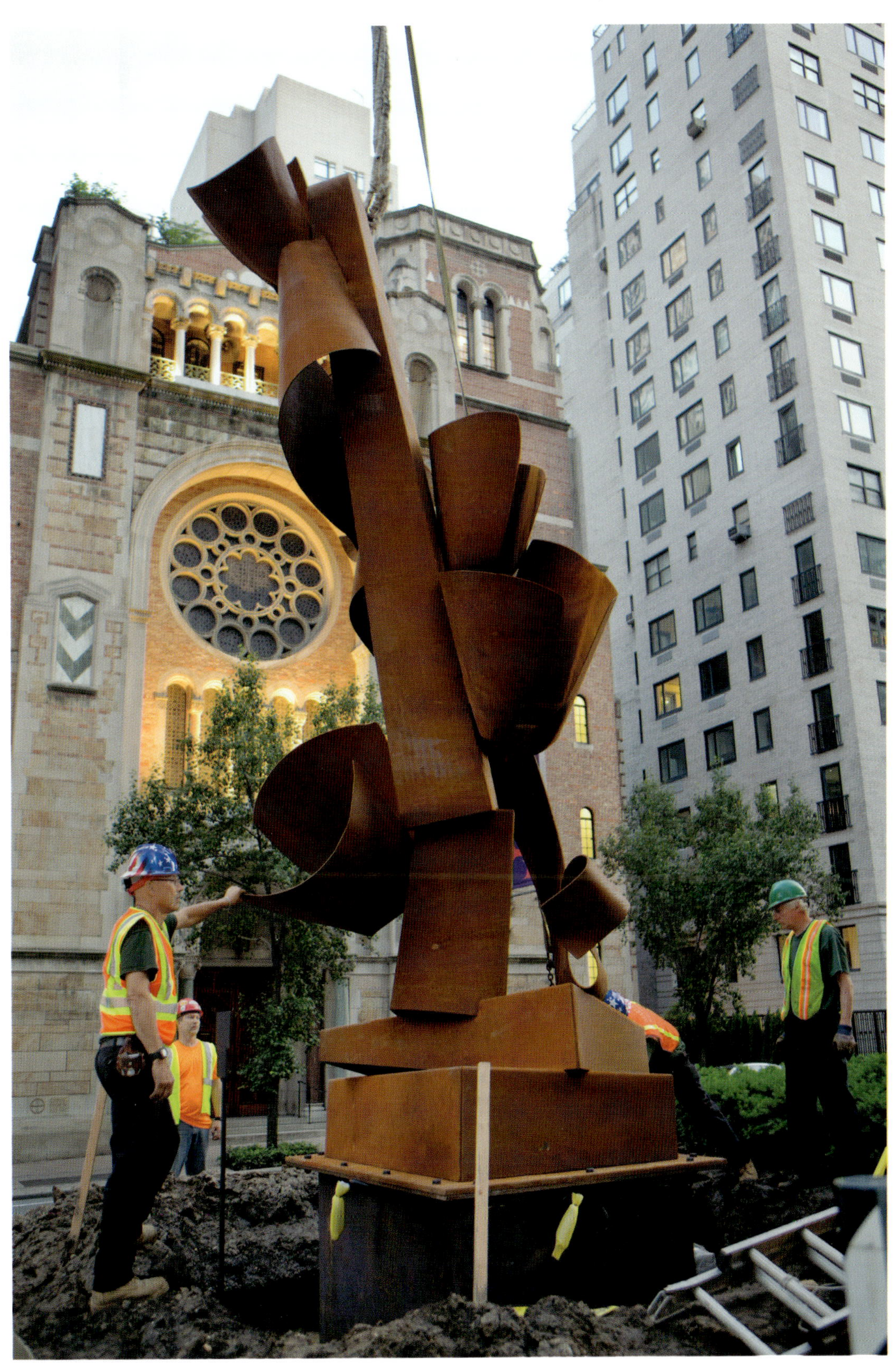

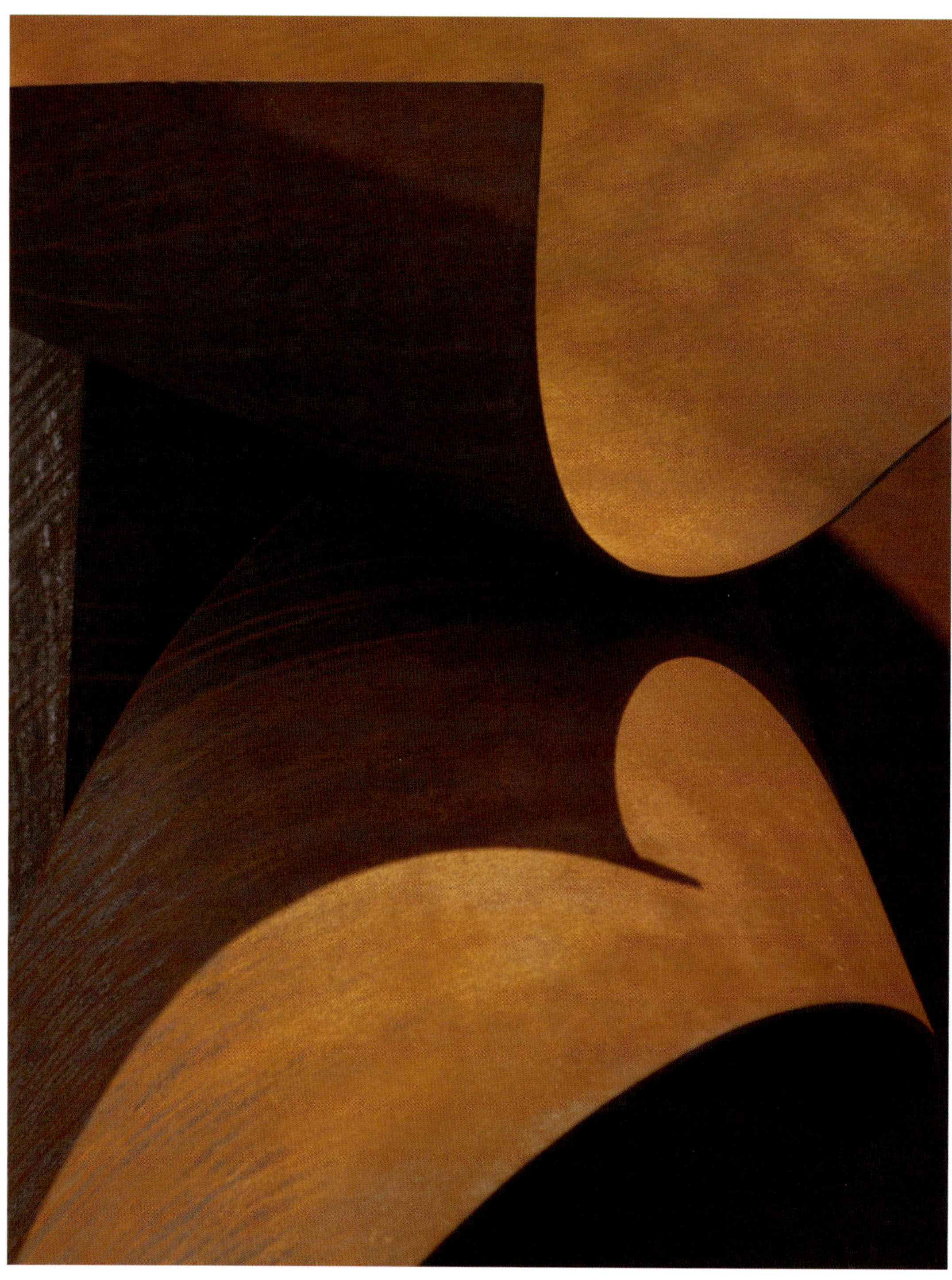

p. 96
Tilted Column
Fabrication
Paley Studios, Lyell Avenue
Rochester, New York

p. 97
Tilted Column
Installation
60th Street and Park
Avenue, New York
June 14, 2013

above
Tilted Column
Detail

right
Tilted Column, 2013
Formed and fabricated
weathering steel
19'10" x 9'5" x 7'11"
60th Street and Park
Avenue, New York

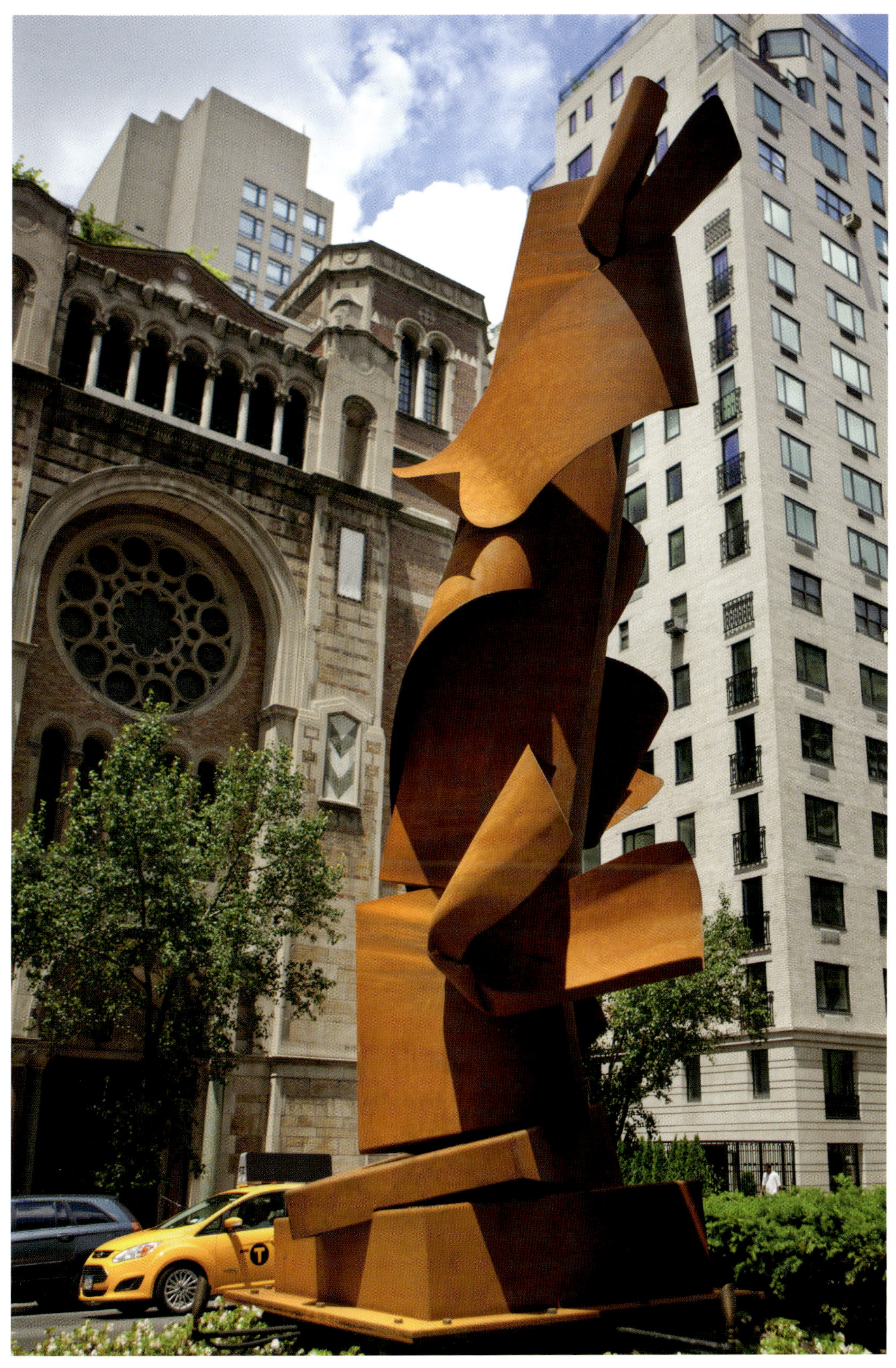

61ST SOUTH
AMBIGUOUS RESPONSE

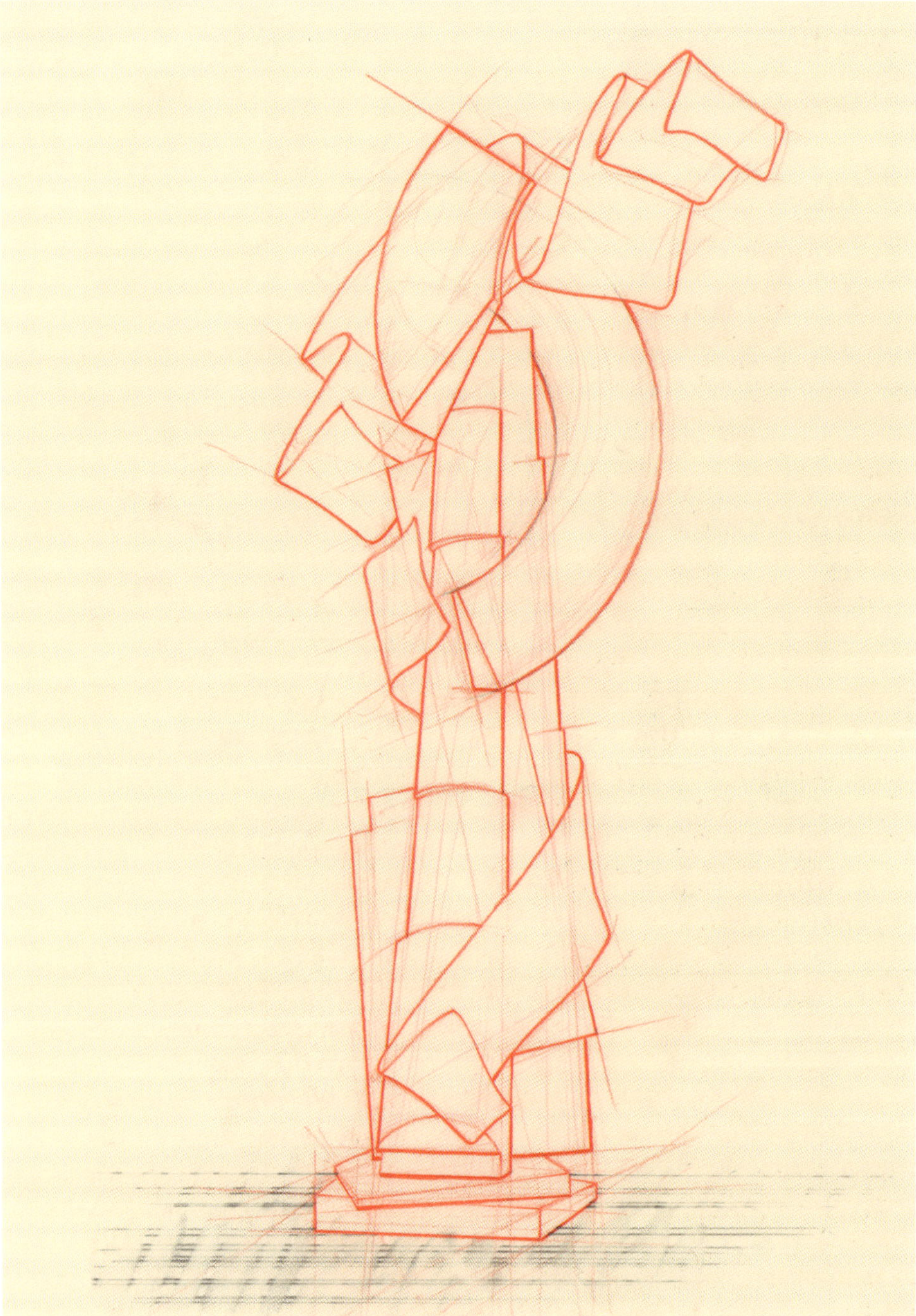

Ambiguous Response
Concept drawing
Graphite and red pencil
on paper
24" x 19"
Paley Studios Archive

Ambiguous Response
Photomontage
10" x 8"
Paley Studios Archive

Ambiguous Response
Maquette
Formed and fabricated
patinated steel with
wood base
39" x 17" dia.
Paley Studios Archive

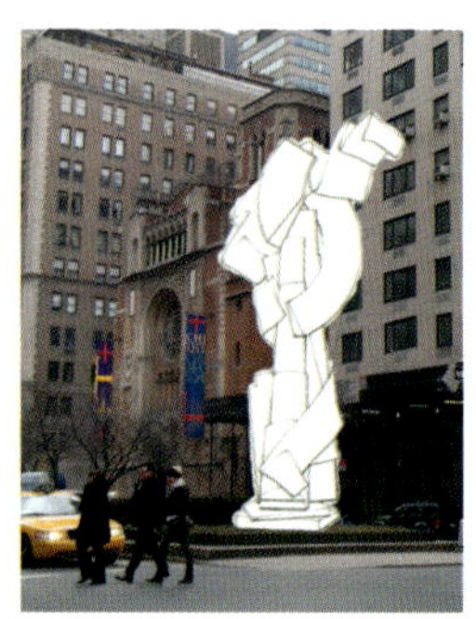

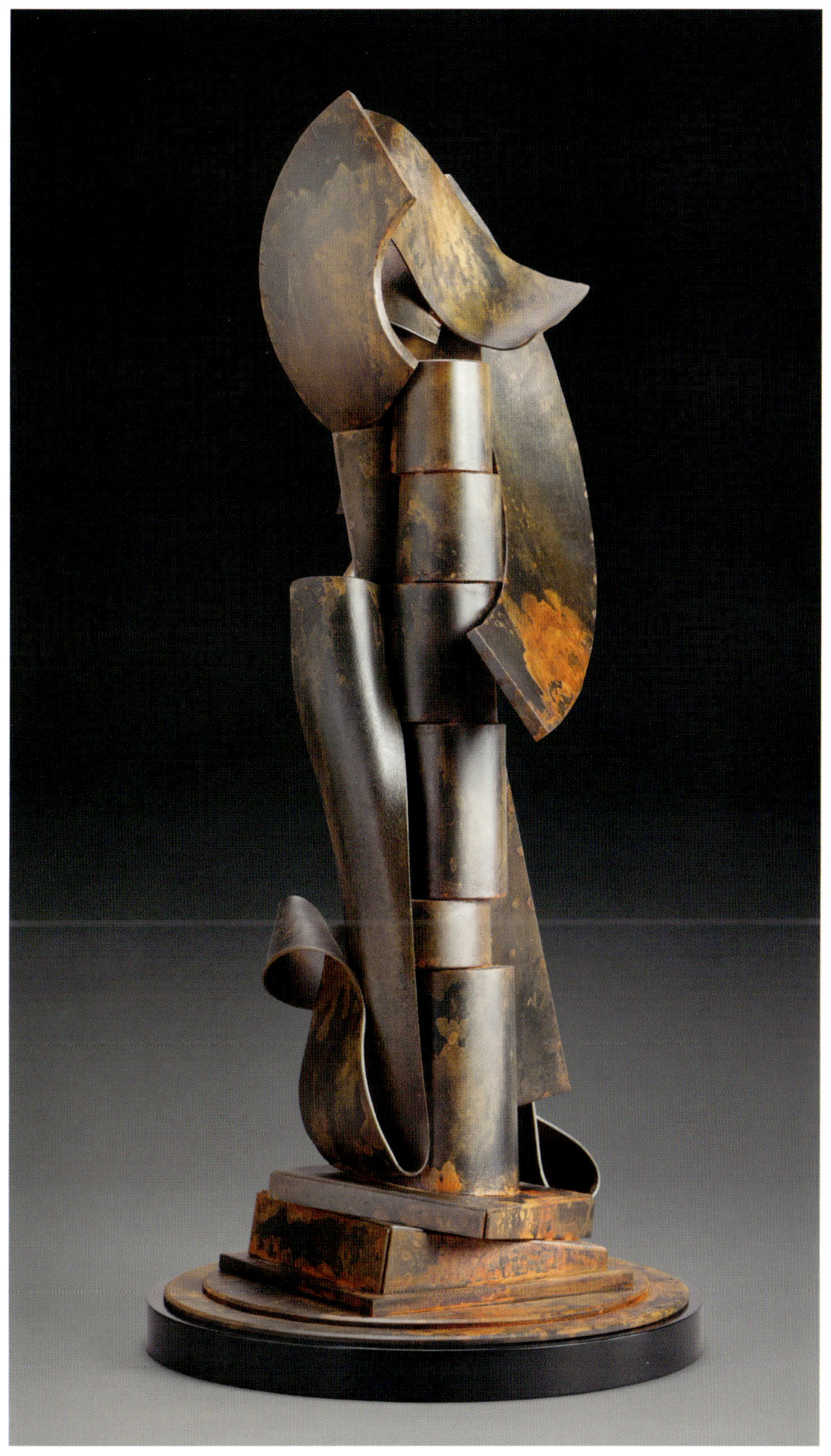

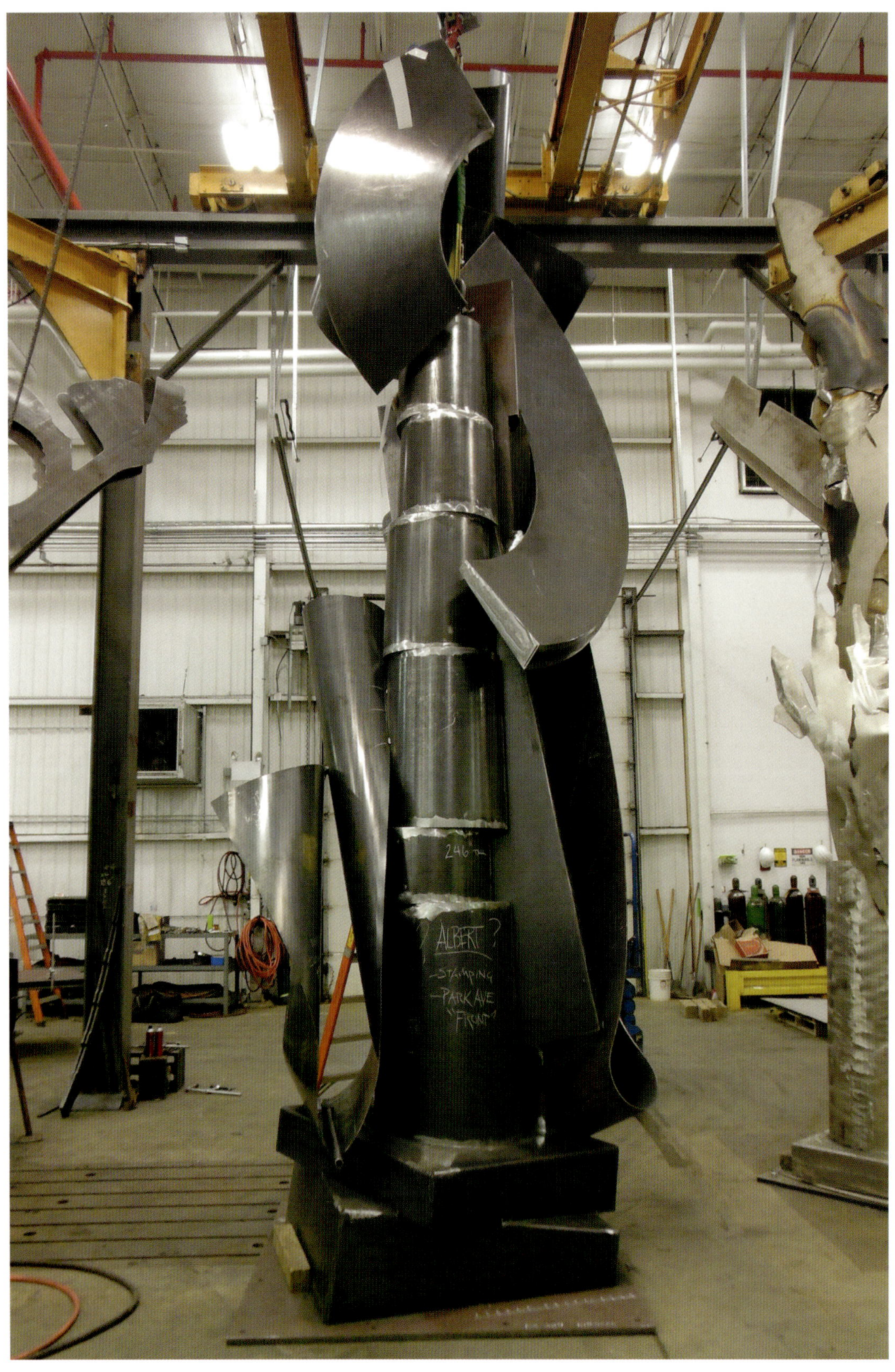

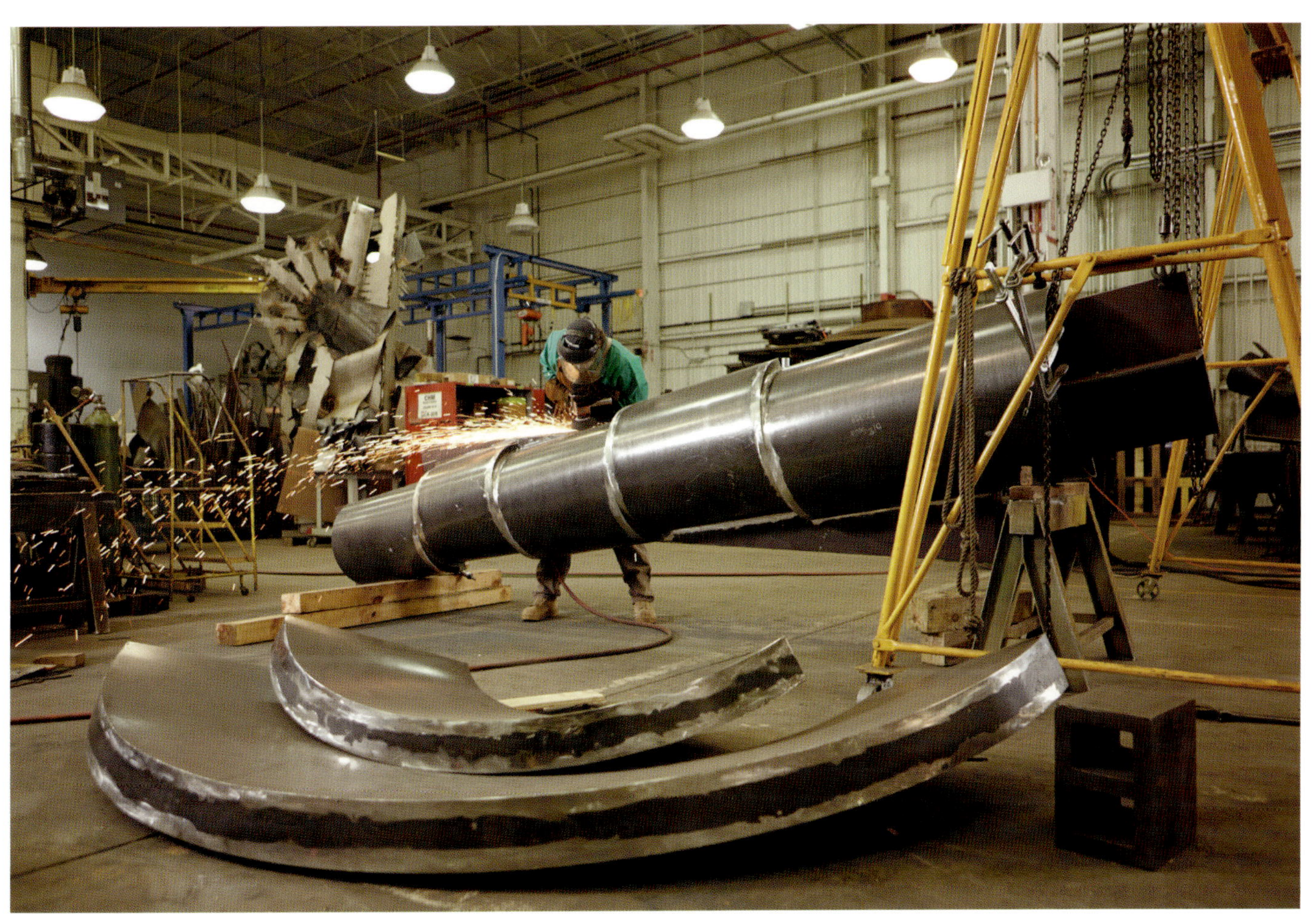

Ambiguous Response
Fabrication
Paley Studios, Lyell Avenue
Rochester, New York

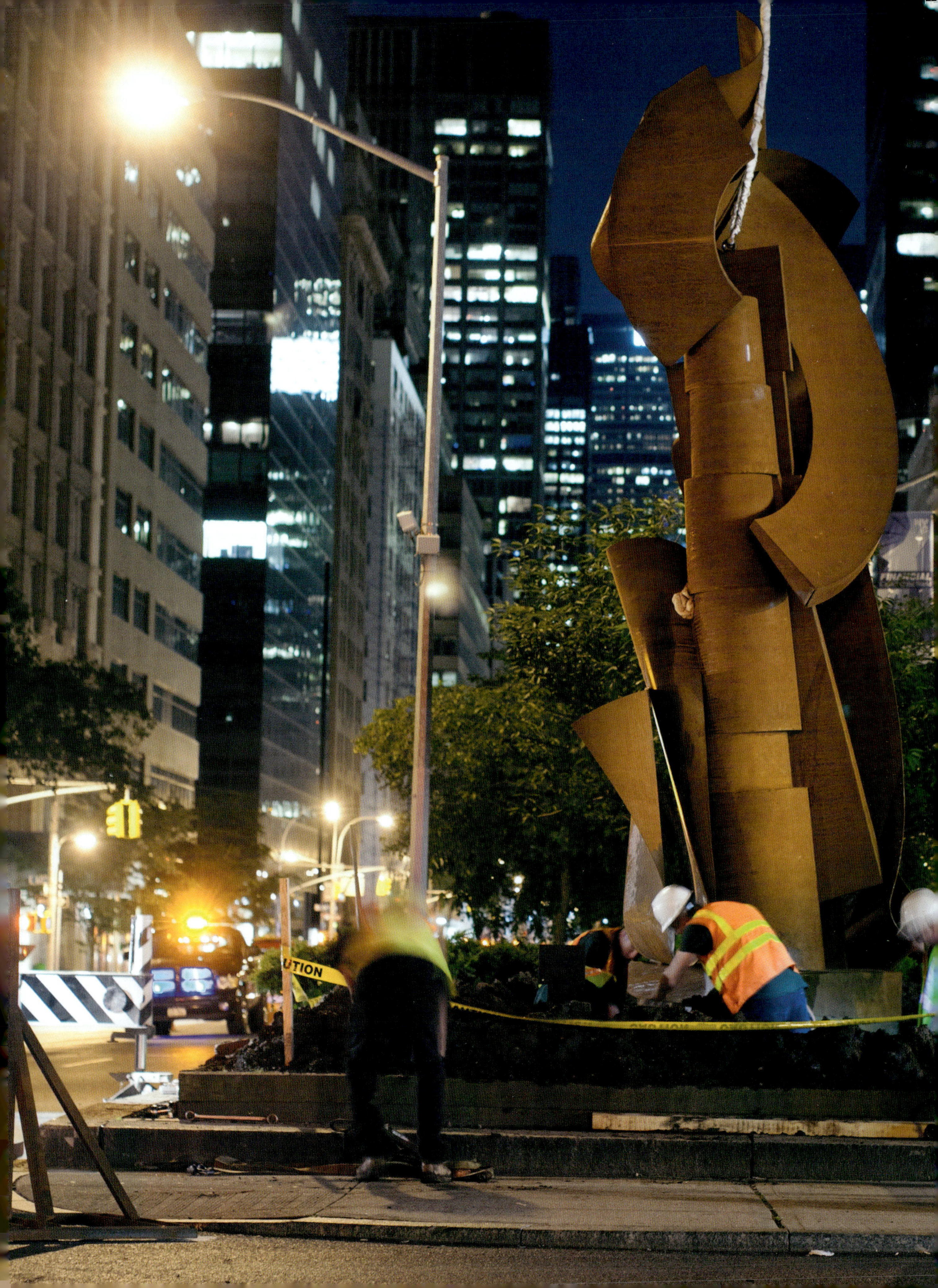

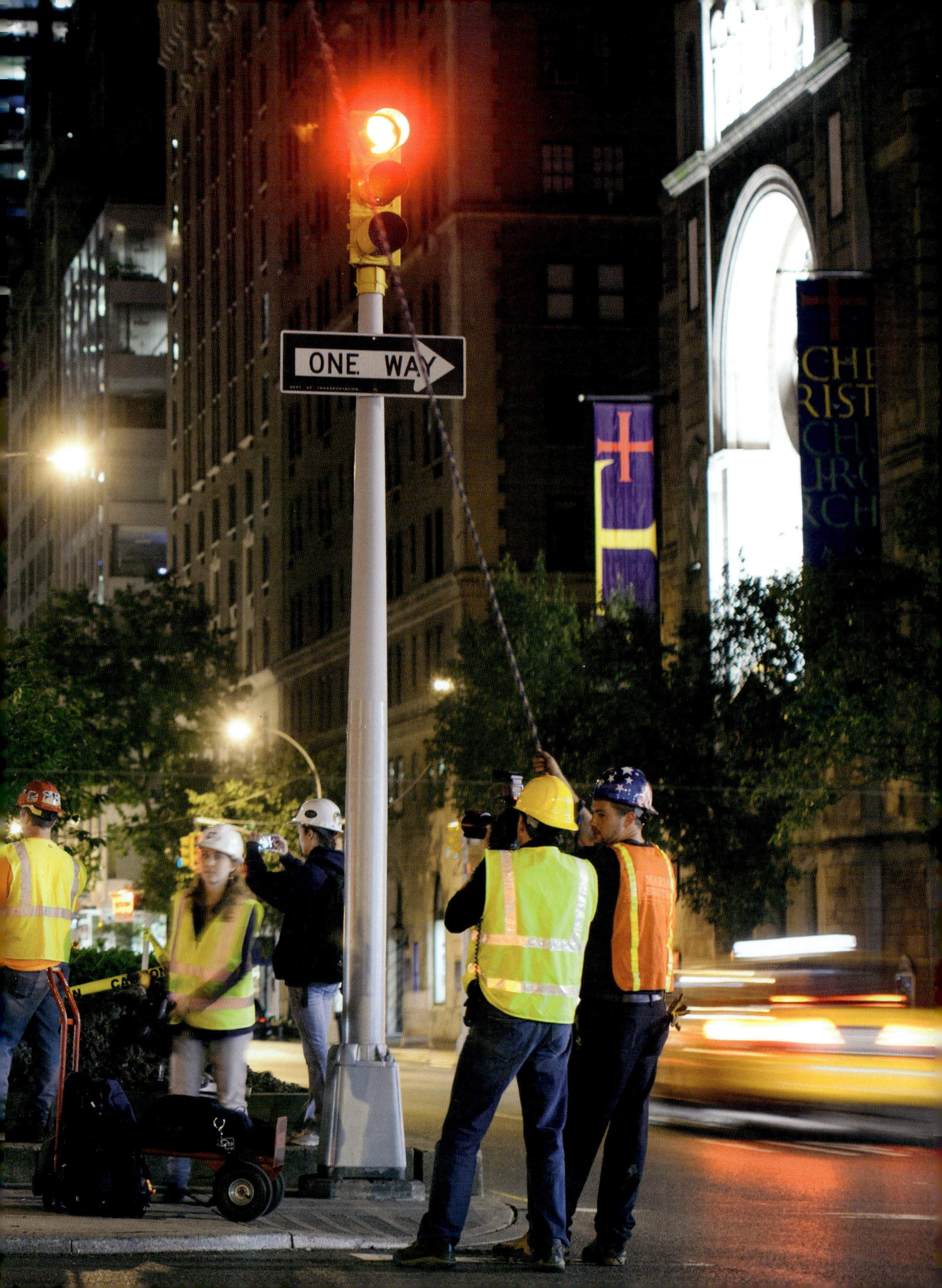

ONE WAY
DEPT. OF TRANSPORTATION

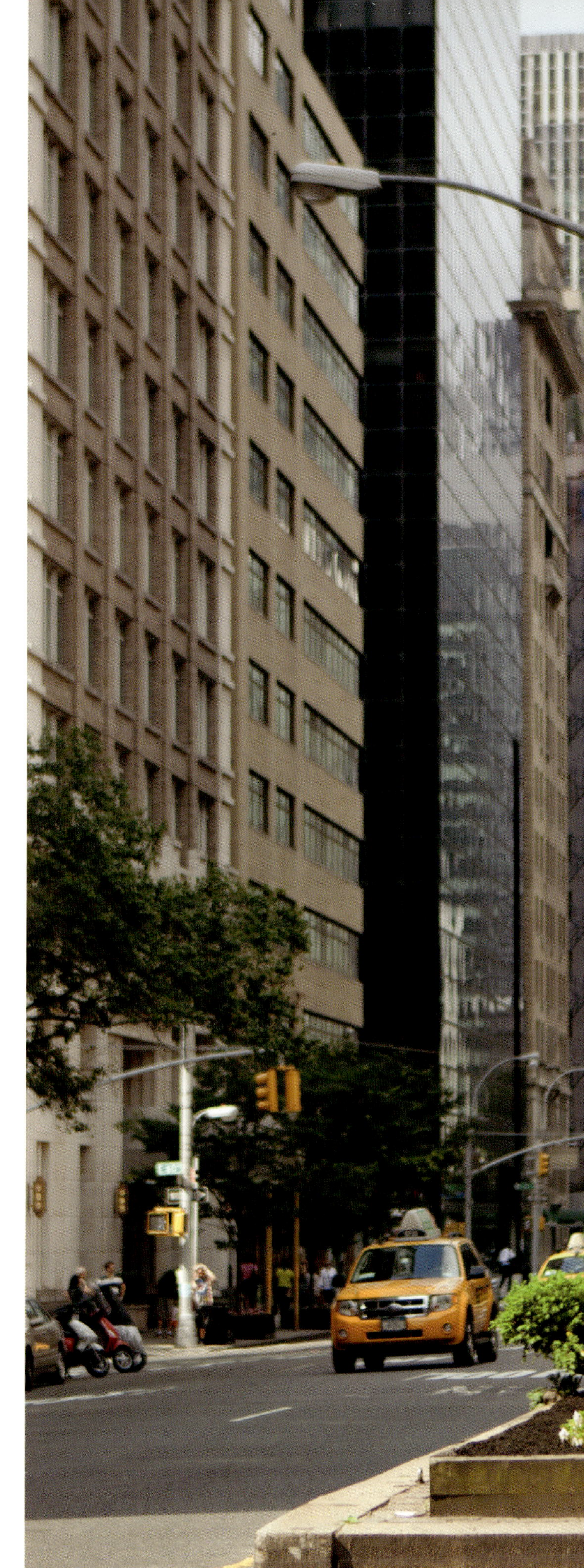

pp. 104-105
Ambiguous Response Installation
61st Street and Park Avenue, New York
June 14, 2013

right
Ambiguous Response
Formed and fabricated weathering steel
20'6" x 6'8" x 7'2"

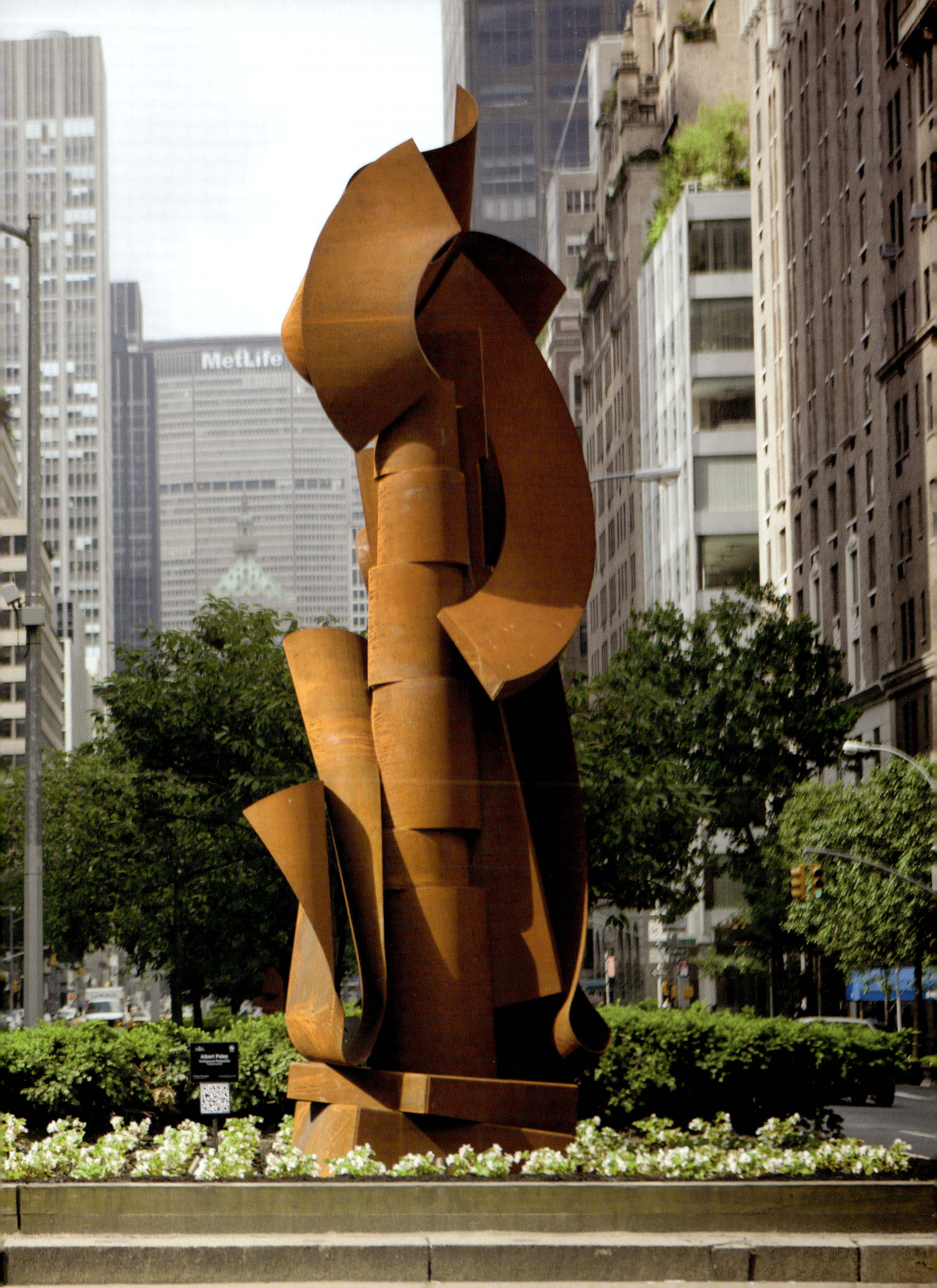

61ST NORTH
CLOAKED INTENTION

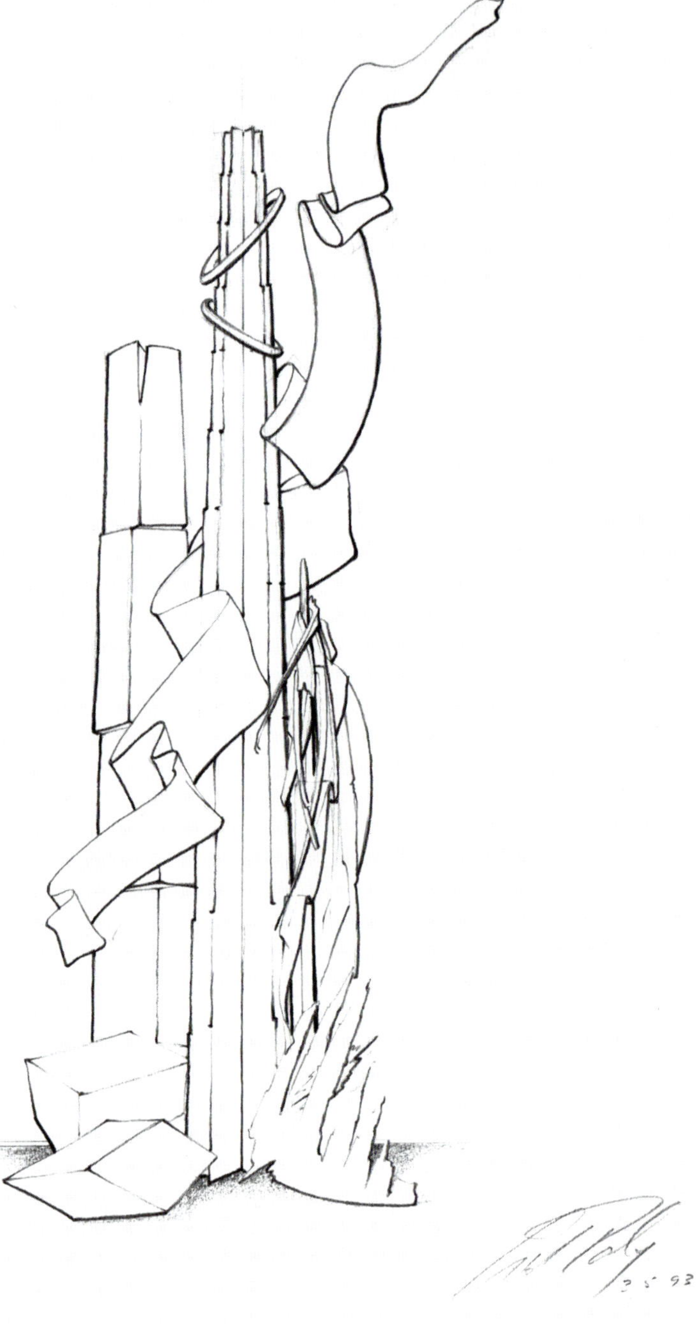

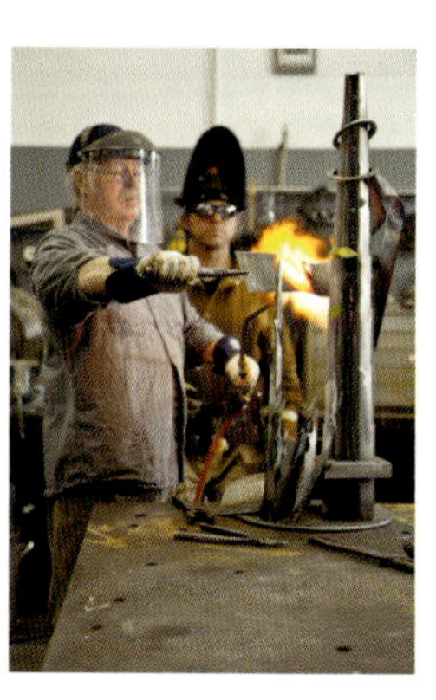

Cloaked Intention
Concept drawing
Graphite on paper
44″ x 30″
Paley Studios Archive

Cloaked Intention
Maquette fabrication
Paley Studios, Lyell Avenue
Rochester, New York

Cloaked Intention
Maquette
Formed and fabricated
patinated steel
38″ x 16½″ x 15¾″
Paley Studios Archive

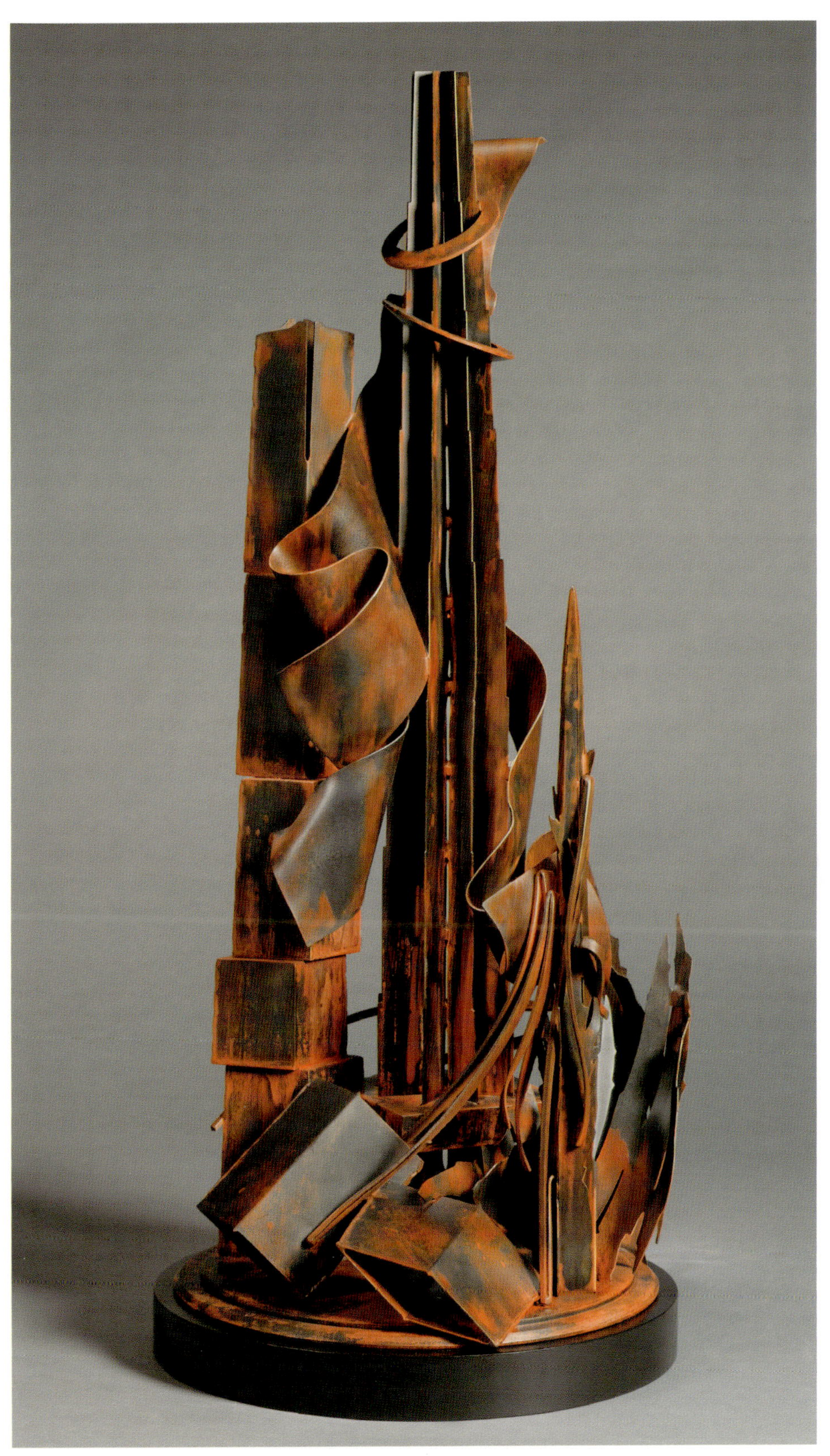

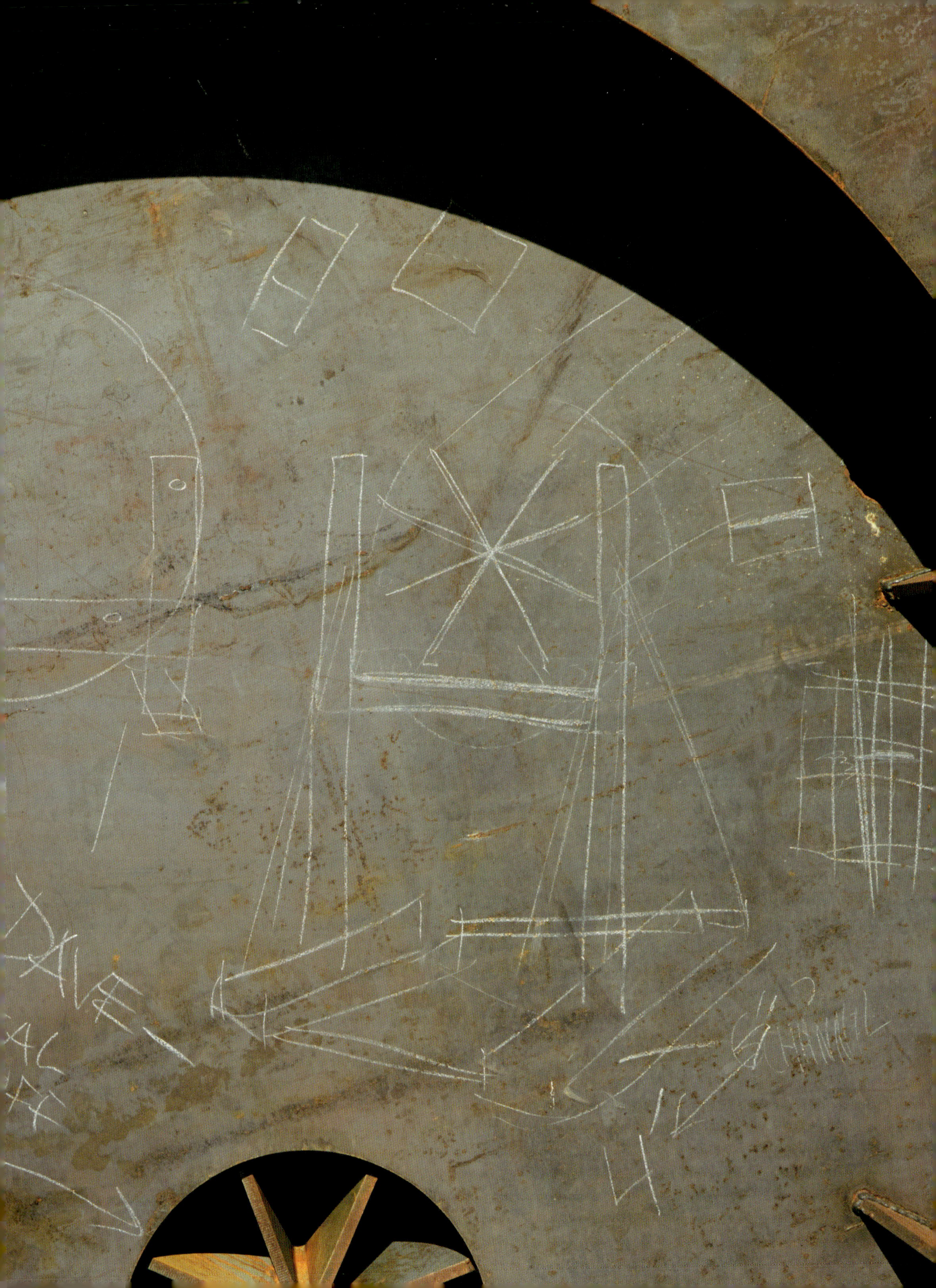

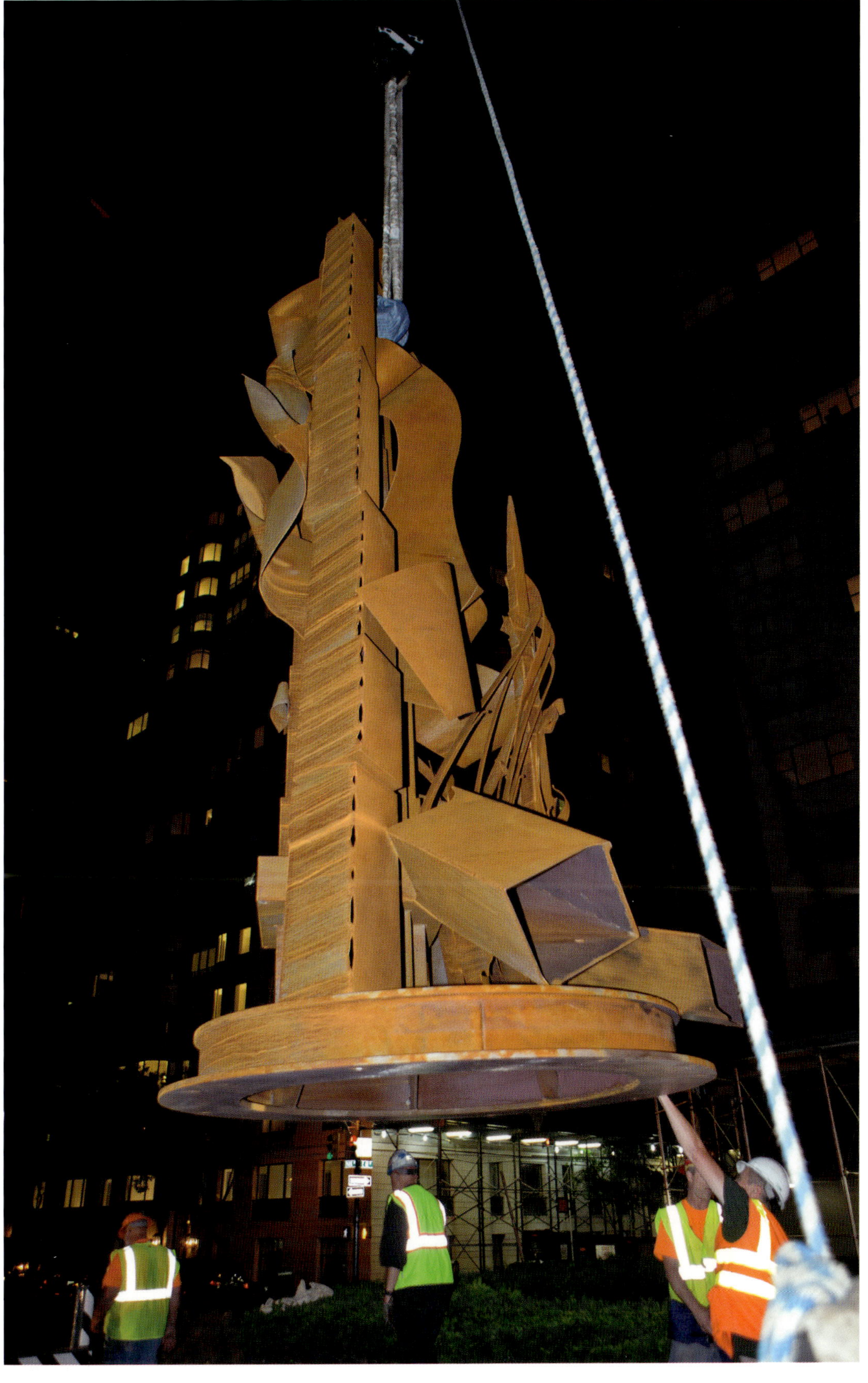

p. 110
Cloaked Intention
Base detail, fabrication
notations
Paley Studios, Lyell Avenue
Rochester, New York

p. 111
Cloaked Intention
Installation
61st Street and Park
Avenue, New York
June 14, 2013

right
Cloaked Intention, 2013
Formed and fabricated
weathering steel
19′8″ x 8′7″ dia.

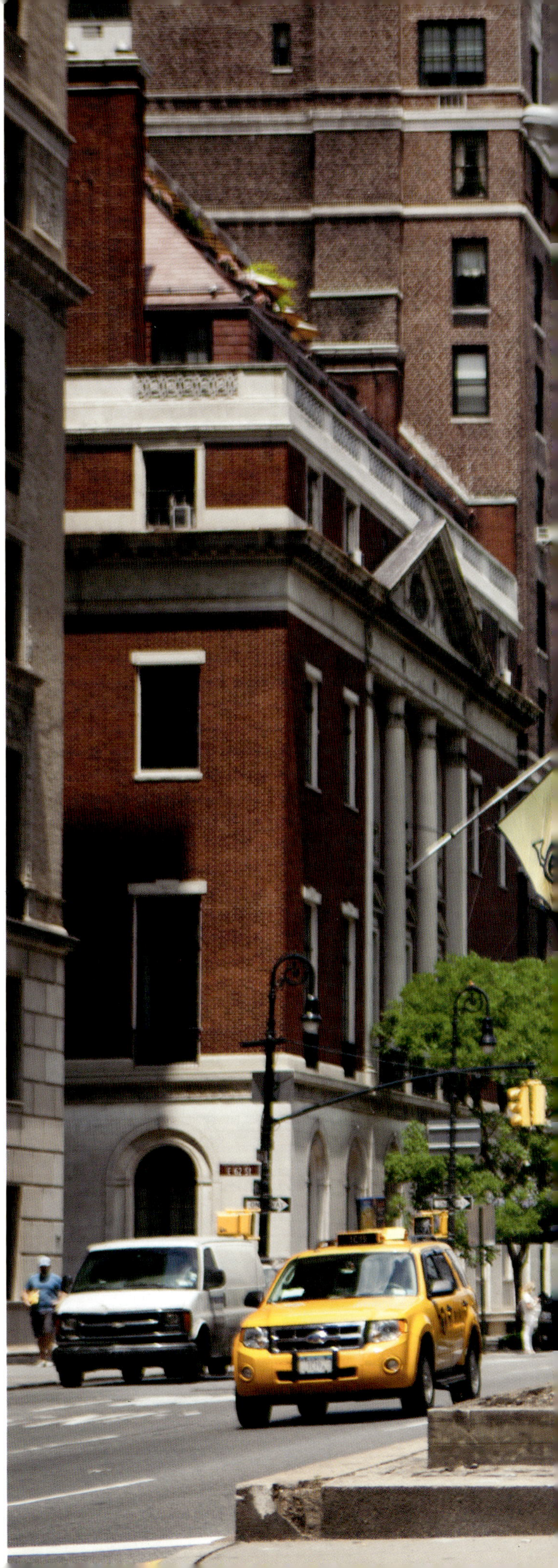

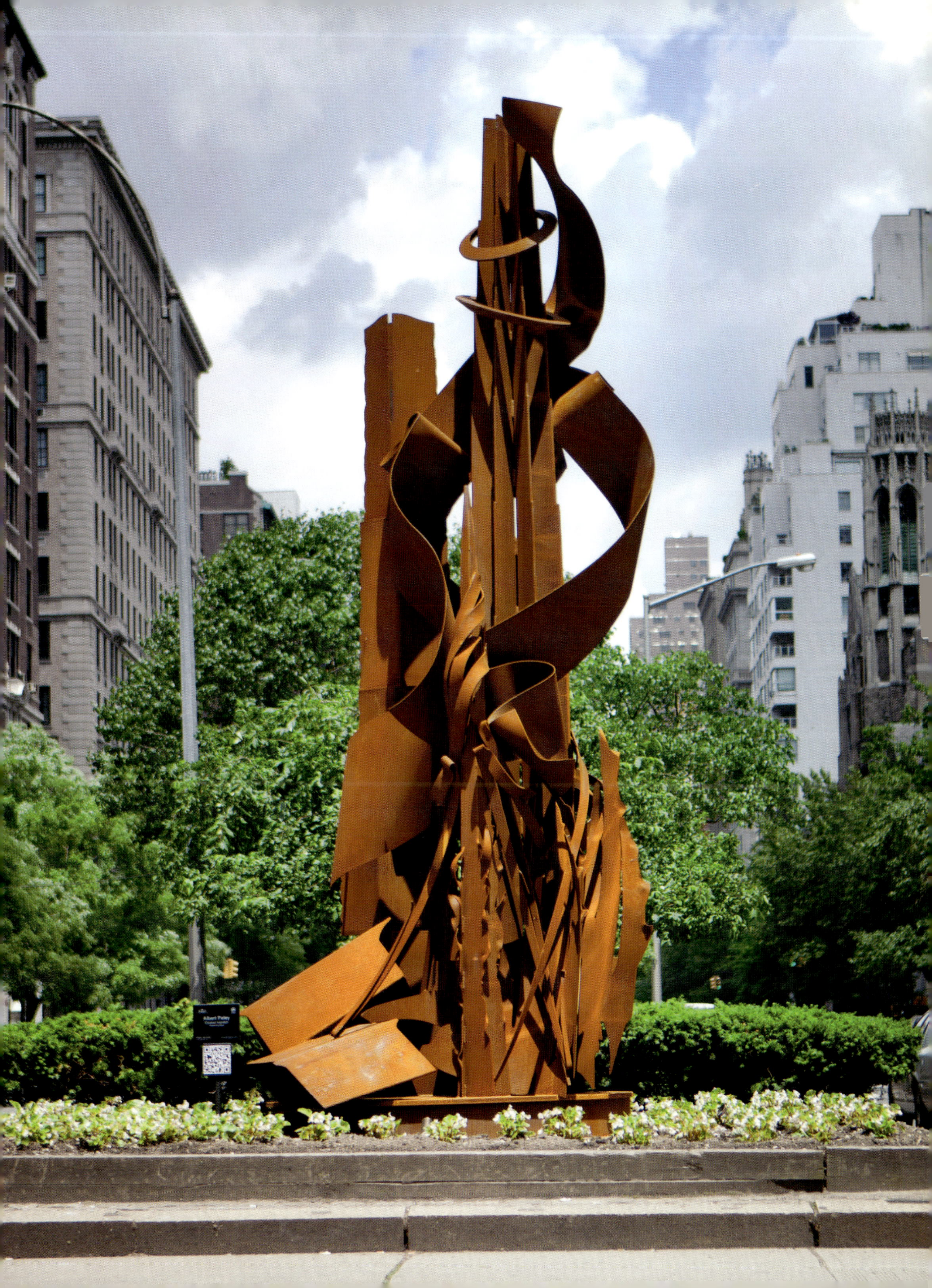
Albert Paley

64TH
COMPOSED PRESENCE

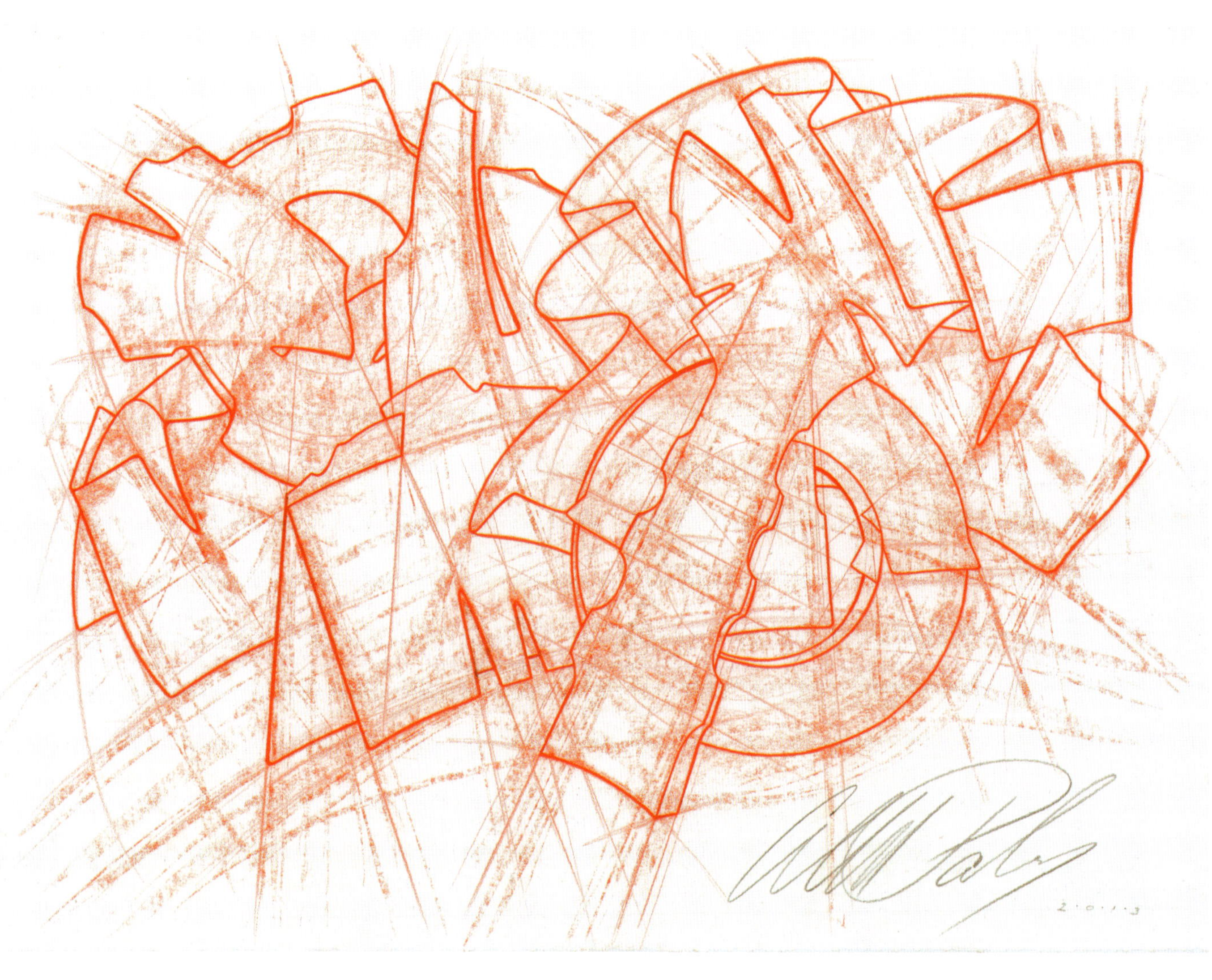

Composed Presence
Concept drawing
Graphite and red pencil
on paper
22 1/8" x 30"
Paley Studios Archive

Composed Presence
Cardboard model
18" x 25" x 13"
Paley Studios Archive

Composed Presence
Maquette
Formed and fabricated
painted steel with stainless
steel base
30½" x 37" x 23"
Paley Studios Archive

pp. 116-117
Composed Presence
Fabrication
Paley Studios, Lyell Avenue
Rochester, New York

pp. 118-119
Composed Presence, 2013
Formed and fabricated
painted steel
in two sections
10' x 13'6½" x 6'10"
64th Street and Park
Avenue, New York

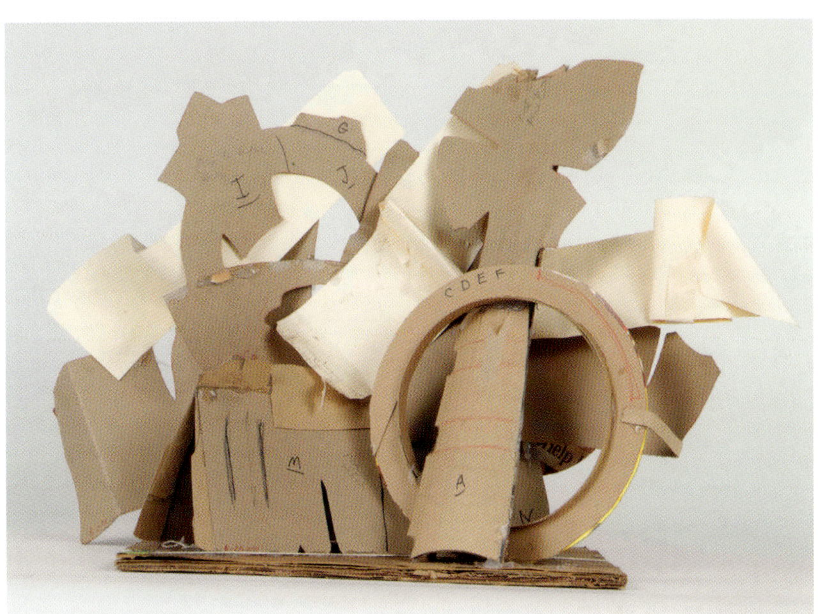

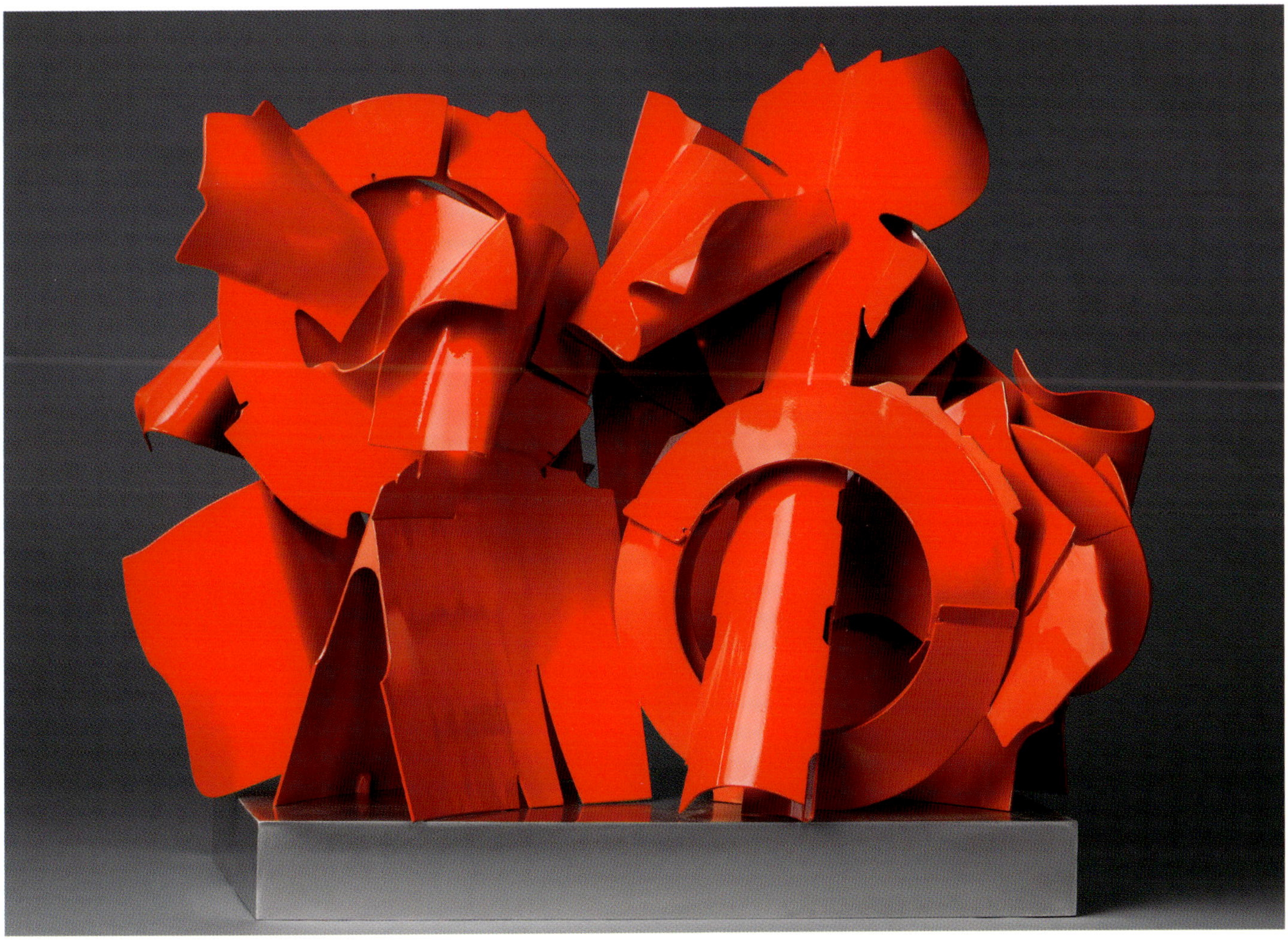

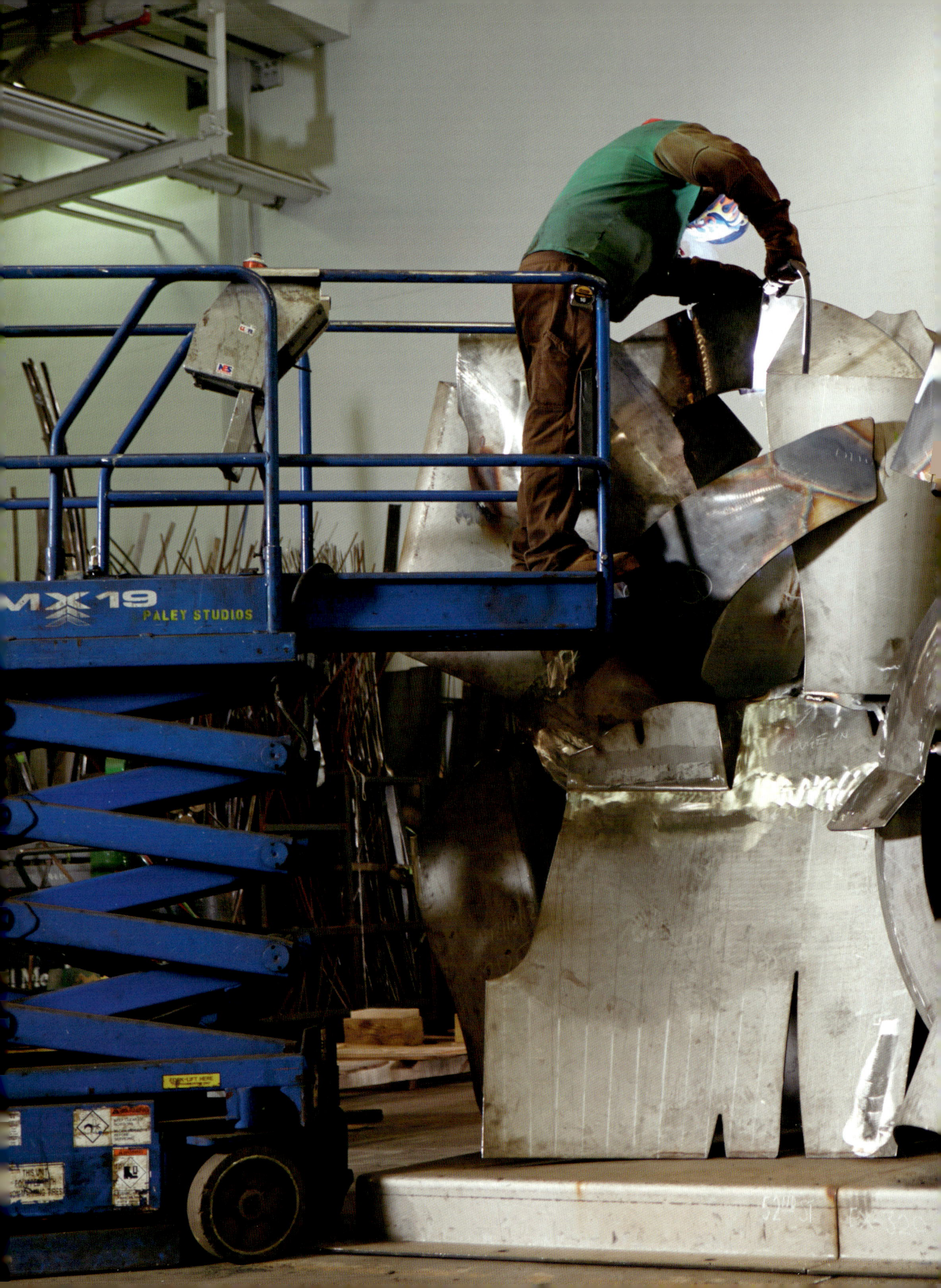
MX19
PALEY STUDIOS

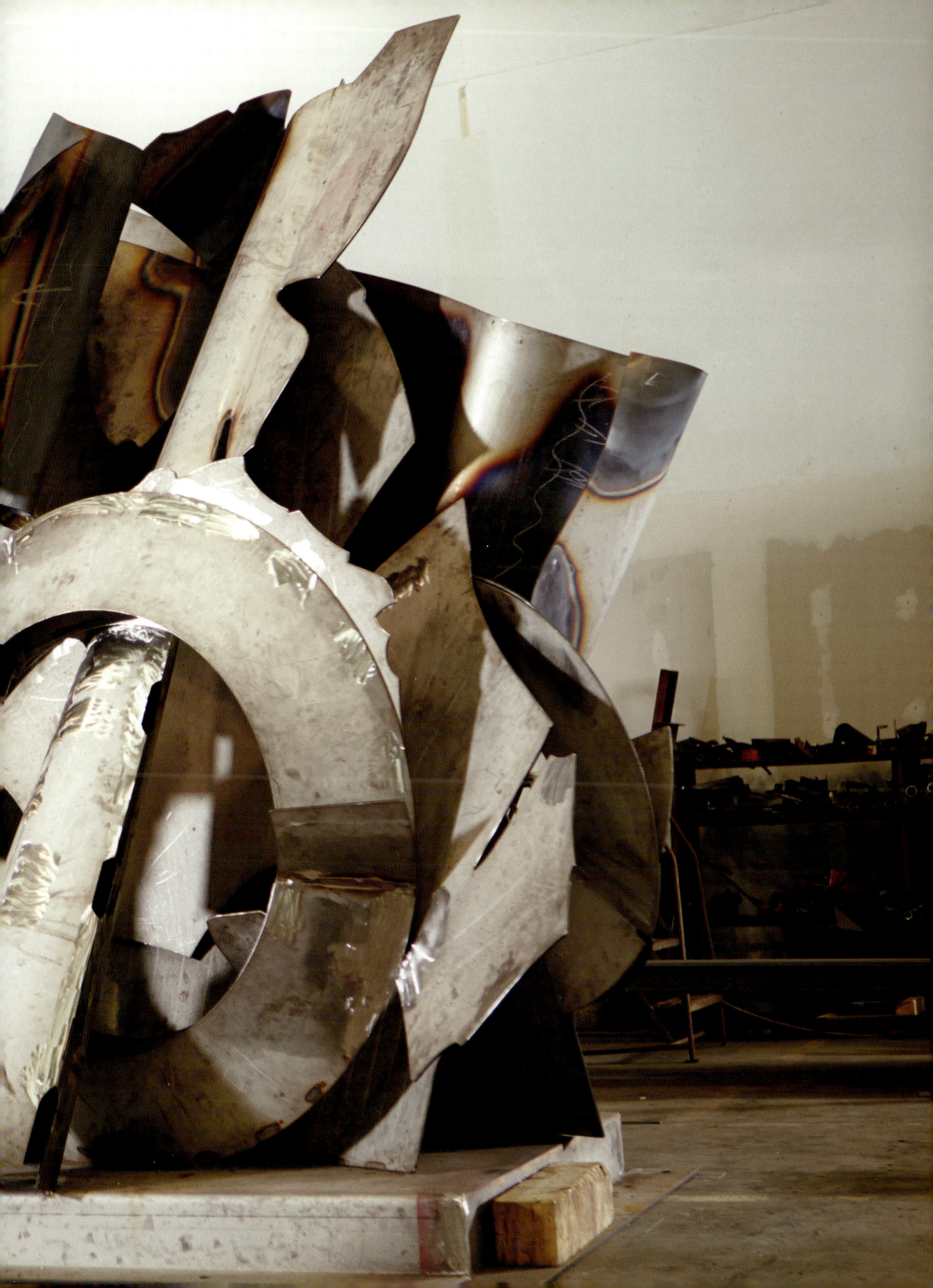

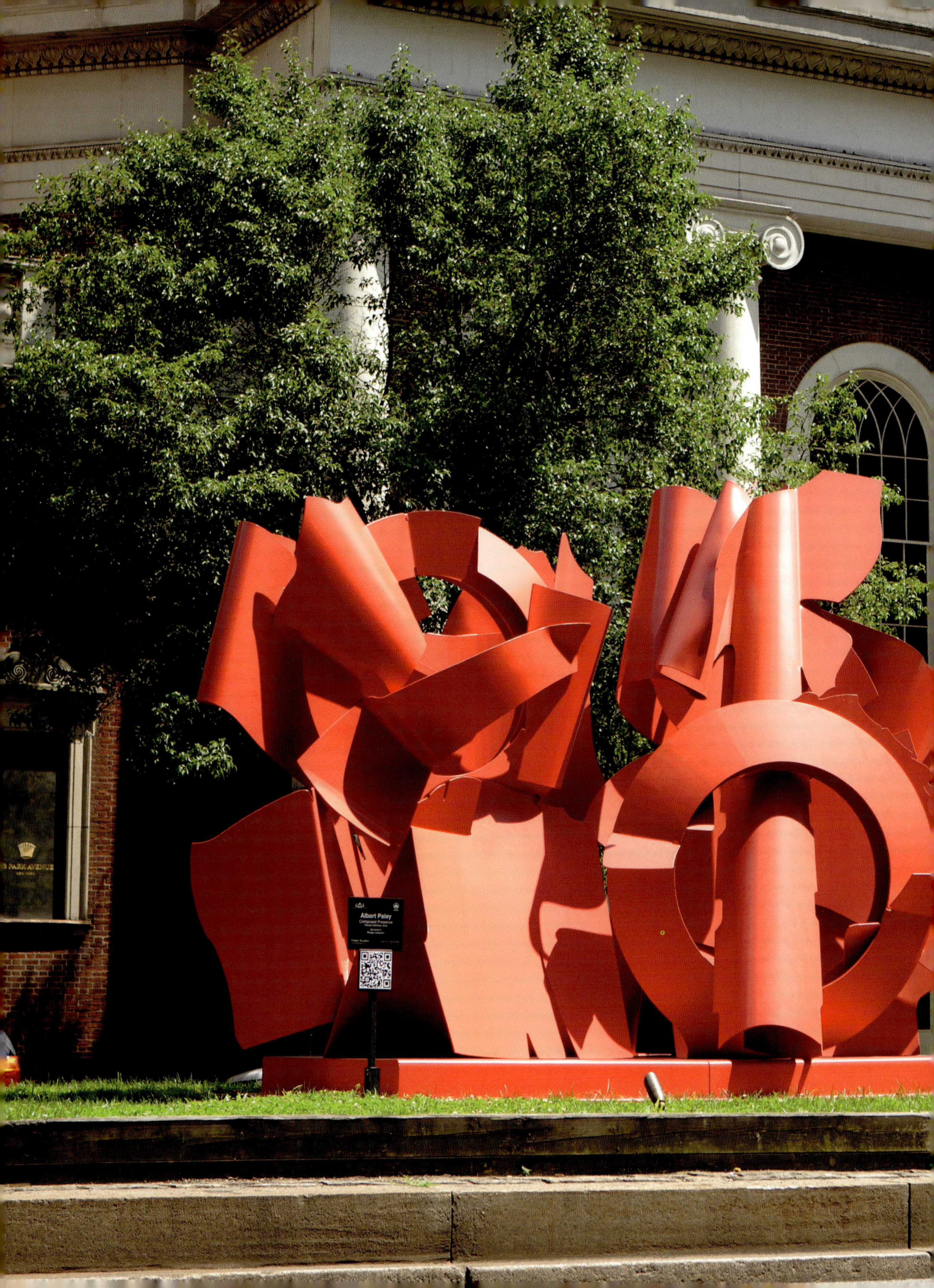

Albert Paley
Composed Presence

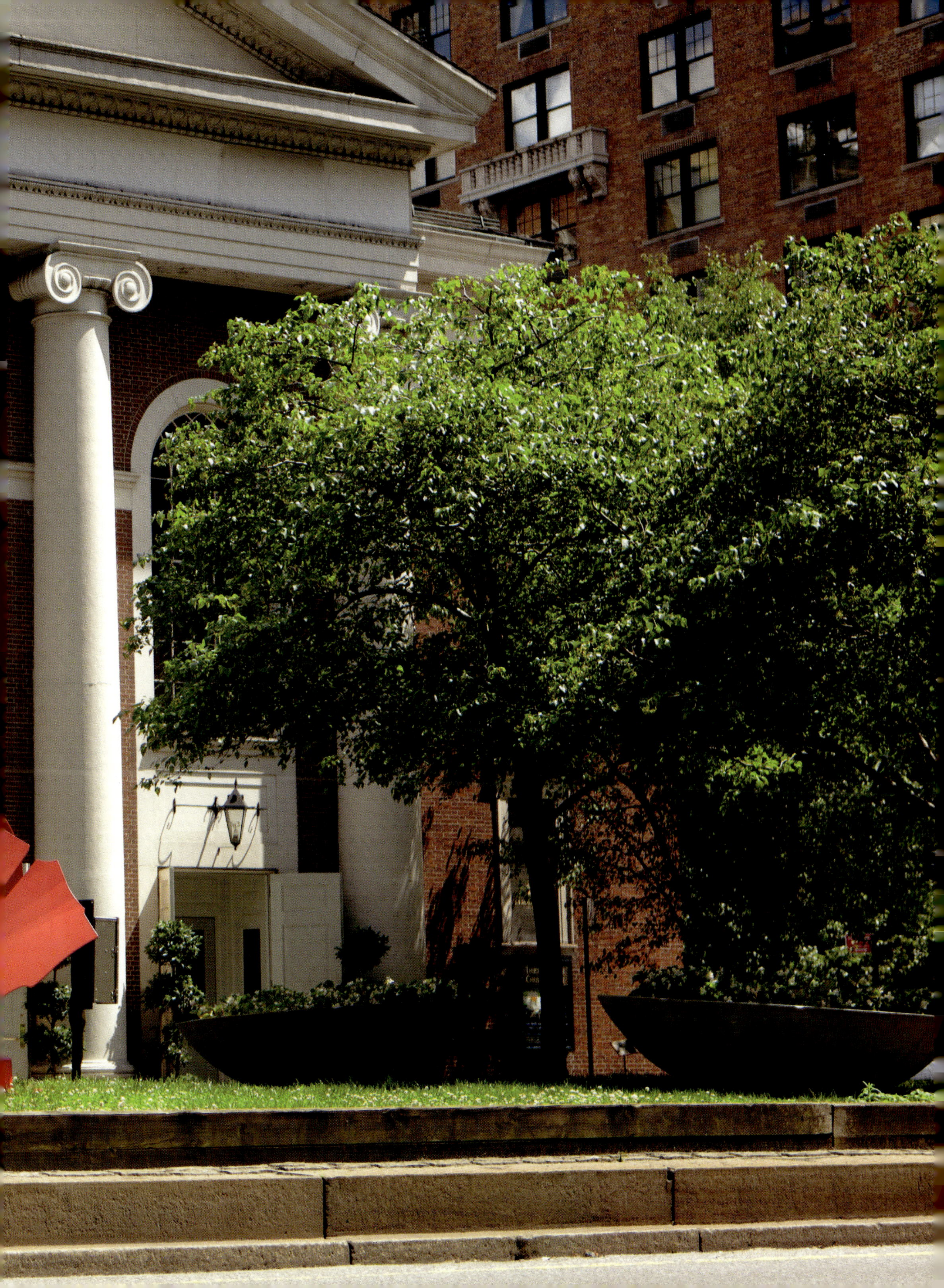

LANGUOROUS REPOSE

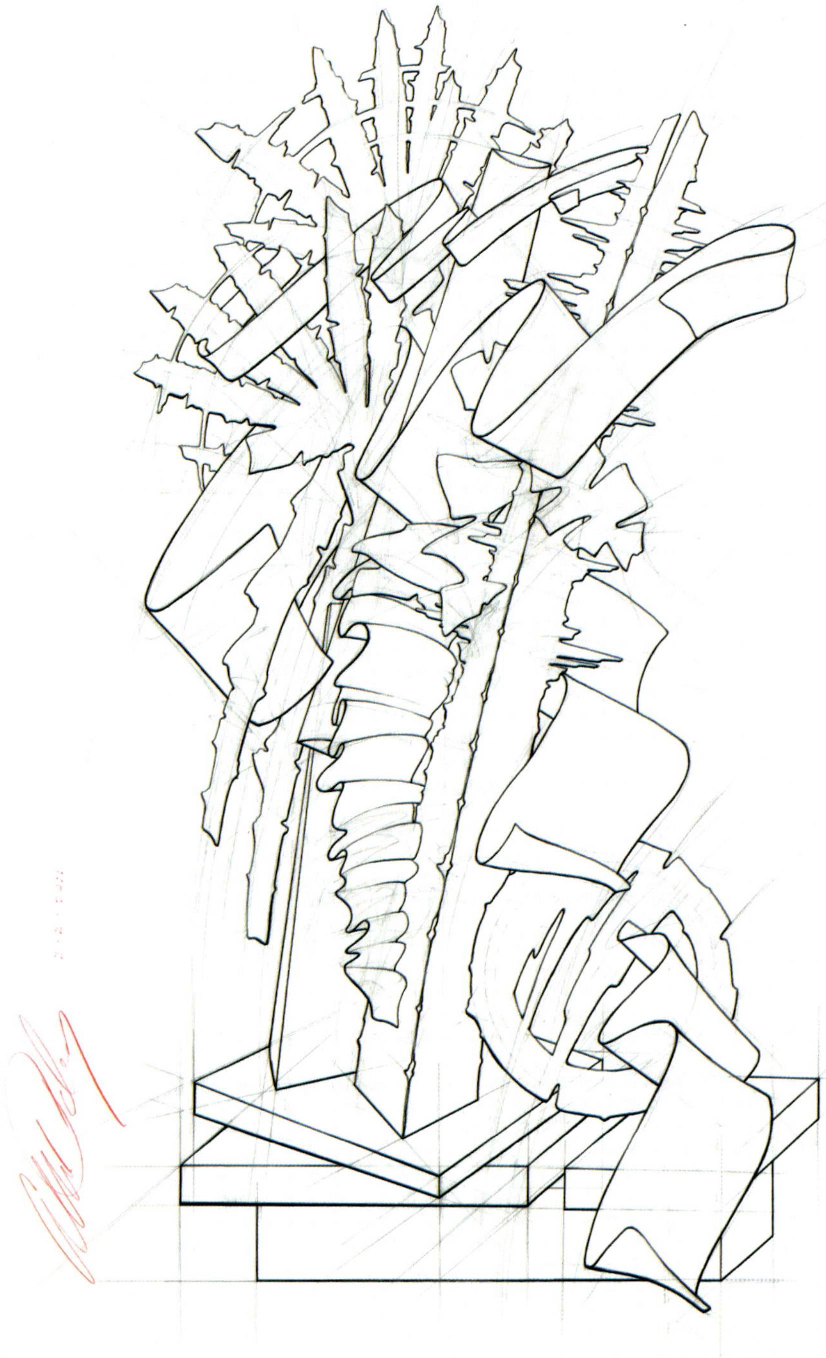

Languorous Repose
Concept drawing
Graphite and red pencil
on paper
40" x 26"
Paley Studios Archive

Languorous Repose
Cardboard model
32" x 16" x 16"
Paley Studios Archive

Languorous Repose
Maquette
Formed and fabricated
painted steel
with wood base
40½" x 22" x 17"
Paley Studios Archive

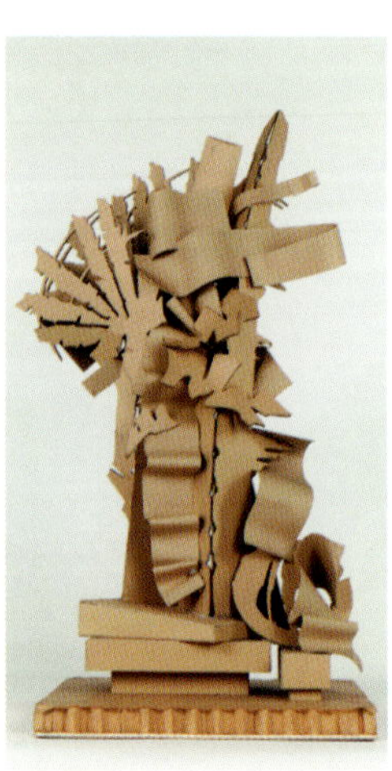

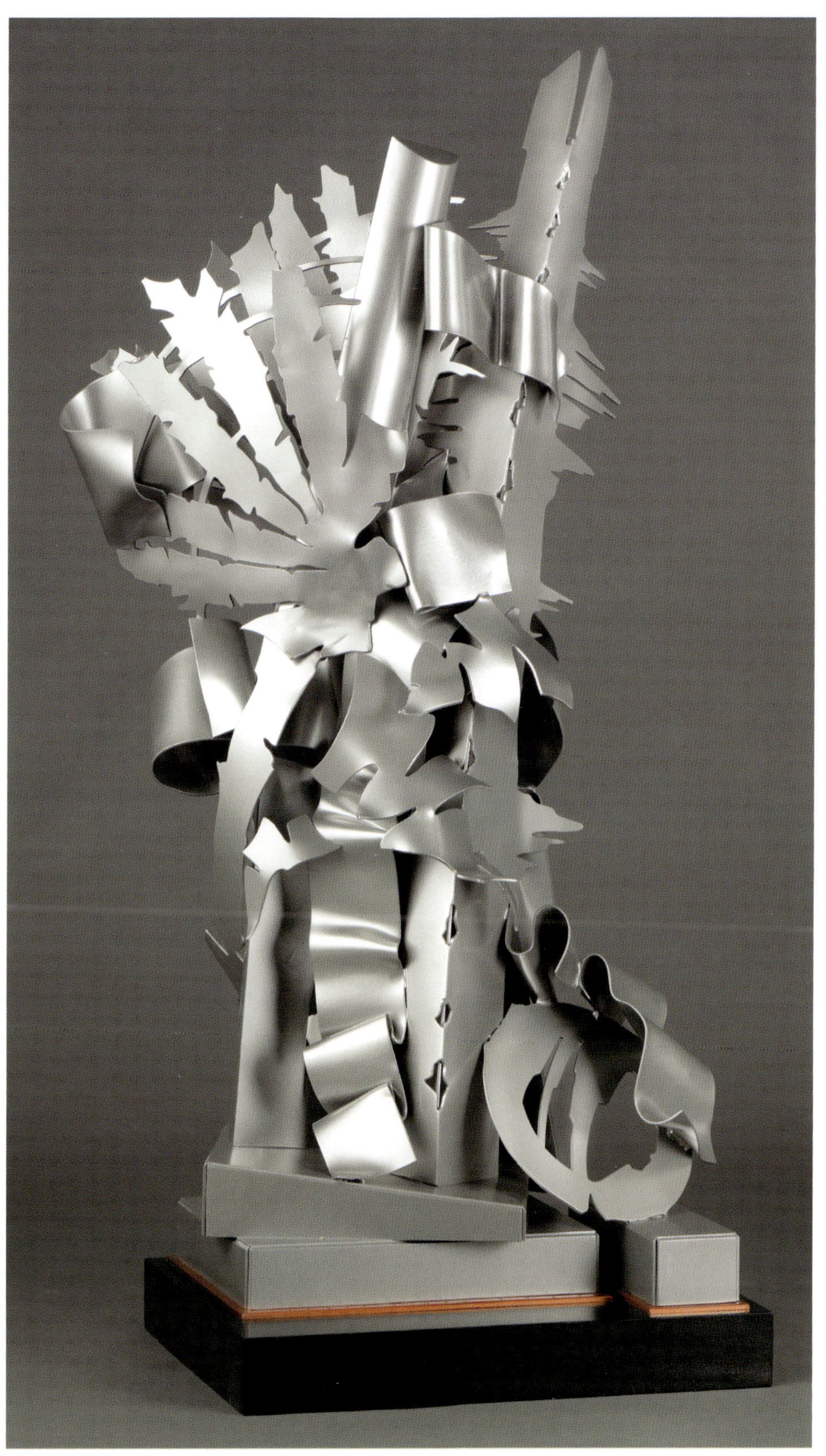

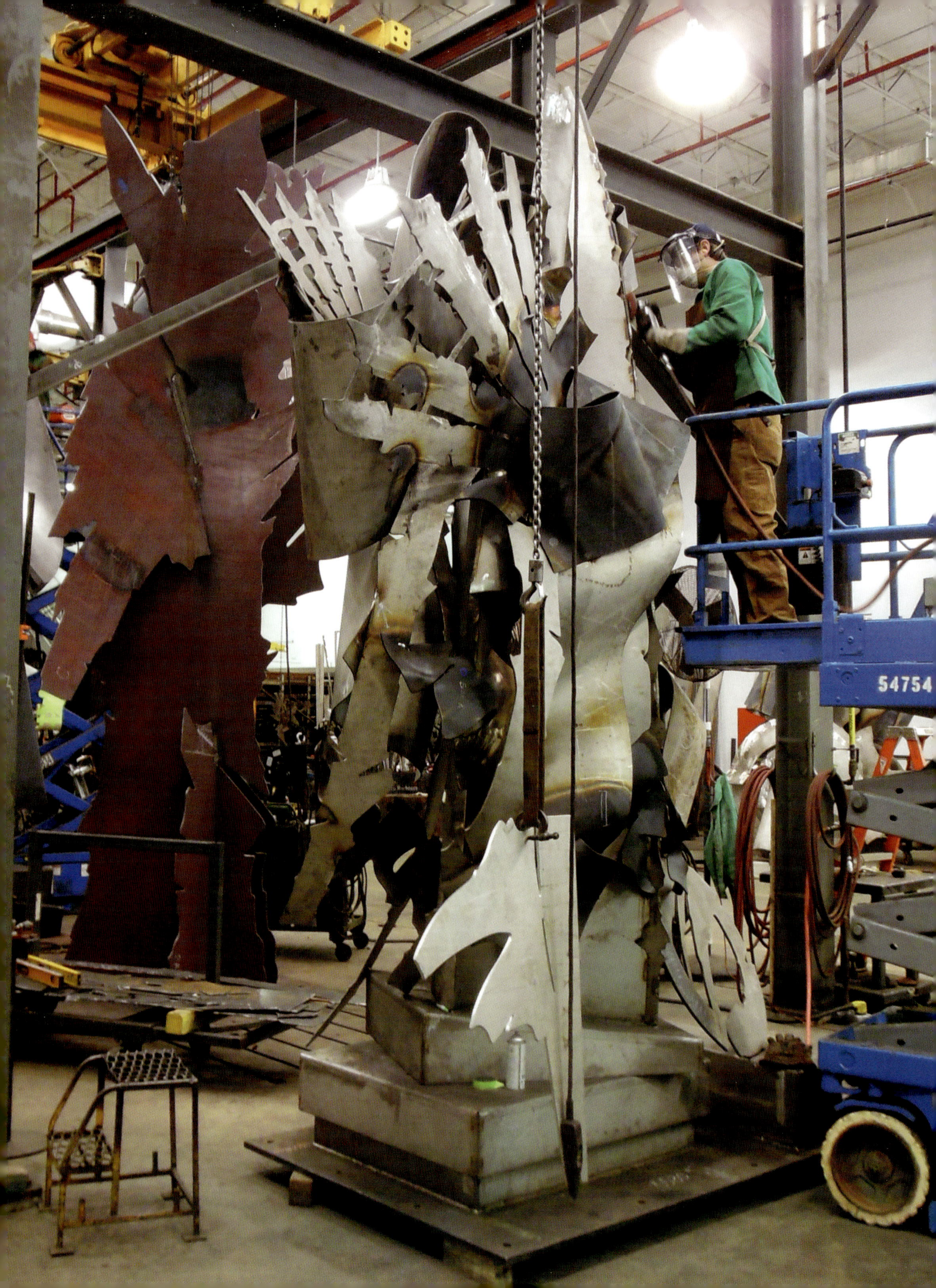

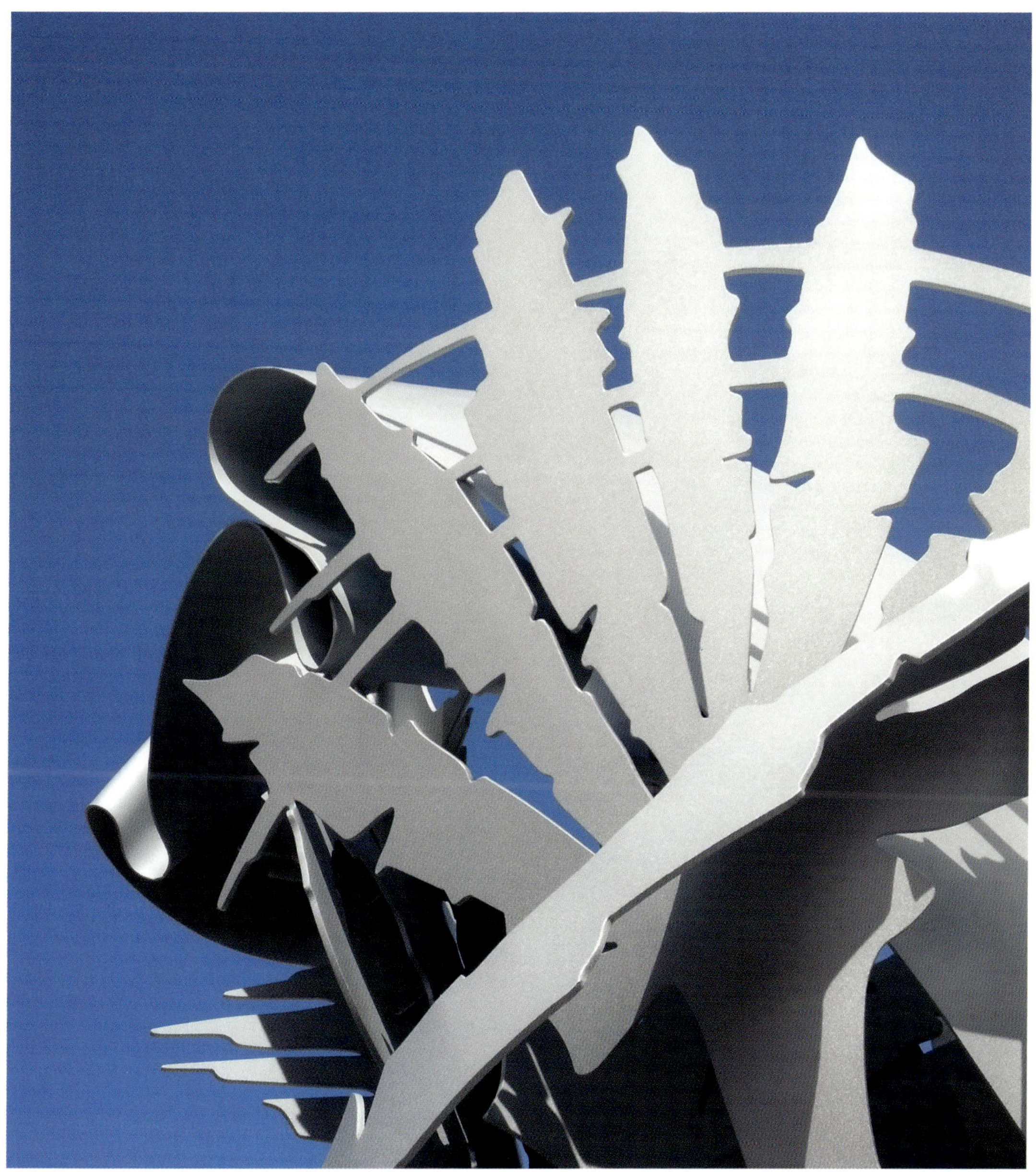

p. 122
Languorous Repose
Fabrication
Paley Studios, Lyell Avenue
Rochester, New York

above
Languorous Repose
Detail

pp. 124-125
Languorous Repose
Formed and fabricated
stainless steel
14'8" x 8'3¾" x 5'9¾"
66th Street and Park
Avenue

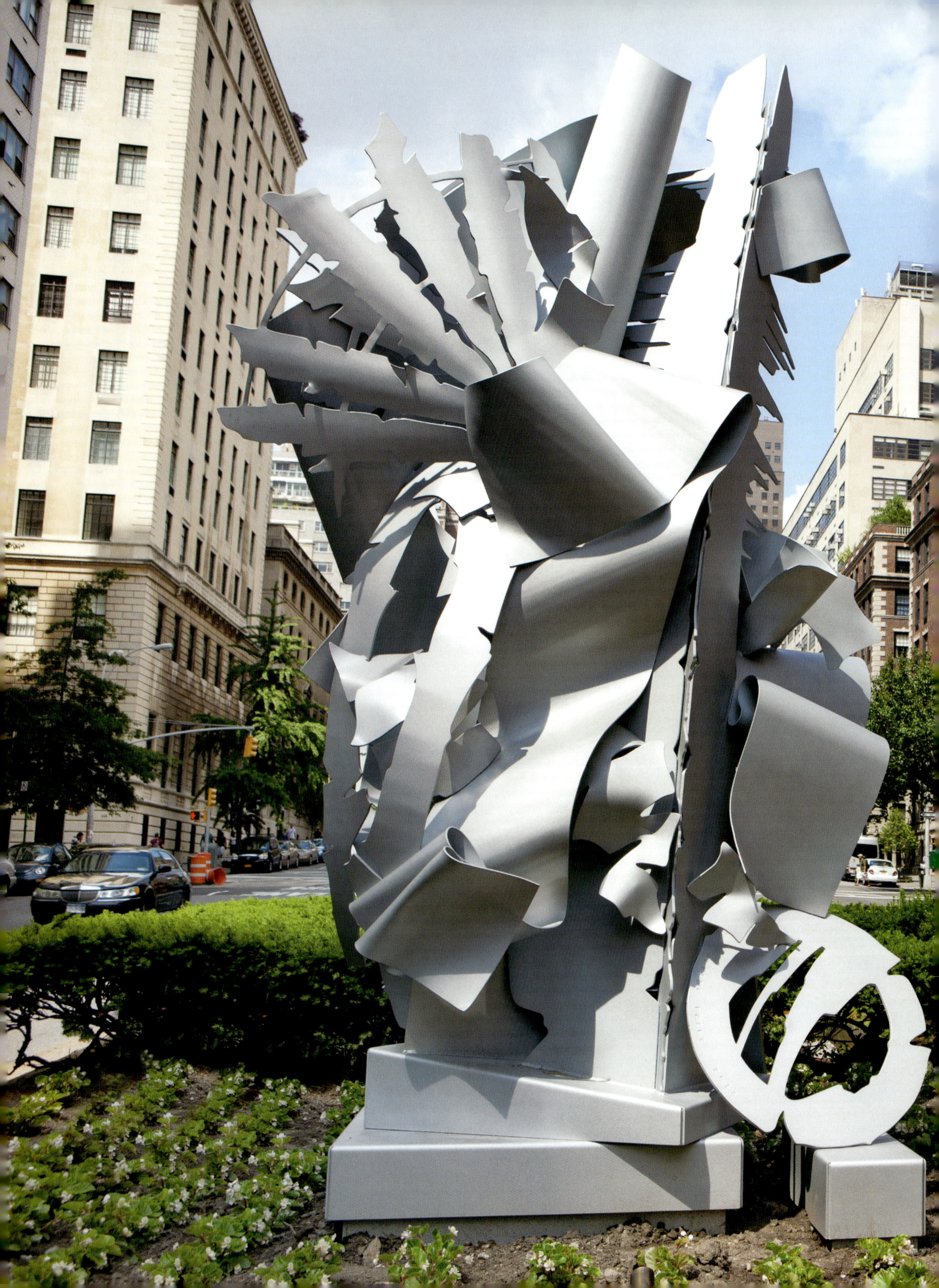

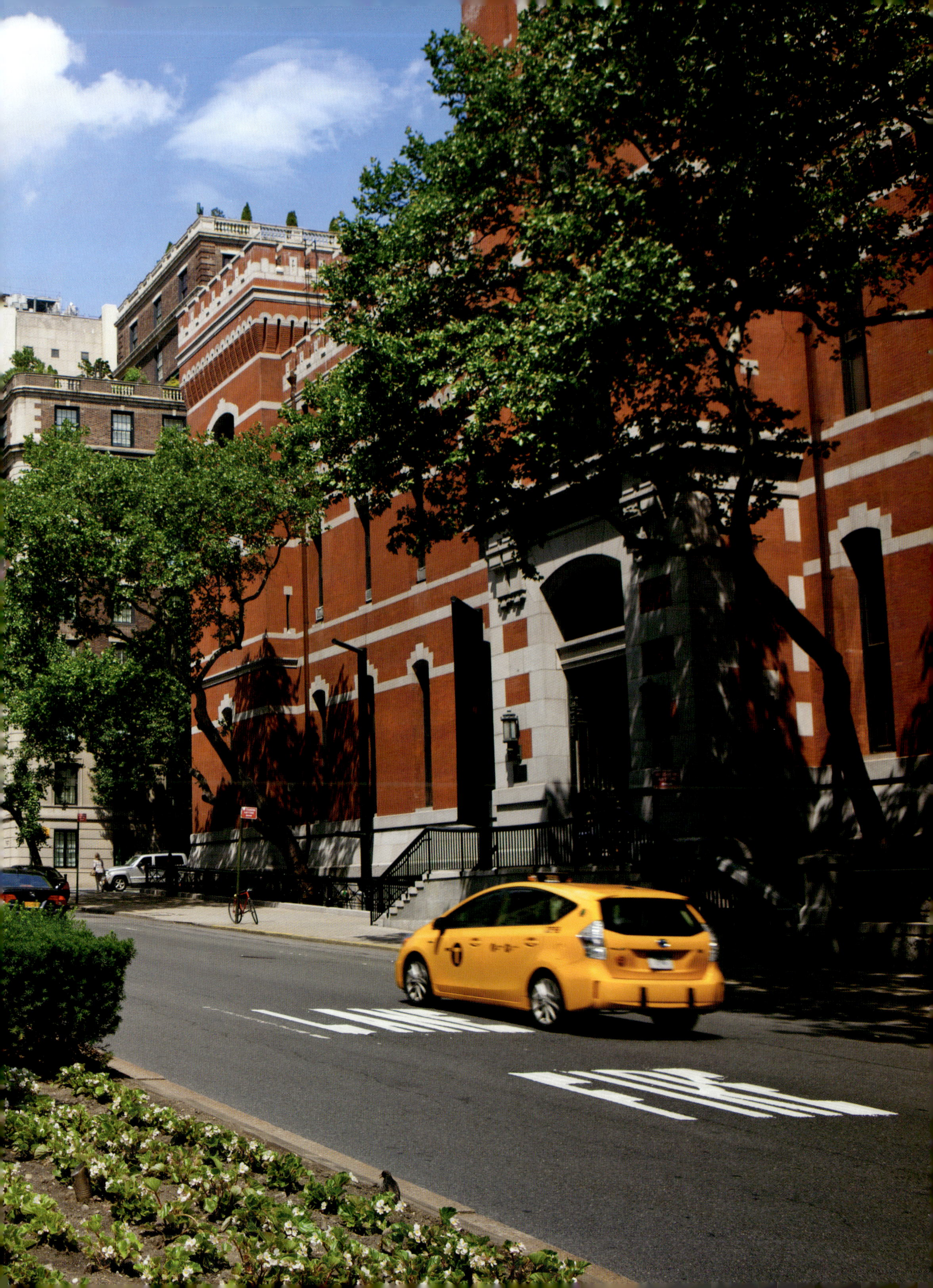

67TH
ENVIOUS COMPOSURE

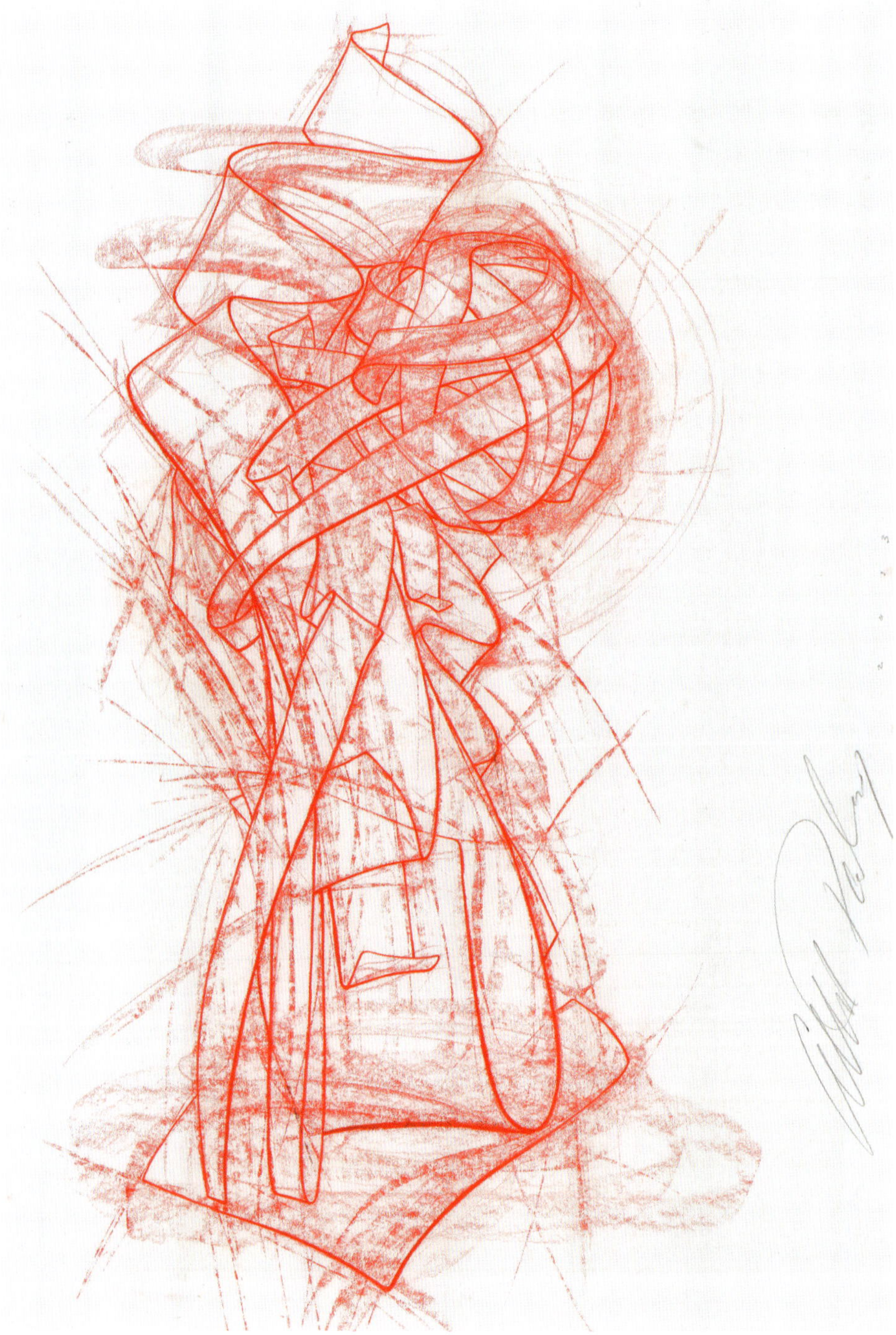

Envious Composure
Concept drawing
Graphite and red pencil
on paper
44" x 30"
Paley Studios Archive

Envious Composure
Cardboard Model
Paley Studios Archive

Envious Composure
Fabrication detail
Paley Studios, Lyell Avenue
Rochester, New York

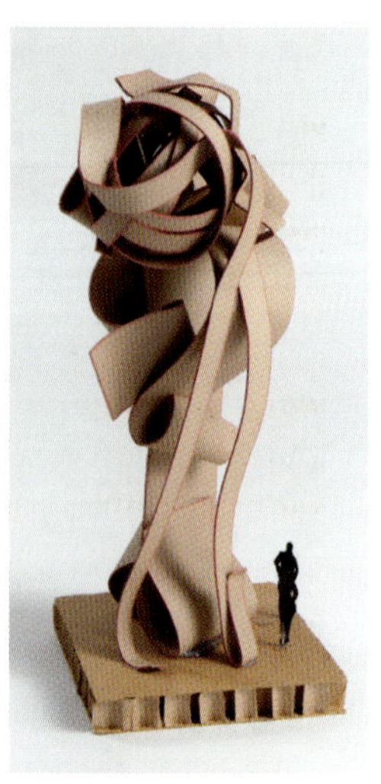

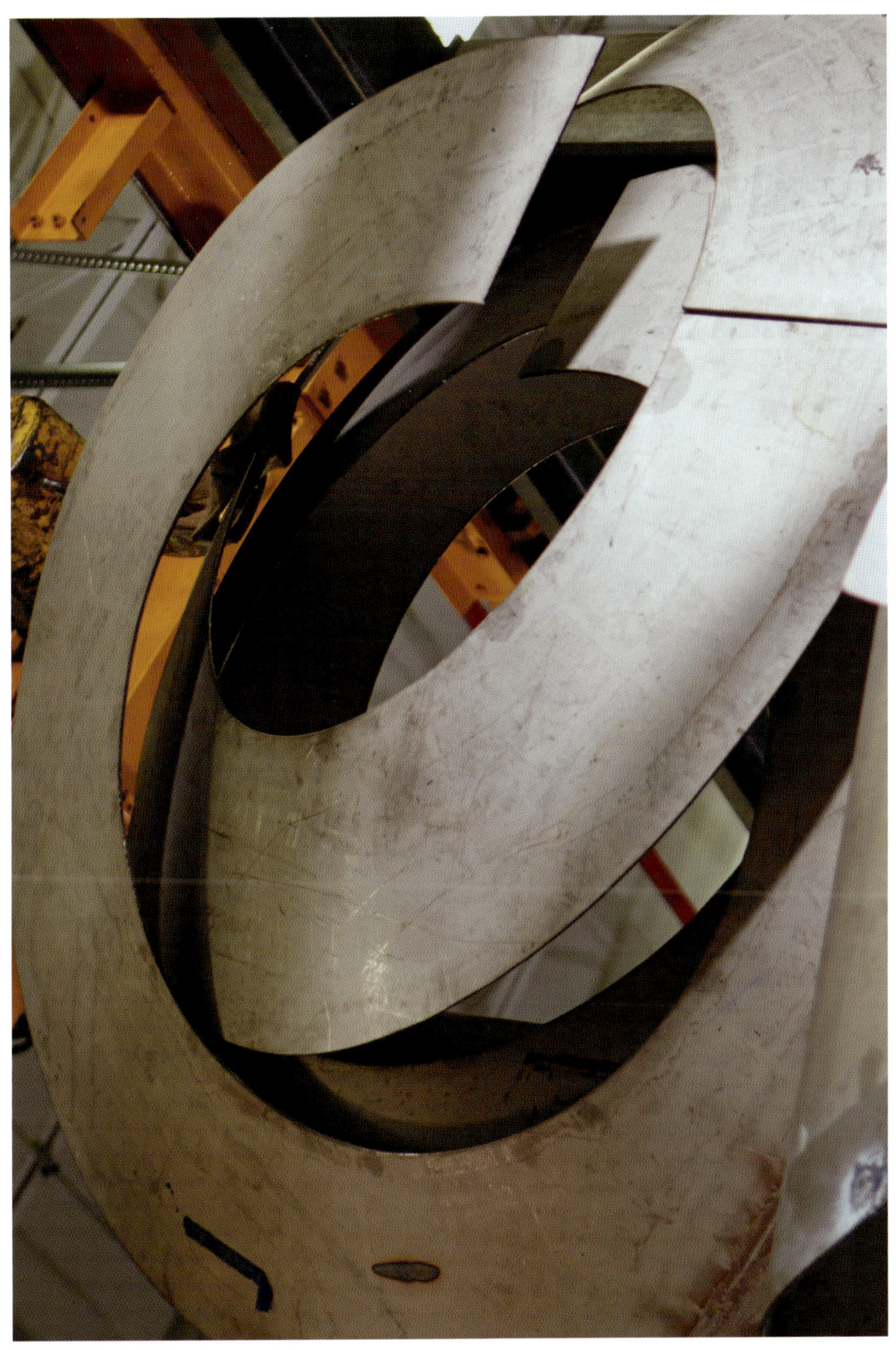

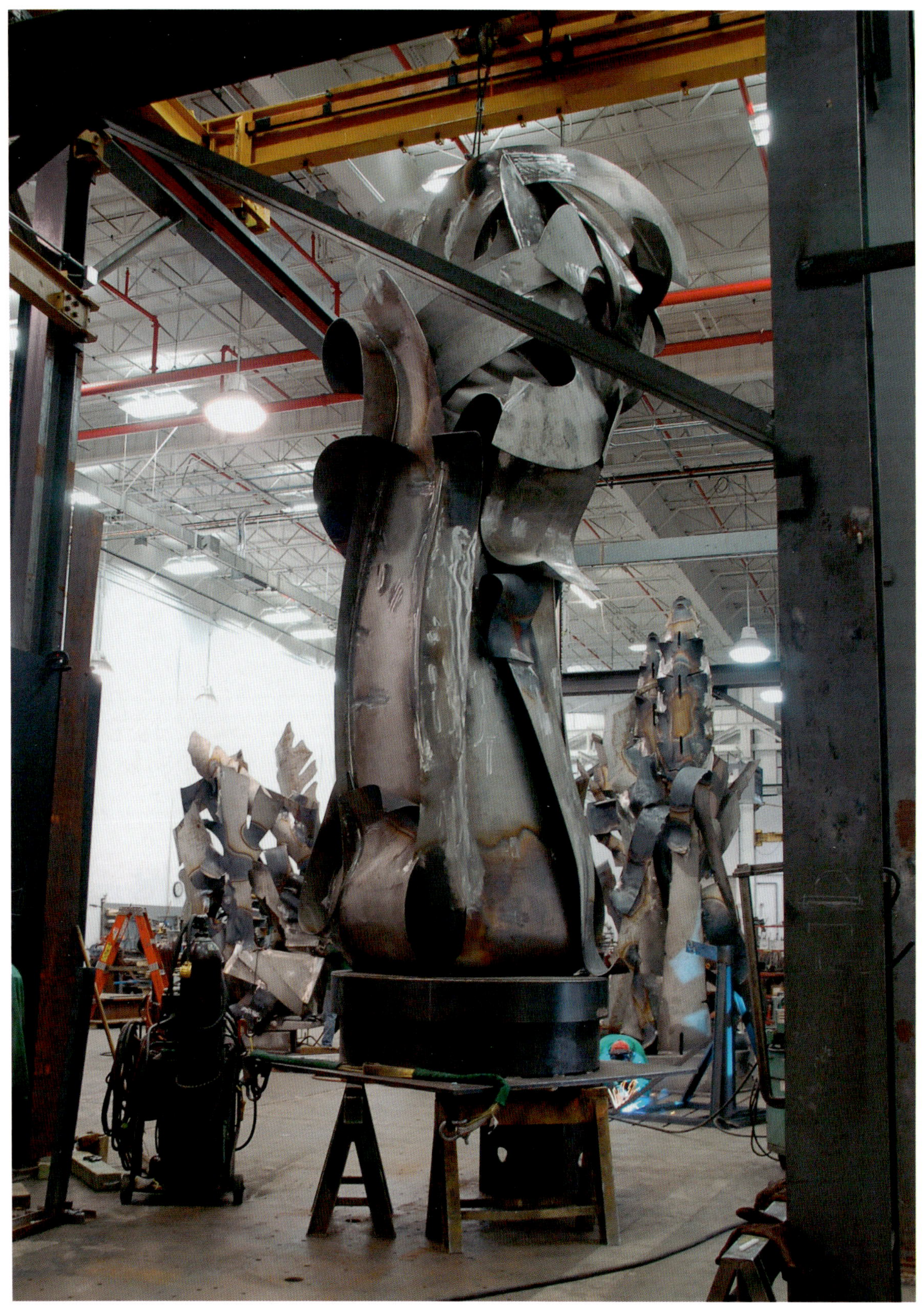

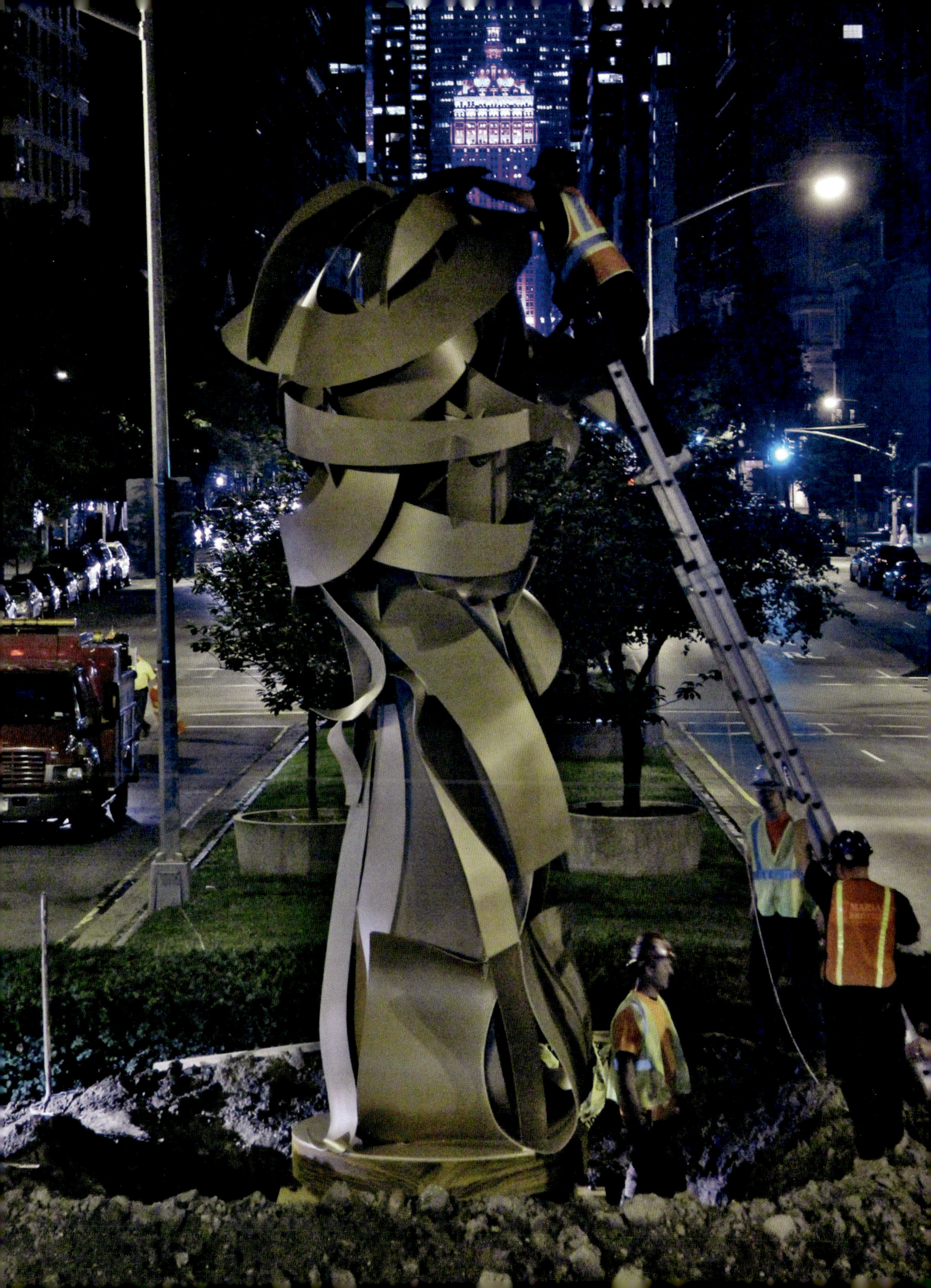

p. 128
Envious Composure
Fabrication
Paley Studios, Lyell Avenue
Rochester, New York

p. 129
Envious Composure
Installation
67th Street and Park
Avenue, New York
June 15, 2013

right
Envious Composure, 2013
Formed and fabricated
painted stainless steel
18'3" x 7'6" x 7'

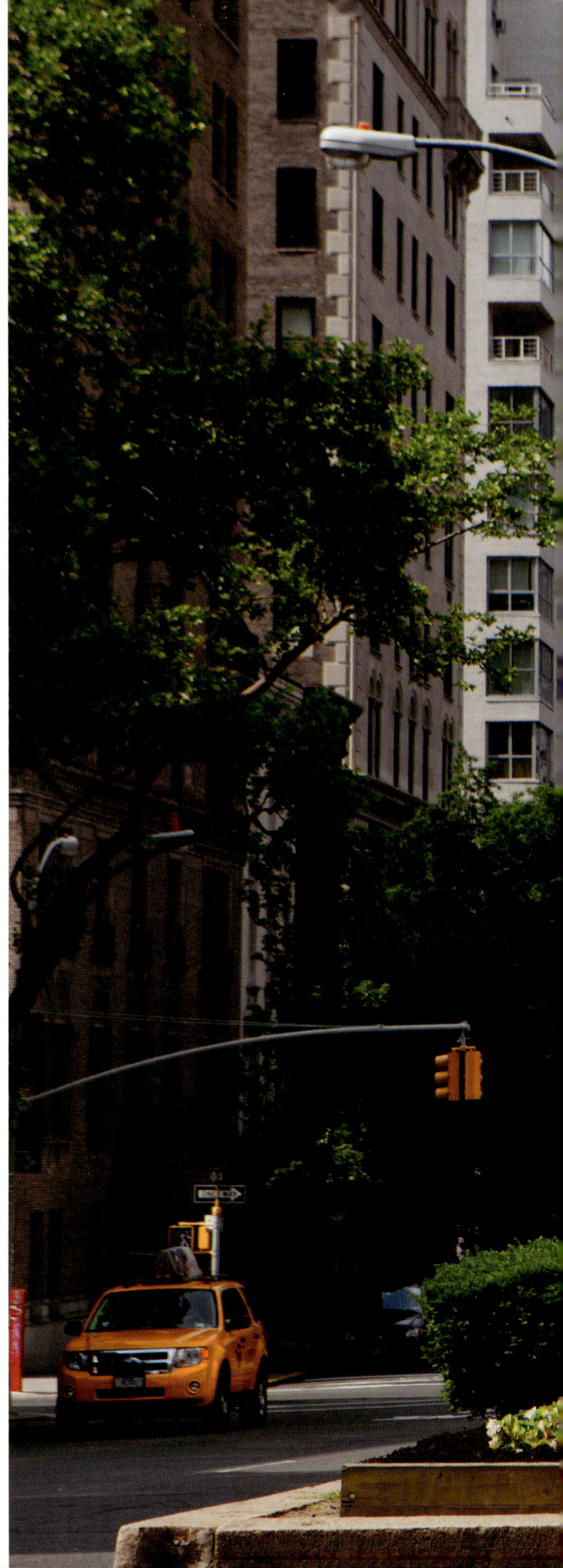

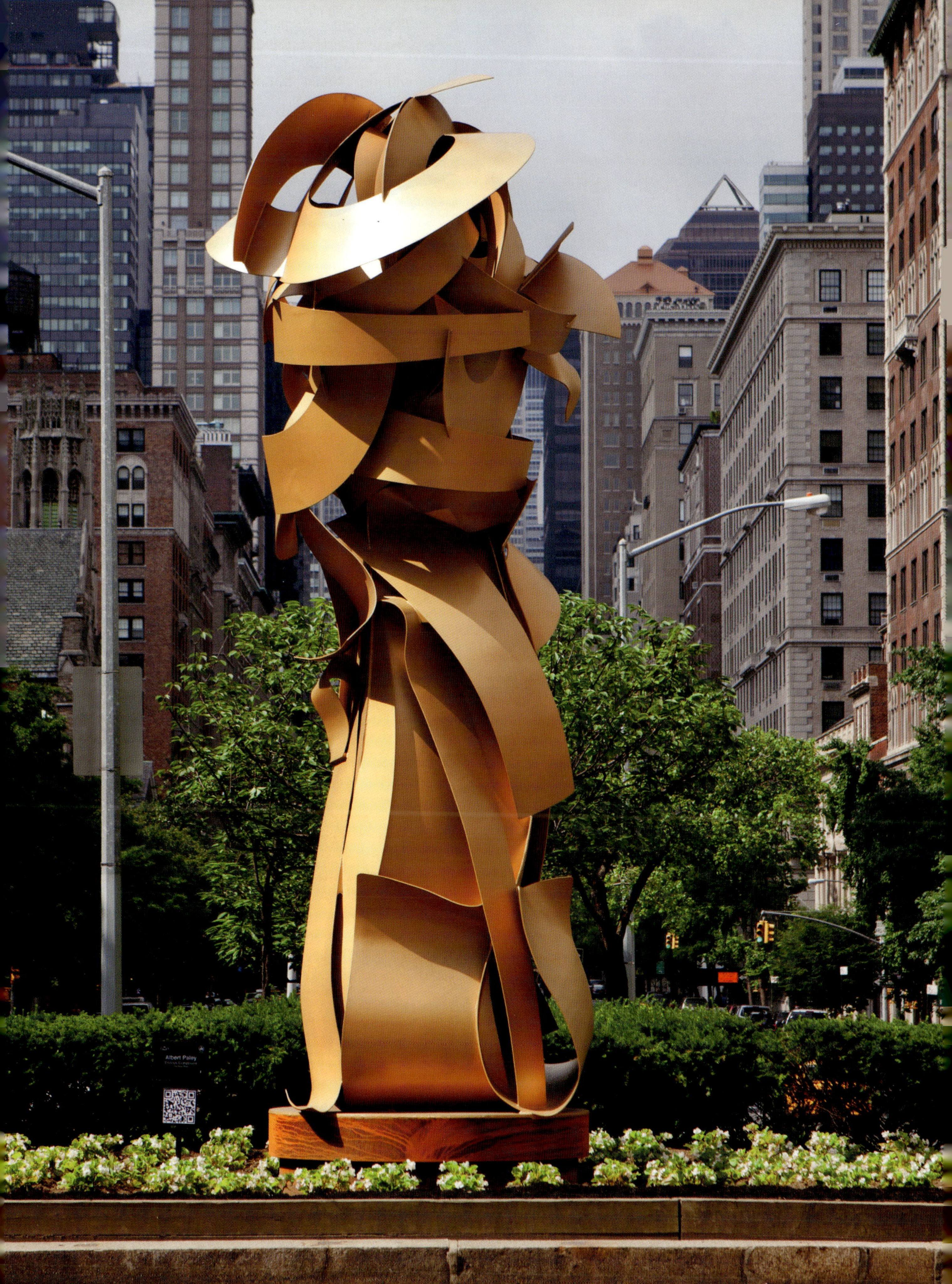

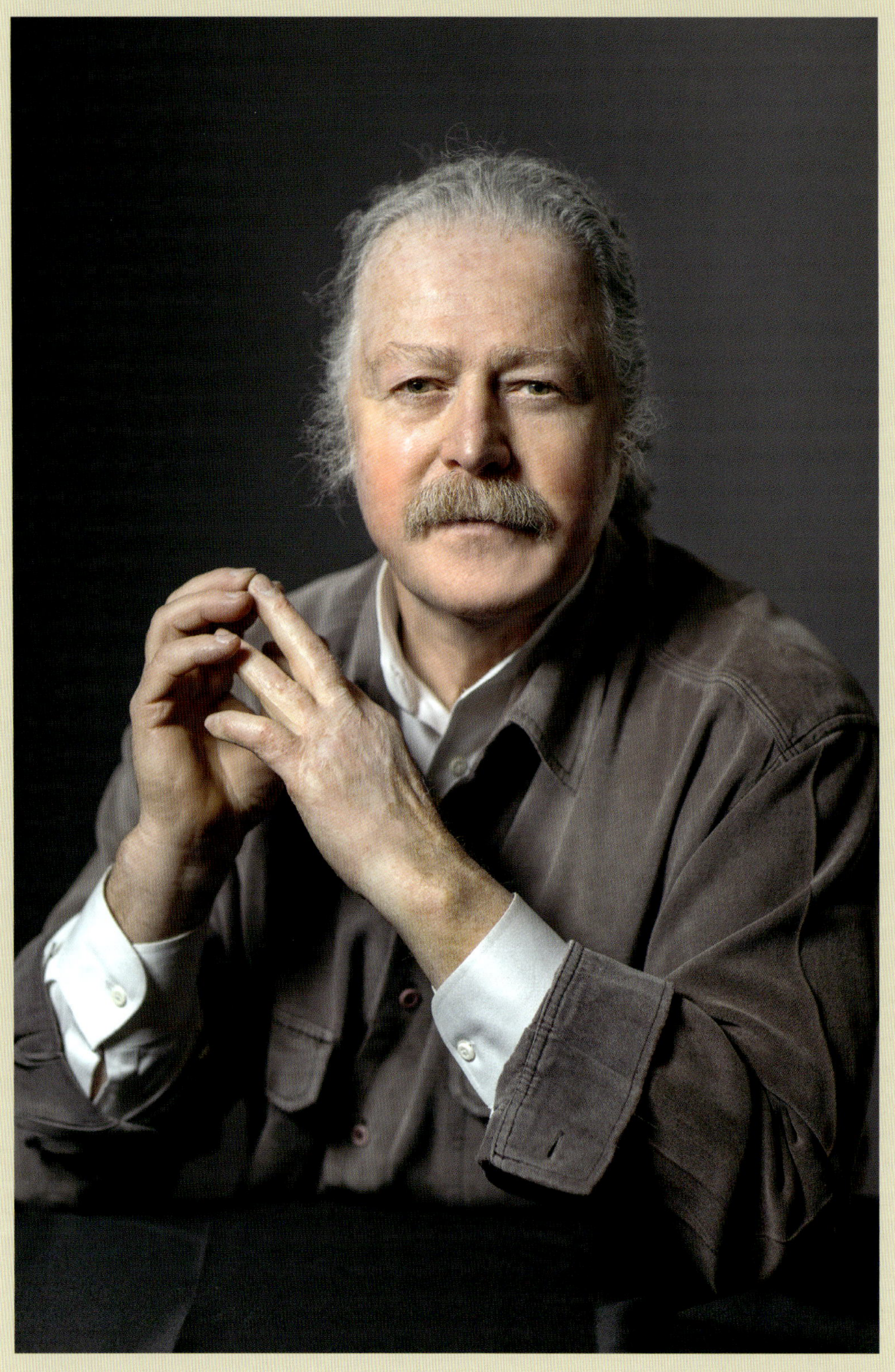

BIOGRAPHY

Albert Paley was born in Philadelphia, Pennsylvania, March 28th 1944.

His studio was first registered in 1963 and he has been an active artist for over 40 years. After formal studies he moved to Rochester, New York, in 1969. The studio was incorporated as Paley Studios in 1986. After several studio locations the current studio in Rochester, employs 16 people in the fabrication and office areas. Paley is the first metal sculptor to receive the coveted Institute Honors awarded by the American Institute of Architects, the AIA's highest award to a non-architect. "The allure of Paley's art comes though its intrinsic sense of integration of art and architecture," as one noted architect stated.

Commissioned by both public institutions and private corporations, Paley has completed more than 60 site-specific works. Some notable examples are the Portal Gates for the Renwick Gallery of the Smithsonian Institution in Washington DC, Synergy, a ceremonial archway in Philadelphia, the Portal Gates for theNew York State Senate Chambers in Albany, New York, Sentinel, a monumental plaza sculpture for Rochester Institute of Technology, as well as a 65-foot sculpture for the entry court of Bausch and Lomb's headquarters in Rochester, NY. Recently completed works include three sculptures for the National Harbor development near Washington DC, a 130' long archway named *Animals Always* for the St. Louis Zoo, a gate for the Cleveland Botanical Gardens in Cleveland, OH, a sculptural relief for Wellington Place, Toronto, Canada, a sculpture named *Threshold* for the Corporate Headquarters of Klein Steel, Rochester, NY, and a ceremonial entrance-way called *Transformation* for Iowa State University in Ames, Iowa.

Pieces by Albert Paley can be found in the permanent collections of many major museums including the Metropolitan Museum of Art in New York, the Museum of Fine Arts in Boston, the Museum of Fine Arts in Houston, and the Victoria and Albert Museum in London.

Broadly published and an international lecturer, Paley received his BFA and MFA from Temple University, Tyler School of Art in Philadelphia, Pennsylvania. He received honorary doctorates from the University of Gothenburg, Gothenburg, Sweden in 2012, the University of Rochester in 1989, the State University of New York at Brockport in 1996, and St. Lawrence University, in Canton, New York in 1997. He presently holds the Charlotte Fredericks Mowris Endowed Chair, College of Imaging Arts and Sciences, Rochester Institute of Technology, Rochester, New York.

The primary focus of Paley's studio activities are in reference to large-scale public sculpture in the A architectural arena.

ALBERT PALEY

Selected Major Commissions

2013
Cedar Rapids Library, Cedar Rapids, Iowa, *Regeneration*, exterior plaza sculpture, formed and fabricated painted steel, 19' 6" H x 43' w x 13' D

Memorial Art Gallery of the University of Rochester, Rochester New York, *Soliloquy*, exterior sculpture, Centennial Sculpture Park, formed and fabricated stainless steel with a polychromed finish, 26' H x 10' Diam.

2012
Hershey Penn State Children's Hospital, Hershey, Pennsylvania, *The Promise*, exterior plaza sculpture, fabricated and polychromed steel, 40' H x 27' w x 17' D

Hilo University, Hilo Hawaii, *Makalii*, exterior entryway sculpture, formed and fabricated weathering steel, stainless steel and bronze, 43' 9" H x 13' D

2011
Michigan State University, East Lansing, Michigan, *Cadence*, relief sculpture, formed and fabricated stainless steel, 25' H x 47' W x 2' D

Wichita Waterwalk, Wichita, Kansas, *Paragon*, exterior plaza sculpture of weathering steel and stainless steel and bronze, 40' H x 16' 6" W x 19' 3" D

2010
24th Street Bridge Project, Iowa West Foundation, Council Bluffs, Iowa, *Odyssey*, four gateway sculptures, formed and fabricated steel, stainless steel and bronze, ranging from 45' H - 60' H

2009
Monterrey, Mexico, Parque Fundidora, *Evanesce*, exterior sculpture, formed and fabricated painted steel, 100' H x 43' W x 48' D

Clay Center for the Arts and Sciences, Charleston, West Virginia, exterior sculpture, formed and fabricated steel, stainless steel and bronze, 68' H x 39' W x 34' D

2008
Jewish Community Center, Cincinnati, Ohio, *The Light*, exterior entrance sculpture, formed and fabricated, stainless steel, 20' H x 7' W x 7' D

New Jersey Transit, Trenton, New Jersey, *Zenith*, exterior sculpture, formed and fabricated polychromed steel, 34' H x 9' W x 8' D

Riviera Complex, Fort Myers, Florida, *Naiad*, sculpture, formed and fabricated polychromed steel, 30' h

Village of Hope, Orange County, California. Entrance Portal, forged and fabricated steel with a natural patina 15' H x 20' W x 1' 6" D

National Harbor, Fort Washington, Maryland, *The Beckoning*, exterior sculpture, formed and fabricated weathering steel and polychromed steel, 85' H x 33' W x 33' D

2007
Iowa State University, Ames, Iowa, *Transformation*, entrance sculpture, formed and fabricated stainless steel, 15' H x 15' W x 2' D / 9' 7" H x 10' W x 2' D

National Cathedral, Washington, DC., Good Shepard Chapel Gates, 8' 10" H x 5' 4" W x 1' 8" D

2006
Klein Steel Corporation, Rochester, New York, *Threshold*, exterior sculpture, fabricated and polychromed steel, 67' H x 40' W x 36' D

St. Louis Zoological Park, St. Louis, Missouri, *Animals Always*, exterior plaza sculpture, 36' H x 130' W x 8' D

2005
Memphis Museum of Art, Memphis Tennessee, *Entrance Portals*, exterior gates, forged and painted steel, 15' 3" H x 1' 6" W x 14' 6" D

2004
North Bridge Commons, Orlando, Florida, *Rhapsody*, exterior sculpture, formed, fabricated and polychromed steel, 26' 7" H x 7' W x 7' D

Monahan Pacific Development Corporation, San Francisco, California, *Volute*, exterior sculpture, formed and fabricated stainless steel, 11' 4" H x 3' 4" W x 3' D

M D Andersen Ambulatory Clinical Building, Houston, Texas, *Tree of Life*, interior sculpture, formed, fabricated and polychromed steel, 22' 6" H x 19' D

D C Commission on the Arts and Humanities, Washington, DC. *Epoch*, exterior sculpture, formed, fabricated and polychromed steel, 24' H x 12' W x 10' 6" D

Lake Mirror Park, Lakeland, Florida, *Tribute to Volunteerism*, exterior sculpture, formed, fabricated and polychromed steel, 41' H x 9' 1" W x 10' 6" D

Cleveland Botanical Garden, Cleveland, Ohio, *Kohl Gate*, ceremonial archway, formed and fabricated weathering steel, 14' 10" H x 55' 3" W x 3' 2"

2003
Rochester Institute of Technology, Rochester, New York, *Sentinel*, exterior sculpture, formed and fabricated weathering steel, stainless steel and bronze, 73' H x 30' Diam.
Syracuse University, Syracuse, New York, *Banner*, exterior sculpture, fabricated weathering steel, 9' 5" H x 2' 3" W x 1' 10" D

2002
Hotel Pattee, Perry, Iowa, *Reconfiguration*, pair of gateway sculpture for city park, fabricated found objects with painted finish, 25' 7" H x 28' W x 7' 4" D and 19' H

x 24' 6" W x 6' 6" D
Wellington Place, Toronto, Canada, *Constellation*, relief façade sculpture, formed and fabricated stainless steel, 15' 10" H x 2' 7" W x 18' D

Columbia Public Library, Columbia, Missouri, *Cypher*, pair of entrance sculptures, formed, fabricated and polychromed steel, 38' 9" H x 18' W x 11' D and 30' 4" H x 11' 6" W x 21' D

2001
Florida Gulf Coast University, Fort Myers, Florida, *Cross Currents*, exterior sculpture, formed, fabricated and polychromed steel, 21' 10" H x 12' W x 8' D

La Cienega Center Beverly Hills, California, *Oblique*, exterior sculpture, formed and fabricated weathering steel, stainless steel and bronze, 23' H x 12' 4" W x 7' 6" D

2000
University of the South, Sewanee, Tennessee, *Relief Sculpture*, formed and fabricated steel and bronze, 8' 3" H x 14' W x 6" D

Naples Philharmonic Center for the Arts, Naples Florida, Portal Gates, formed and fabricated steel, stainless steel, and bronze, 20' H x 10' 7" W x 1' 4" D

1999
Florida State University, Tallahassee, Florida, Stadium Entrance Gates, formed and fabricated weathering steel, stainless steel and bronze, 12' 6" H x 36' W x 6" D

Toledo Museum of Art, Toledo, Ohio, design public space, wall sculpture and interior furnishings, formed and fabricated stainless steel, 12' H x 12' 6" W

1998
Adobe Systems, Inc., San Jose, California, *Horizon*, exterior plaza sculpture, formed and fabricated weathering steel, stainless steel, bronze, 28' H x 37' W x 7' D / 9' H x 7' W x 7' 6" D

The Municipality of Anchorage, Anchorage, Alaska, *Solstice*, exterior sculpture, formed and fabricated weathering steel and stainless steel with polychrome finish, 25' 6" H x 8' 6" W x 7' 6" D

The University of Toledo, Toledo, Ohio, *Symbion*, exterior plaza sculpture, formed, fabricated and polychromed weathering and stainless steel, 27' 9" H x 11' 7" W x 8' D

1997
San Francisco Art Commission, California, for the Civic Center Courthouse, Exterior Entrance Doors, Rotunda Lobby Gates, Elevator Doors, formed and fabricated stainless steel, 10' 4" H x 6' 9" W

The Ohio State University, Columbus, Ohio, *Gnomon*, exterior sculpture, formed and fabricated weathering steel, 19' 6" H x 8' 6" W x 8' D

Canandaigua Wine Company, Canandaigua, New York, *Helix*, exterior sculpture, formed and fabricated weathering steel, 16' H x 15' W x 38' 6" D

American Bankers Insurance Group, Miami, Florida, Exterior Sculpture, formed, fabricated and polychromed steel, 17' 6" H x 8' 4" W x 5' 5" D

Miami University, Oxford, Ohio, Library Entrance Doors, for Alumni Hall, formed and fabricated bronze, 6' H x 1' W x 6" D

1996
Bausch and Lomb, Rochester, New York, *Genesee Passage*, exterior sculpture, formed and fabricated weathering steel, 60' H x 16' W x 12'

Sony Pictures Entertainment, Culver Studios Office Building, Culver City, California, *Primordial Reflections*, exterior relief panels, formed, fabricated and painted steel, 6' 7" H x 21' 5" W x 10" D

Congregation Adath Jeshurun, Elkins Park, Pennsylvania, *Revelation*, temple tabernacle doors, formed and fabricated steel, 24' 5" H x 12' 9" W x 3' 3" D

1995
General Services Administration, Washington, D.C. for the New Federal Building, Asheville, North Carolina, *Passage*, exterior sculpture, formed and fabricated weathering steel, 37' H x 23' W x 16' D

1994
General Services Administration, Washington, D.C. for the Federal Courthouse, Camden, New Jersey, *Metamorphosis*, interior rotunda sculpture, formed, fabricated and polychromed steel, 9' H x 11' W x 1' 6" D

Temple Israel, Dayton, Ohio, *Tabernacle Screen*, formed, fabricated and polychromed steel, 7' 8" H x 8' 8" W x 4" D

1992
Montgomery County, Silver Springs, Maryland, *Criss-Cross*, exterior sculpture, formed, fabricated and polychromed steel, 20' H x 30' W x 10' D

1991
Arizona State University, Tempe, Arizona, *Ceremonial Gates*, exterior gate, formed, fabricated and polychromed steel, 12' H x 8' W x 1' 6" D

1990
The Landmarks Group, Promenade Two Building, Atlanta, Georgia, *Olympia*, exterior sculpture, formed, fabricated and polychromed steel, 29' H x 14' W x 8' D

Arts Council of Roanoke Valley, Roanoke Airport Authority, Roanoke Regional Airport, Roanoke, Virginia, *Aurora*, exterior sculpture, forged, fabricated and polychromed steel, 18' h x 12' W x 6' D

Birmingham Museum of Art, Birmingham, Alabama, *Confluence*, exterior sculpture, formed and fabricated weathering steel, 18' H x 10' W x 4' D

1988
Cornell University Medical College, Lasdon Biomedical Research Building, New York, New York, Architectural Screen, forged, fabricated and polychromed steel, 8' W x 6' H x 1' D

Memorial Art Gallery of the University of Rochester, Rochester, New York, *Convergence*, interior sculpture, forged, fabricated and painted steel, 8' H x 6' W x 3' D

State of Connecticut, Bureau of Public Works, for the Hartford Superior Court Building, Hartford, Connecticut, *Hexad*, interior sculpture, forged and fabricated painted steel and bronze, 21' H x 12' D

1987
Houston Lyric Theater Foundation, Inc., Houston, Texas, Wortham Center for the Performing Arts, Houston, Texas, eight Stairway Sculptures, interior sculptures, formed, fabricated and polychromed steel, varying in height from 15' H to 30' H

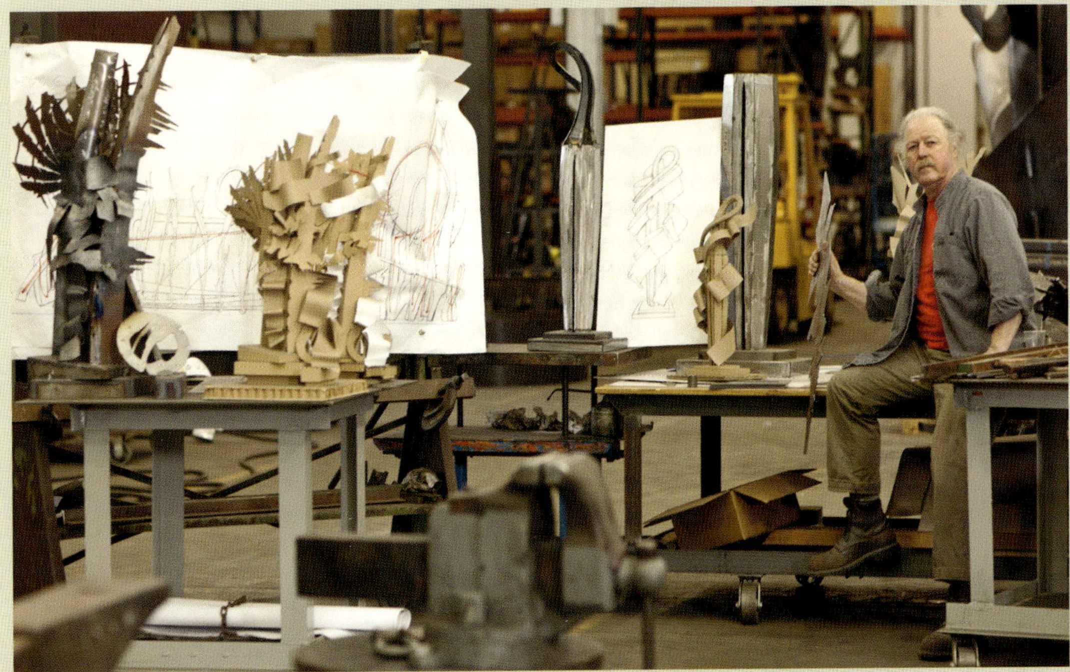

Paley in design area, Paley Studios, Lyell Avenue, Rochester, New York

Massachusetts Bay Transit Authority, Milk Street Station, Boston, Massachusetts, Entrance Gateway, forged, fabricated and painted steel, 10' H x 10' W

Redevelopment Authority of the City of Philadelphia for Museum Towers, Philadelphia, Pennsylvania, *Synergy*, archway exterior sculpture, formed, fabricated and polychromed steel, 25' H x 60' W x 6' D

1986
Gannett Publishing Corporation, Washington, D.C., Bronze Relief, forged and fabricated bronze, 6' H x 15' W x 1' D

Virginia Museum of Fine Art, Richmond, Virginia, Pedestrian Entrance Gate, forged, fabricated and painted steel, 8' h x 8' W; Vehicular Entrance Gate, formed, fabricated and painted steel, 11' 6" H x 32' W

The Willard Building, Washington, DC, interior Sculpture, forged and fabricated steel and bronze, 8' H x 6' W x 1' 6" D

1984
Harro Theater East, Rochester, New York, *Conclave*, exterior sculpture, formed, fabricated and painted steel, 30' H x 22' W x 10' D

1983
The Hyatt Corporation, for the Hyatt Grand Cypress Hotel, Orlando, Florida, Entrance Sculpture, forged and fabricated steel and bronze, 25' H x 54' W x 8' D

1982
Strong Museum, Rochester, New York, exterior Sculpture, hollow formed and fabricated weathering steel, 15' 6" H x 31' 6" W x 6' D

1980
New York State Senate, Albany, New York for State Senate Chambers, Capitol Building, two pair Portal Gates, forged and fabricated steel, brass, and bronze, 13' 6" H x 9' W x 6" D each

1978
Redevelopment Authority of the City of Philadelphia, Philadelphia, Pennsylvania, Sculpture Screens, forged and fabricated steel, 6' h x 4' W; Two Gates, forged and fabricated steel, 3' H x 8' W

1975
Hunter Museum of Art, Chattanooga, Tennessee, exterior Sculpture Court Enclosure, forged, fabricated and painted steel, 12' H x 87' 6" W 6' D

1974
Renwick Gallery, National Museum of American Art, Smithsonian Institution, Washington, DC, interior Portal Gates, forged and fabricated steel, brass, and bronze. 7' 6' H x 6' W x 6" D

Selected Permanent Collections

Arizona State University, Tempe, Arizona
Art Gallery of Western Australia, Perth, Australia
The Birmingham Museum of Art, Birmingham, Alabama
The British Museum, London, England
The Brooks Museum of Art, Memphis, Tennessee
Columbia Library, Columbia, Missouri
The Columbus Museum of Art, Columbus, Ohio
Cooper-Hewitt, Smithsonian Institution, Washington, DC
Delaware Art Museum, Wilmington, Delaware
Detroit Institute of Arts, Detroit, Michigan
Earlham College, Richmond, Indiana
The Fitzwilliam Museum, Cambridge University, England
Gannett Publishing Corporation, Washington, DC
High Museum of Art, Atlanta, Georgia
Hunter Museum of Art, Chattanooga, Tennessee
International Sculpture Center's Collection II, Hamilton, New Jersey
Iowa State University, Ames, Iowa
Iris and B. Gerald Cantor Center for Visual Arts, Stanford University, California
Memorial Art Gallery, University of Rochester, Rochester, New York
Museum of Arts And Design, New York City
Metropolitan Museum of Art, New York, New York
Minneapolis Institute of Arts, Minneapolis, Minnesota
Minnesota Museum of American Art, St. Paul, Minnesota
Mint Museum of Art and Design, Charlotte, North Carolina
Museum of Art, Brigham Young University, Provo, Utah
Museum of Fine Arts, Boston, Massachusetts
Museum of Fine Arts, Springfield, Massachusetts
The Museum of Fine Arts Houston, Houston, Texas
The Newark Museum, Newark, New Jersey
Penn State University, Hershey, Pensylvania

Philadelphia Archdiocese, Philadelphia, Pennsylvania
Philadelphia Museum of Art, Philadelphia, Pennsylvania
Pilchuck Glass School Seattle, Washington

Polk Museum of Art, Lakeland, Florida
Racine Art Museum, Racine, Wisconsin
Renwick Gallery, Smithsonian Institution, Washington, DC
San Jose University, San Jose, California

State Capitol, Albany, New York
Strong Museum, Rochester, New York
Syracuse University, Syracuse, New York
Temple University, Philadelphia, Pennsylvania
Toledo Museum of Art, Toledo, Ohio
University of Hawaii at Hilo, Hilo, Hawaii
University of Illinois, Normal, Illinois
University of North Texas P.R.I.N.T. Collection, Denton, Texas
Virginia Museum of Fine Arts, Richmond, Virginia
The White House, Washington, D.C.
Victoria & Albert Museum, London, England
Worcester Art Museum, Worcester, Massachusetts
Yale University Art Gallery, New Haven, Connecticut

Selected Awards and Grants

2013
George Eastman Award, the University of Rochester, Rochester, New York

2011
Rochester Institute of Technology Innovation Hall of Fame Inductee, Rochester, New York

2010
American Craft Council Gold Metal for Consummate Craftsmanship Award, Minneapolis, Minnesota

1997
Masters of the Medium Award, James Renwick Alliance, Renwick Gallery, Smithsonian Institute, Washington, DC

1995
Citations and Fellowship Award, National Association of Schools of Art and Design (NASAD)

Institute Honors, Lifetime Achievement Award for dialog of Art and Architecture, The American Institute of Architects (AIA), National Committee on Design

1982
Award of Excellence, American Institute of Architects: Art in Architecture (Portal Gates, New York State Senate Chambers, Albany, New York)

1979
Master Apprenticeship Grant, National Endowment for the Arts, Washington, D.C.

1978
Fullbright Fellowship/New Zealand, Washington, D.C.

1976
International Design Exhibition, Zlatarna Celije, Celije, Yugoslavia, Design Award

Selected Exhibitions

2014
Albert Paley Retrospective, The Corcoran Gallery, Washington D.C.

2013
Albert Paley on Park Avenue, The Fund for Park Sculpture Advisory Committee, Park Avenue, New York, New York

2012
Albert Paley Sculpture, Rohsska Museet, Goteborg, Sweden.

2010
Albert Paley in the 21st Century, Memorial Art Gallery of the University of Rochester, Rochester, New York.

Albert Paley: Celebrating a Contemporary American Sculptor, Joslyn Museum of Art, Omaha, Nebraska

2009
Albert Paley, One Man Show Grounds for Sculpture, Hamilton, New Jersey.

American Sculptors, St. Urban, Switzerland

Open Spaces, Vancouver Sculpture Biennale, 2005-2006, Vancouver, British Columbia, Canada

2003
Second International Sculpture Exhibition, Chetumal, Mexico

2002
First International Sculpture Exhibition, Colima, Mexico

1997
Albert Paley: Selected Works, Fine Art Society, London, England.

1996
Age of Steel: Recent Sculpture by Albert Paley, Museum of Art, Brigham Young University, Provo, Utah

1995
Albert Paley: Sculpture & Drawings, Chang Gallery, Kansas State University, Manhattan, Kansas

1992
Albert Paley: Recent Sculpture, Samuel P. Harn Museum of Art, University of Florida, Gainesville, Florida

"Design Visions", Exhibition ,The Second Australian International Triennial, Museum of Western Australia, Perth, Australia.

Tokyo Art Expo, Exhibition of sculpture and project documentation. Tokyo, Japan

Albert Paley: Sculpture, One Man Show, University of the Arts, Philadelphia, Pennsylvania

1989
Albert Paley, One Man Show, National Museum of Wales, Cardiff, Wales

1986
First World Congress of Iron, Aachen, West Germany

1985-86
Albert Paley: The Art of Metal (Traveling Retrospective Exhibition, 1972-1986)

1983
Towards a New Iron Age, Victoria and Albert Museum, London, England

1980
The Metalwork of Albert Paley (Traveling Retrospective Exhibition, 1962-1975)

1978
Art and Religion, Vatican Museum and Galleries, Rome, Italy

1977
Recent Works in Metal by Albert Paley, Renwick Gallery, Smithsonian Institution, Washington, DC

1976
Invitational Design Exhibition, Zlatarna, Celje, Yugoslavia. Merit Award.

1970
Nova Scotia College of Art and Design, Halifax, Nova Scotia

1969
Philadelphia Art Alliance, Philadelphia, Pennsylvania

Education

2012
Honorary Doctorate of Fine Arts, The University of Gothenburg, Gothenburg, Sweden

1997
Honorary Doctorate of Fine Arts, State University of New York at Brockport, Brockport, New York

1996
Honorary Doctorate of Fine Arts, St. Lawrence University, Canton, New York

Honorary Doctorate of Fine Arts, University of Rochester, Rochester, New York

1966-69
Master of Fine Arts, Tyler School of Art, Temple University, Philadelphia, Pennsylvania

1962-66
Bachelor of Fine Arts, Tyler School of Art, Temple University, Philadelphia, Pennsylvania

Monographs

Hesselbom, Ted. *Albert Paley Steneby & Rohsska Museet*. Gothenburg, Sweden: Rohsska Museet, 2012.

Ratcliff, Carter. *Albert Paley In The 21st. Century*. New York: University of Rochester, Memorial Art Gallery, 2010.

Shearer, Linda. *Threshold*. Milan, Italy: Skira, 2008.

Rowe, M. Jessica. *Albert Paley Portals & Gates*. Ames, Iowa: University Museums, 2007

Kuspit, Donald. *Albert Paley: Sculpture*. Milan, Italy: Skira, 2006.

Yarrington, James. *Sentinel, the Design Fabrication, & Installation of the Monumental Sculpture by Albert Paley at the Rochester Institute of Technology*. Rochester, New York: Rochester Institute of Technology Cary Press, 2005.

Lucie-Smith, Edward. *The Art of Albert Paley*. New York: Harry N. Abrams Inc., 1996.

Selected Publications

Clarke, Mathew S. *From Fire to Form: Sculpture from the Modern Blacksmith and Metalsmith*. New York: Schiffer Publishing, 2009.

Holzman, Malcolm. *A Material Life*. Victoria, Australia: Images Publishing, 2009.

McCreight, Tim. *Design Language*. Maine: Brynmorgen Press, 2006.

Greenhalgh, Paul. *The Persistence of Craft*. A & C Black: London, 2002.

Trilling, James. *The Language of Ornament*. Thames and Hudson, 2001.

Fox & Fowle: *Function, Structure, Beauty*. Milano: L'arca, 1999.

Horn, Robyn. *Living with Form: The Horn Collection*. Little Rock, AR: Bradley Publishing, 1999.

Meilach, Dona Z. *Decorative and Sculptural Ironwork, 2nd Edition*. Atglen, PA: Schiffer Publishing, 1999.

Renwick Gallery. *Skilled Work: American Craft in the Renwick Gallery*. Washington D. C.: Renwick Gallery and Smithsonian Institution Press, 1998.

English, Helen Drutt. *Jewelry of Our Time: Art, Ornament and Obsession*. New York: Rizzoli, 1995.

Lucie-Smith, Edward. *Art Today*. London: Phaidon Press Limited, 1995.

Monroe, Michael W. *The White House Collection of American Crafts*. New York: Harry N. Abrams Inc., 1995.

National Museum of American Art. *National Museum of American Art*. Washington, D.C.: National Museum of American Art, Smithsonian Institution, 1995.

Bach, Penny Balkin. *Public Art in Philadelphia*. Philadelphia, PA: Temple University Press, 1992.

Miller, R. Craig. *Modern Design – In the Metropolitan Museum of Art: 1890-1990*. New York: Harry N. Abrams Inc., 1990.

Minamizawa, Hiroshi. *The World of Decorative & Architectural Wrought Iron*. Kyoto, Japan: Yoshiyo Kobo Co., Ltd., 1990.

Smithsonian Institution. *A Picture Tour of the Smithsonian*. Washington, D.C.: Smithsonian Institution Press, 1990.

Carlock, Marty. *A Guide to Public Art in Greater Boston*. Boston, MA: The Harvard Common Press, 1988.

Verlag, Julius Hoffmann. *Kunst aus dem Feuer (Art from the Fire)*. Stüttgart, Germany: Hoffmann, 1987.

Meilach, Dona Z. *Decorative and Sculptural Ironwork*. New York: Crown, 1977.

Selected Film and Video

2013
Albert Paley on Park Avenue, Produced by Brianna Byrne, WXXI, Local Broadcast and international Internet distribution May – June 2013.

2006
Machi, Tony, Albert Paley: Sentinel. Produced and directed by Tony Machi, Machi and Machi Productions. (Approx. 60 min. High Definition video) PBS National Broadcast.

Machi, Tony, Albert Paley: Man of Steel. Produced and directed by Tony Machi, Machi and Machi Productions. (Approx. 57 min. video color/sound) PBS National Broadcast, January 12, 2001.

1994
Albert Paley - Metal Artist. NHK TV (Japanese Public Television). In Japanese (Approx. 20 min., HDTV color/sound).

1987
Albert Paley's Albany Gates. Produced and directed by Bill Rowley (58 min., 16mm color/sound).

1986
Albert Paley: Architectural Metal Sculptor. Produced and directed by John P. Dworak, Virginia Museum of Fine Arts, Richmond, Virginia. Aired on Public Broadcasting System (28 min. 30 sec.).

1983
Hand and Eye ("Against Oblivion"). Canadian Broadcasting Company.

1982
Handmade in America: Interview with Albert Paley. Produced by Barbara Lee Diamondstein for ABC Video Enterprises, American Broadcasting Corporation, New York (23 min., color, sound).

1976
Behind the Fence: Albert Paley, Metalworker. Produced by David Darby. Viewed - National Public Broadcasting (30 min., color, sound). Award, 2nd International Film Festival, New York State Council of the Arts, New York, New York.

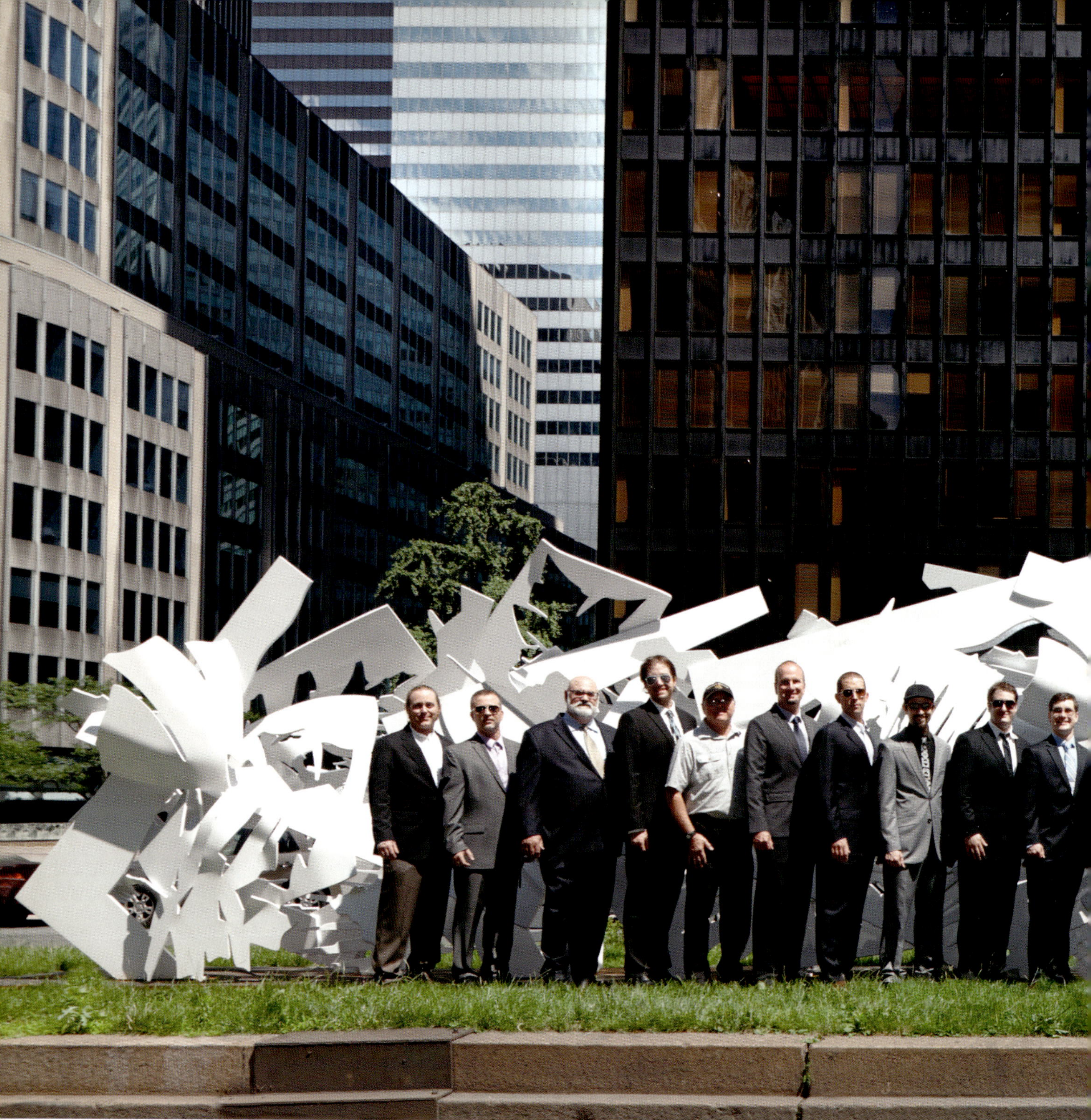

Albert Paley and the Paley Studios team at the Paley on Park Avenue exhibition opening celebration. New York, New York June 29, 2013

Left to right:
Sam Castner,
David Owens,
Jeff Jubenville,
Peter Chapman,
Ron Herrick,
John Lang,

Chris Malloy,
Blake Terzini,
Matt Shafir,
Tyler Guay,
Albert Paley,
Frances Paley,
Jennifer Laemlein,

Gina Foster,
Darcy Hart,
Elizabeth Cameron,
Hannah Lightbody,
Erin Gillaspy

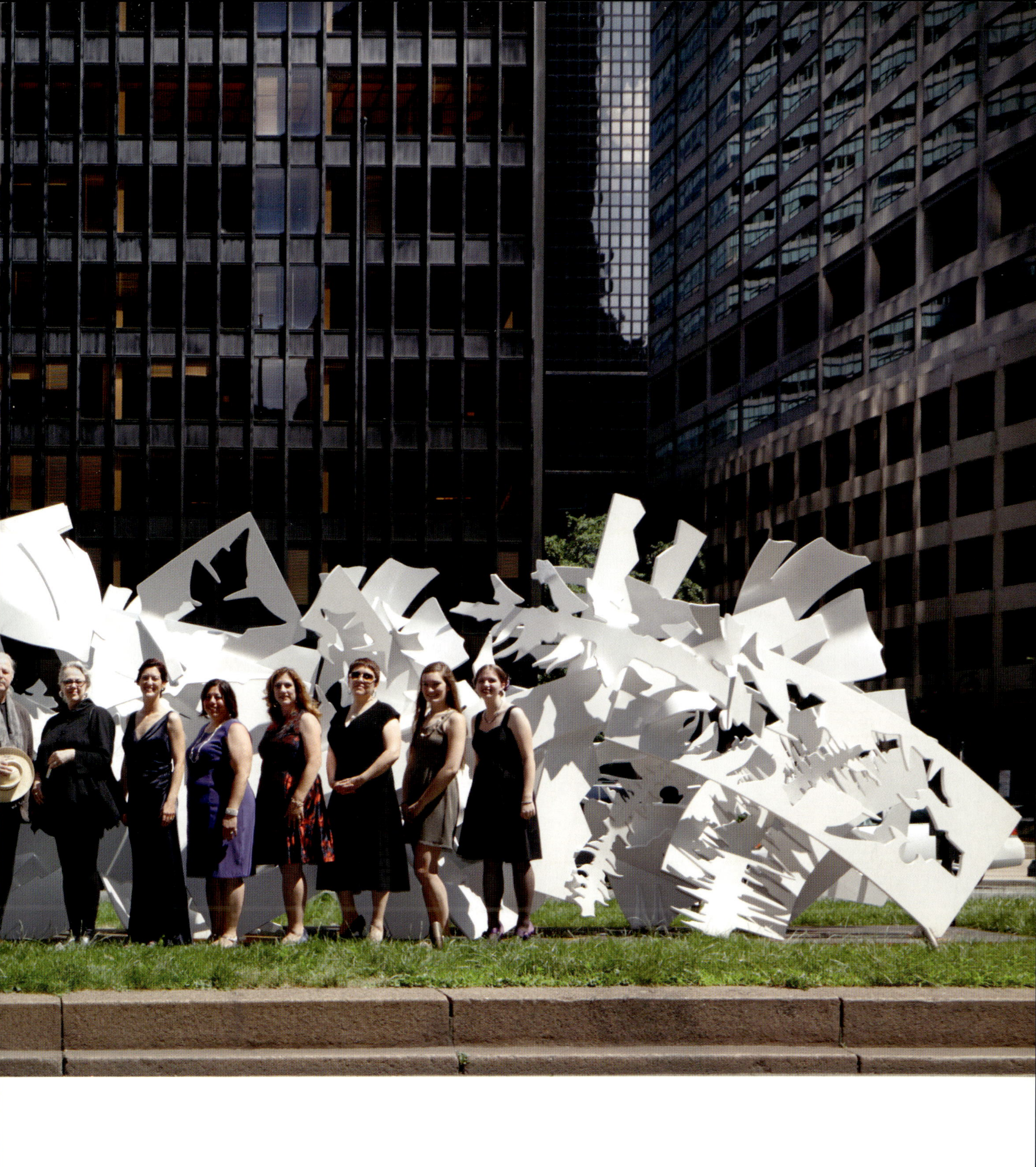

Photo Credits

Jim Day
129

Bill Dubois
76, 92, 115, 120, 126

Peter Fellows
24

Craig Kuhner
14

Hannah Lightbody
32-33, 123

Bruce Miller
10, 15,

Myers Creative Imaging
2, 36-37, 38, 39, 40-41, 42-43, 45, 46, 47, 50-51, 53, 55, 56, 58-
59, 60-61, 63, 64-65, 66-67, 68, 69, 71, 72, 73, 74, 75, 77, 78,
79, 80-81, 82, 83, 85, 87, 88-89, 90-91, 93, 94-95, 96, 97, 98,
99, 101, 103, 104-105, 106-107, 108, 109, 110, 111, 112-113,
115, 116-117, 118-119, 121, 124-125, 127, 130-131, 132, 135,
142-143

Paley Studios Archive
8, 12, 18, 30-31, 34, 35, 39, 44, 48-49, 52, 54, 57, 62, 70, 76,
84, 86, 92, 100, 102, 108, 114, 120, 122, 126, 128

Toledo Museum of Art, Frederick B. and Kate L. Shoemaker
Fund
22

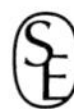

Silvana Editoriale S.p.A.
via Margherita De Vizzi, 86
20092 Cinisello Balsamo, Milano
tel. 02 61 83 63 37
fax 02 61 72 464
www.silvanaeditoriale.it

Reproductions, printing and binding by
Arti Grafiche Amilcare Pizzi S.p.A.
Cinisello Balsamo, Milan
Printed August 2013